Advance Praise for *Head First Excel*

"*Head First Excel* is awesome! Like other Head First books, it's a very approachable mix of knowledge, business situations, and humor. Not only do you learn all you need to know about Excel, but you also get to learn some real business lingo and smarts as well. Need to create formulas? Need to make reports, charts, or pivot tables? This is the book for you. *Head First Excel* gives you the goods and will help you excel at Excel!"

— **Ken Bluttman, *www.kenbluttman.com***

"*Head First Excel* shows how to fully utilize some of the best features Excel has to offer to improve productivity and data analysis skills. If I've been using Excel for over 10 years and still found many useful topics, so can you, regardless of your experience level."

— **Anthony Rose, President, Support Analytics**

"Do you use Excel to keep lists and calculate the occasional budget? Would you like to dive deeper and learn how Excel can give you an edge in your daily workflow? Unlock your Excel superpowers with Michael Milton's *Head First Excel*. You'll learn to create data visualizations and design spreadsheets that make your point and get you noticed. Discover how to easily audit complex formulas written by others, so you can quickly validate (or call 'B.S.' on) their calculations. Build models that optimize your business and/or finances based on all possible scenarios. Excel's many features can seem intimidating; Michael cuts through the complexity and teaches you to bend Excel to your will."

— **Bill Mietelski, software engineer**

Praise for other *Head First* books

"Kathy and Bert's *Head First Java* transforms the printed page into the closest thing to a GUI you've ever seen. In a wry, hip manner, the authors make learning Java an engaging 'what're they gonna do next?' experience."

—Warren Keuffel, *Software Development Magazine*

"Beyond the engaging style that drags you forward from know-nothing into exalted Java warrior status, *Head First Java* covers a huge amount of practical matters that other texts leave as the dreaded 'exercise for the reader.' It's clever, wry, hip and practical—there aren't a lot of textbooks that can make that claim and live up to it while also teaching you about object serialization and network launch protocols."

—Dr. Dan Russell, Director of User Sciences and Experience Research IBM Almaden Research Center (and teaches Artificial Intelligence at Stanford University)

"It's fast, irreverent, fun, and engaging. Be careful—you might actually learn something!"

—Ken Arnold, former senior engineer at Sun Microsystems Coauthor (with James Gosling, creator of Java), *The Java Programming Language*

"I feel like a thousand pounds of books have just been lifted off of my head."

—Ward Cunningham, inventor of the Wiki and founder of the Hillside Group

"Just the right tone for the geeked-out, casual-cool guru coder in all of us. The right reference for practical development strategies—gets my brain going without having to slog through a bunch of tired, stale professor-speak."

—Travis Kalanick, founder of Scour and Red Swoosh Member of the MIT TR100

"There are books you buy, books you keep, books you keep on your desk, and thanks to O'Reilly and the Head First crew, there is the penultimate category, Head First books. They're the ones that are dog-eared, mangled, and carried everywhere. *Head First SQL* is at the top of my stack. Heck, even the PDF I have for review is tattered and torn."

— Bill Sawyer, ATG Curriculum Manager, Oracle

"This book's admirable clarity, humor, and substantial doses of clever make it the sort of book that helps even nonprogrammers think well about problem solving."

—Cory Doctorow, co-editor of Boing Boing Author, *Down and Out in the Magic Kingdom* and *Someone Comes to Town, Someone Leaves Town*

"I received the book yesterday and started to read it…and I couldn't stop. This is definitely très 'cool.' It is fun, but they cover a lot of ground and they are right to the point. I'm really impressed."

> — **Erich Gamma, IBM Distinguished Engineer**
> **Coauthor, *Design Patterns***

"One of the funniest and smartest books on software design I've ever read."

> — **Aaron LaBerge, VP Technology, ESPN.com**

"What used to be a long, trial-and-error learning process has now been reduced neatly into an engaging paperback."

> — **Mike Davidson, CEO, Newsvine, Inc.**

"Elegant design is at the core of every chapter here, each concept conveyed with equal doses of pragmatism and wit."

> — **Ken Goldstein, Executive Vice President, Disney Online**

"I ♥ *Head First HTML with CSS & XHTML*—it teaches you everything you need to learn in a 'fun coated' format."

> — **Sally Applin, UI designer and artist**

"Usually when reading through a book or article on design patterns, I'd have to occasionally stick myself in the eye with something just to make sure I was paying attention. Not with this book. Odd as it may sound, this book makes learning about design patterns fun.

"While other books on design patterns are saying, 'Bueller… Bueller… Bueller,' this book is on the float belting out 'Shake it up, baby!'"

> — **Eric Wuehler**

"I literally love this book. In fact, I kissed this book in front of my wife."

> — **Satish Kumar**

Other related books from O'Reilly

Head First Data Analysis

Analyzing Business Data with Excel

Excel Scientific and Engineering Cookbook

Access Data Analysis Cookbook

Other books in O'Reilly's *Head First* series

Head First Java™

Head First Object-Oriented Analysis and Design (OOA&D)

Head First HTML with CSS and XHTML

Head First Design Patterns

Head First Servlets and JSP

Head First EJB

Head First PMP

Head First SQL

Head First Software Development

Head First JavaScript

Head First Ajax

Head First Physics

Head First Statistics

Head First Rails

Head First PHP & MySQL

Head First Algebra

Head First Web Design

Head First Networking

Head First Data Analysis

Head First 2D Geometry

Head First Programming

Head First Excel

Wouldn't it be dreamy if there was a book on Excel that could turn me into an expert while keeping me engaged and entertained? But it's probably just a fantasy....

Michael Milton

O'REILLY®

Beijing • Cambridge • Farnham • Köln • Sebastopol • Taipei • Tokyo

Head First Excel

by Michael Milton

Printed in the United States of America.

Published by O'Reilly Media, Inc., 1005 Gravenstein Highway North, Sebastopol, CA 95472.

O'Reilly Media books may be purchased for educational, business, or sales promotional use. Online editions are also available for most titles (*http://my.safaribooksonline.com*). For more information, contact our corporate/institutional sales department: (800) 998-9938 or *corporate@oreilly.com*.

Series Creators:	Kathy Sierra, Bert Bates
Series Editor:	Brett D. McLaughlin
Editor:	Brian Sawyer
Cover Designers:	Louise Barr, Steve Fehler
Production Editor:	Rachel Monaghan
Indexer:	Angela Howard
Proofreader:	Colleen Toporek
Page Viewers:	Mandarin, the fam, and Preston

Printing History:

March 2010: First Edition.

Mandarin

The fam

Preston

RepKover™ This book uses RepKover™, a durable and flexible lay-flat binding.

ISBN: 978-0-596-80769-6

Author of Head First Excel

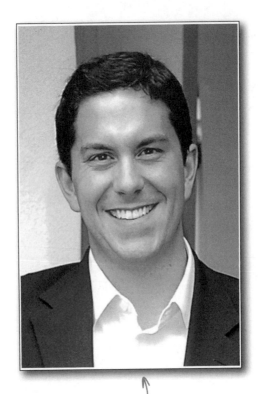

Michael Milton

When **Michael Milton**'s friends were programming in BASIC and playing Leisure Suit Larry back in the 80s, he was creating charts in SuperCalc.

His career has consisted mainly of helping people out by showing up with the right spreadsheet at the right moment, and he hopes that after reading *Head First Excel,* you'll have the same experience.

When he's not in the library or the bookstore, you can find him running, taking pictures, brewing beer, or blogging at michaelmilton.net.

Table of Contents (Summary)

Table of Contents (the real thing)

Intro

Your brain on Excel. Here *you* are trying to *learn* something, while here your *brain* is doing you a favor by making sure the learning doesn't *stick*. Your brain's thinking, "Better leave room for more important things, like which wild animals to avoid and whether naked snowboarding is a bad idea." So how *do* you trick your brain into thinking that your life depends on knowing spreadsheets?

Introduction to formulas

Excel's real power

We all use Excel to keep lists.

And when it comes to lists, Excel does a great job. But the real Excel ninjas are people who have mastered the world of formulas. Using data well is all about executing the **calculations** that will tell you what you need to know, and **formulas** do those calculations, molding your data into something useful and illuminating. If you know your formulas, you can really make your numbers *sing*.

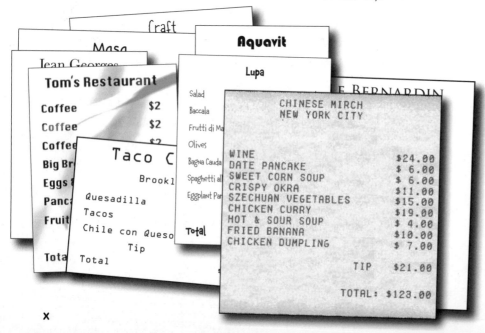

visual design

Spreadsheets as art

2

Most people usually use Excel for page layout.

A lot of formula-writing masters, who are familiar with just how powerful Excel can be, are shocked that people "just" use the software for showing information with a grid. But Excel, especially in its more recent versions, has become quite handy as a page layout tool. You're about to get comfortable with some important and not-so-obvious Excel tools for serious visual design.

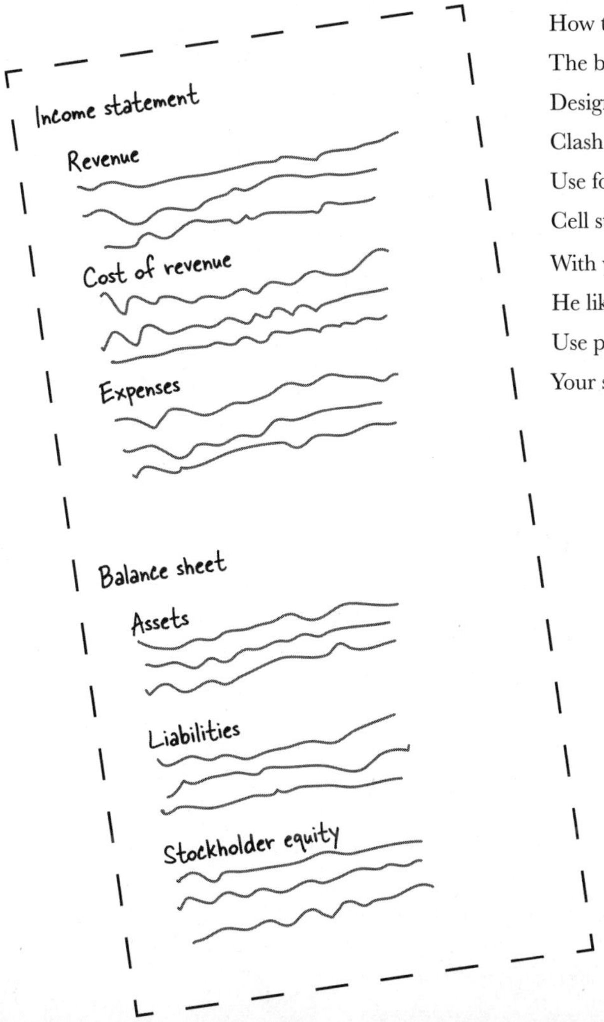

Income statement

Revenue

Cost of revenue

Expenses

Balance sheet

Assets

Liabilities

Stockholder equity

references

Point in the right direction

A formula is only as good as its references.

No matter how creative and brilliant your formula is, it won't do you much good if it does not point to the correct data. It's easy to get references right for short, individual formulas, but once those formulas get long and need to be copied, the chance of reference mistakes increases dramatically. In this chapter, you'll exploit **absolute and relative references** as well as Excel's advanced new **structured reference** feature, ensuring that no matter how big and numerous your references are, your formulas will stay tight and accurate.

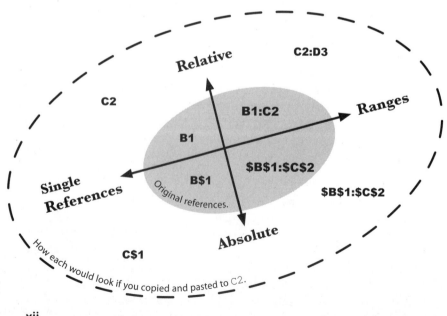

change your point of view

Sort, zoom, and filter

4

The details of your data are tantalizing.

But only if you know *how* to look at them. In this chapter, you'll forget about formatting and functions and just focus on how to change your perspective on your data. When you are exploring your data, looking for issues to investigate, the **sort, zoom, and filter** tools offer surprising versatility to help you get a grip on what your data contains.

Sort by donation

E	F	G
ZIP	Donation	
10012	$ 50,000	
10012	$ 10,000	
20817	$ 10,000	
06511	$ 10,000	
78723	$ 10,000	
34234	$ 10,000	
06511	$ 5,000	
20817	$ 5,000	
10012	$ 5,000	
10012	$ 5,000	
90210	$ 5,000	
10012	$ 5,000	
10012	$ 5,000	
06511	$ 5,000	
20817	$ 5,000	
90210	$ 5,000	
34234	$ 5,000	
90210	$ 5,000	
10012	$ 5,000	
10012	$ 5,000	
10012	$ 5,000	
78723	$ 5,000	
10012	$ 5,000	
06511	$ 5,000	
10012	$ 5,000	
10012	$ 5,000	
10012	$ 5,000	

Sort by ZIP

D	E	F
t Name	ZIP	Donation
/a	06511	$ 10,000
by	06511	$ 5,000
n	06511	$ 5,000
ey	06511	$ 5,000
son	06511	$ 3,000
na	06511	$ 3,000
ob	06511	$ 2,500
oine	06511	$ 2,500
lee	06511	$ 2,500
lisyn	06511	$ 2,500
rad	06511	$ 2,500
an	06511	$ 2,000
o	06511	$ 2,000
in	06511	$ 1,000
lyah	06511	$ 1,000
ie	06511	$ 1,000
	06511	$ 1,000
	06511	$ 1,000
as	06511	$ 1,000
y	06511	$ 1,000
ur	06511	$ 1,000
nael	06511	$ 1,000
juin	06511	$ 1,000
son	06511	$ 1,000
	06511	$ 1,000
lynn	06511	$ 1,000
	06511	$ 750

Sort by name

C	D
Last Name	First Name
Abbott	Corinne
Abbott	Ingrid
Abbott	Kaylie
Abbott	Rashad
Acevedo	Aima
Acevedo	Dante
Acevedo	Jeremiah
Acevedo	Natalie
Acosta	Alan
Acosta	Dayami
Acosta	Jaylin
Adams	Diamond
Adams	Hana
Adams	Jayce
Adams	Jaylan
Adams	Lewis
Adkins	Alvin
Adkins	Braxton
Adkins	Coby
Adkins	Danny
Adkins	Hanna
Aguilar	Dax
Aguilar	Isabelle
Aguilar	Mary
Aguilar	Meghan
Aguilar	Owen
Aguirre	Carlo
Aguirre	Sergio
Aguirre	Sloane

5

data types

Make Excel value your values

Excel doesn't always show you what it's thinking.

Sometimes, Excel will show you a number but think of it as text. Or it might show you some text that it sees as a number. Excel will even show you data that is neither number nor text! In this chapter, you're going to **learn how to see data the way Excel sees it**, no matter how it's displayed. Not only will this knowledge give you greater control over your data (and fewer "What the #$%! is going on?" experiences), but it will also help you unlock the whole universe of formulas.

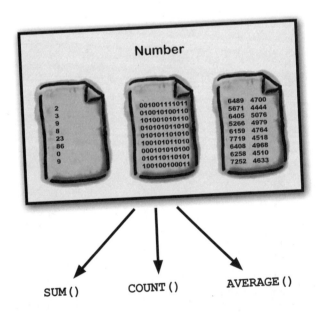

dates and times

Stay on time

Dates and times in Excel are hard.

Unless you understand *how Excel represents them* internally. All of us at one point or another have had to do calculations involving these types of figures, and this chapter will give you the **keys to figuring out** how many days, months, years, and even seconds there are between two dates. The simple truth is that dates and times are a really **special case** of the data types and formatting that you already know. Once you master a couple of basic concepts, you'll be able to use Excel to *manage scheduling flawlessly*.

6

You give the formula your text.

=VALUE(**A4**)

Excel reads the text value and sees that it's really a number

Jun 12, 2010

The formula returns a number.

40341

finding functions

7

Mine Excel's features on your own

Excel has more functions than you will ever use.

Over many years and many versions, the program has accumulated specialized functions that are terribly important to the small group of people who use them. That's not a problem for you. But what *is* a problem for you is the group of functions **that you don't know** but that **are useful in your work**. Which functions are we talking about? Only you can know for sure, and you're about to learn some tips and techniques to finding quickly the formulas you need to get your work done efficiently.

Excellent!

8

formula auditing
Visualize your formulas

Excel formulas can get really complicated.

And that is the point, right? If all you wanted to do was simple calculation, you'd be fine with a paper, pen, and calculator. But those complicated formulas can get unwieldy—especially ones written by other people, which can be almost impossible to decipher if you don't know what they were thinking. In this chapter, you'll learn to use a simple but powerful graphical feature of Excel called **formula auditing**, which will dramatically illustrate the flow of data throughout the *models* in your spreadsheet.

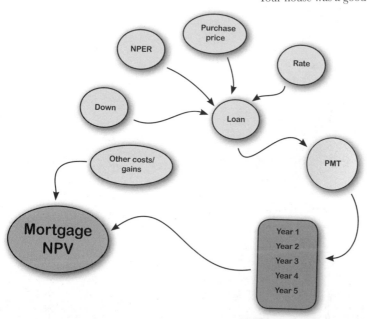

charts

Graph your data

9

Who wants to look at numbers all the time?

Very often a nice graphic is a more engaging way to present data. And sometimes you have so much data that you actually can't see it all without a nice graphic. Excel has extensive charting facilities, and if you just know where to click, you'll unlock the power to make charts and graphs to display your data with drama and lucidity.

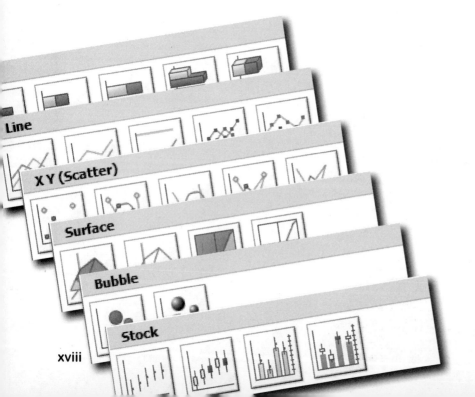

Line

X Y (Scatter)

Surface

Bubble

Stock

what if analysis

Alternate realities

10

Things could go many different ways.

There are all sorts of *quantitative factors* that can affect how your business will work, how your finances will fare, how your schedule will manage, and so forth. Excel excels at helping you model and manage all your *projections*, evaluating how changes in those factors will affect the variables you care about most. In this chapter, you'll learn about three key features—**scenarios**, **Goal Seek**, and **Solver**—that are designed to make assessing all your "what ifs" a breeze.

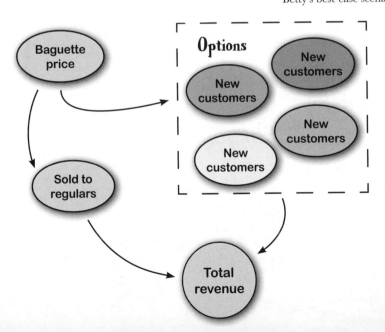

text functions

Letters as data

Excel loves your numbers, but it can also handle your text.

It contains a suite of functions designed to enable you to manipulate **text data**. There are many applications to these functions, but one that all data people must deal with is what to do with *messy* data. A lot of times, you'll receive data that isn't at all in the format you need it to be in—it might come out of a strange database, for example. Text functions shine at letting you pull elements out of messy data so that you can make analytic use of it, as you're about to find out....

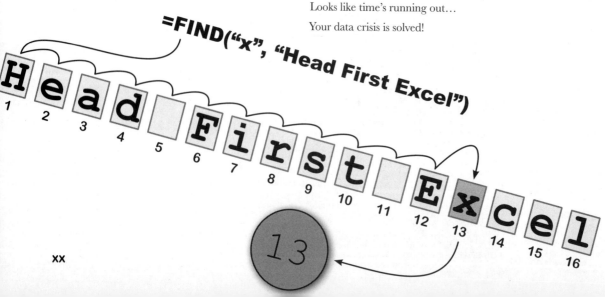

=FIND("x", "Head First Excel")

H e a d   F i r s t   E x c e l
1 2 3 4 5 6 7 8 9 10 11 12 13 14 15 16

13

pivot tables
Hardcore grouping

12

Pivot tables are among Excel's most powerful features.

But what are they? And why should we care? For Excel newbies, pivot tables can also be among Excel's most *intimidating* features. But their purpose is quite simple: **to group data quickly** so that you can analyze it. And as you're about to see, grouping and summarizing data using pivot tables is ***much faster*** than creating the same groupings using formulas alone. By the time you finish this chapter, you'll be slicing and dicing your data in Excel faster than you'd ever thought possible.

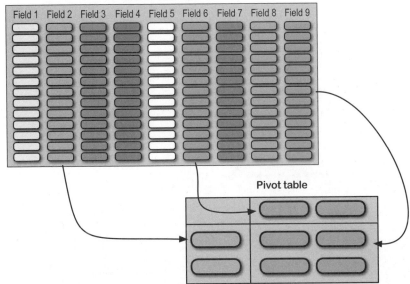

Lots of raw data

Field 1 Field 2 Field 3 Field 4 Field 5 Field 6 Field 7 Field 8 Field 9

Pivot table

booleans

13 TRUE and FALSE

There's a deceptively simple data type available in Excel.

They're called **Boolean values**, and they're just plain ol' TRUE and FALSE. You might think that they are too basic and elementary to be useful in serious data analysis, but nothing could be further from the truth. In this chapter, you'll plug Boolean values into **logical formulas** to do a variety of tasks, from cleaning up data to making whole new data points.

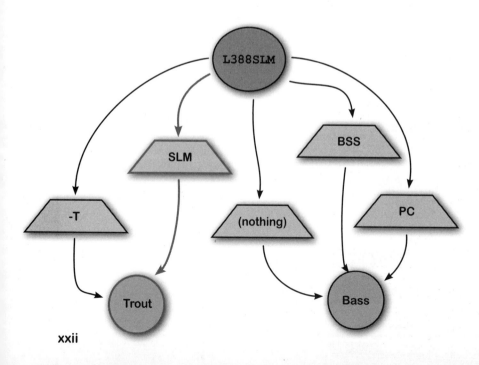

segmentation

Slice and dice

Get creative with your tools.

You've developed a formidable knowledge of Excel in the past 13 chapters, and by now you know (or know how to find) most of the tools that fit your data problems. But what if your problems *don't fit those tools*? What if you don't even have the data you need all in one place, or your data is divided into categories that don't fit your analytical objectives? In this final chapter, you'll use **lookup functions** along with some of the tools you already know to slice new **segments** out of your data and get really creative with Excel's tools.

14

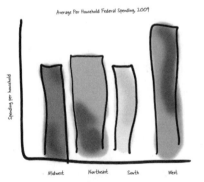

Average Per Household Federal Spending, 2009

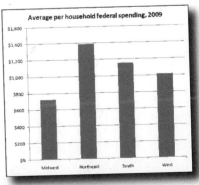

leftovers
The Top Ten Things (we didn't cover)

You've come a long way.

But Excel is a complicated program, and there's so much left to learn. In this appendix, we'll go over 10 items that there wasn't enough room to cover in this book, but should be high on your list of topics to learn about next.

install excel's solver
The Solver

Some of the best features of Excel aren't installed by default.

That's right, in order to run the optimization from Chapter 10, you need to activate the **Solver**, an add-in that is included in Excel by default but not activated without your initiative.

Intro

In this section we answer the burning question:
"So why DID they put that in an Excel book?"

Who is this book for?

If you can answer "yes" to all of these:

1 Have you never used Excel at all, or used it a little but never done anything powerful with it?

2 Do you have **basic** software skills like opening and closing files, and copying and pasting text?

3 Do you prefer stimulating dinner party conversation to dry, dull, academic lectures?

this book is for you.

Who should probably back away from this book?

If you can answer "yes" to any of these:

1 Have you already learned most of Excel's functions but need a solid reference?

2 Are you looking to do higher-level programming in Excel with macros and Visual Basic for Applications?

3 Are you afraid to try something different? Would you rather have a root canal than mix stripes with plaid? Do you believe that a technical book can't be serious if it anthropomorphizes Boolean functions and pivot tables?

this book is **not** for you.

[Note from marketing: this book is for anyone with a credit card.]

We know what you're thinking

"How can *this* be a serious Excel book?"

"What's with all the graphics?"

"Can I actually *learn* it this way?"

We know what your *brain* is thinking

Your brain craves novelty. It's always searching, scanning, *waiting* for something unusual. It was built that way, and it helps you stay alive.

So what does your brain do with all the routine, ordinary, normal things you encounter? Everything it *can* to stop them from interfering with the brain's *real* job—recording things that *matter*. It doesn't bother saving the boring things; they never make it past the "this is obviously not important" filter.

How does your brain *know* what's important? Suppose you're out for a day hike and a tiger jumps in front of you, what happens inside your head and body?

Neurons fire. Emotions crank up. *Chemicals surge.*

And that's how your brain knows…

This must be important! Don't forget it!

But imagine you're at home, or in a library. It's a safe, warm, tiger-free zone. You're studying. Getting ready for an exam. Or trying to learn some tough technical topic your boss thinks will take a week, 10 days at the most.

Just one problem. Your brain's trying to do you a big favor. It's trying to make sure that this *obviously* non-important content doesn't clutter up scarce resources. Resources that are better spent storing the really *big* things. Like tigers. Like the danger of fire. Like how you should never have posted those "party" photos on your Facebook page. And there's no simple way to tell your brain, "Hey brain, thank you very much, but no matter how dull this book is, and how little I'm registering on the emotional Richter scale right now, I really *do* want you to keep this stuff around."

Your brain thinks THIS is important.

Great. Only 400 more dull, dry, boring pages.

Your brain thinks THIS isn't worth saving.

We think of a "Head First" reader as a <u>learner</u>.

So what does it take to *learn* something? First, you have to *get* it, then make sure you don't *forget* it. It's not about pushing facts into your head. Based on the latest research in cognitive science, neurobiology, and educational psychology, *learning* takes a lot more than text on a page. We know what turns your brain on.

Some of the Head First learning principles:

Make it visual. Images are far more memorable than words alone, and make learning much more effective (up to 89% improvement in recall and transfer studies). It also makes things more understandable. **Put the words within or near the graphics** they relate to, rather than on the bottom or on another page, and learners will be up to *twice* as likely to solve problems related to the content.

Use a conversational and personalized style. In recent studies, students performed up to 40% better on post-learning tests if the content spoke directly to the reader, using a first-person, conversational style rather than taking a formal tone. Tell stories instead of lecturing. Use casual language. Don't take yourself too seriously. Which would *you* pay more attention to: a stimulating dinner party companion, or a lecture?

Get the learner to think more deeply. In other words, unless you actively flex your neurons, nothing much happens in your head. A reader has to be motivated, engaged, curious, and inspired to solve problems, draw conclusions, and generate new knowledge. And for that, you need challenges, exercises, and thought-provoking questions, and activities that involve both sides of the brain and multiple senses.

Get—and keep—the reader's attention. We've all had the "I really want to learn this but I can't stay awake past page one" experience. Your brain pays attention to things that are out of the ordinary, interesting, strange, eye-catching, unexpected. Learning a new, tough, technical topic doesn't have to be boring. Your brain will learn much more quickly if it's not.

Touch their emotions. We now know that your ability to remember something is largely dependent on its emotional content. You remember what you care about. You remember when you *feel* something. No, we're not talking heart-wrenching stories about a boy and his dog. We're talking emotions like surprise, curiosity, fun, "what the…?", and the feeling of "I Rule!" that comes when you solve a puzzle, learn something everybody else thinks is hard, or realize you know something that "I'm more technical than thou" Bob from engineering *doesn't*.

Metacognition: thinking about thinking

If you really want to learn, and you want to learn more quickly and more deeply, pay attention to how you pay attention. Think about how you think. Learn how you learn.

Most of us did not take courses on metacognition or learning theory when we were growing up. We were *expected* to learn, but rarely *taught* to learn.

But we assume that if you're holding this book, you really want to learn about Excel. And you probably don't want to spend a lot of time. If you want to use what you read in this book, you need to *remember* what you read. And for that, you've got to *understand* it. To get the most from this book, or *any* book or learning experience, take responsibility for your brain. Your brain on *this* content.

The trick is to get your brain to see the new material you're learning as Really Important. Crucial to your well-being. As important as a tiger. Otherwise, you're in for a constant battle, with your brain doing its best to keep the new content from sticking.

I wonder how I can trick my brain into remembering this stuff....

So just how *DO* you get your brain to treat Excel like it was a hungry tiger?

There's the slow, tedious way, or the faster, more effective way. The slow way is about sheer repetition. You obviously know that you *are* able to learn and remember even the dullest of topics if you keep pounding the same thing into your brain. With enough repetition, your brain says, "This doesn't *feel* important to him, but he keeps looking at the same thing *over* and *over* and *over*, so I suppose it must be."

The faster way is to do **anything that increases brain activity,** especially different *types* of brain activity. The things on the previous page are a big part of the solution, and they're all things that have been proven to help your brain work in your favor. For example, studies show that putting words *within* the pictures they describe (as opposed to somewhere else on the page, like a caption or in the body text) causes your brain to try to make sense of how the words and picture relate, and this causes more neurons to fire. More neurons firing = more chances for your brain to *get* that this is something worth paying attention to, and possibly recording.

A conversational style helps because people tend to pay more attention when they perceive that they're in a conversation, since they're expected to follow along and hold up their end. The amazing thing is, your brain doesn't necessarily *care* that the "conversation" is between you and a book! On the other hand, if the writing style is formal and dry, your brain perceives it the same way you experience being lectured to while sitting in a roomful of passive attendees. No need to stay awake.

But pictures and conversational style are just the beginning....

Here's what WE did:

We used ***pictures***, because your brain is tuned for visuals, not text. As far as your brain's concerned, a picture really *is* worth a thousand words. And when text and pictures work together, we embedded the text *in* the pictures because your brain works more effectively when the text is *within* the thing the text refers to, as opposed to in a caption or buried in the text somewhere.

We used ***redundancy***, saying the same thing in *different* ways and with different media types, and *multiple senses*, to increase the chance that the content gets coded into more than one area of your brain.

We used concepts and pictures in ***unexpected*** ways because your brain is tuned for novelty, and we used pictures and ideas with at least *some **emotional*** *content*, because your brain is tuned to pay attention to the biochemistry of emotions. That which causes you to *feel* something is more likely to be remembered, even if that feeling is nothing more than a little ***humor***, ***surprise***, or ***interest***.

We used a personalized, ***conversational style***, because your brain is tuned to pay more attention when it believes you're in a conversation than if it thinks you're passively listening to a presentation. Your brain does this even when you're *reading*.

We included more than 80 ***activities***, because your brain is tuned to learn and remember more when you ***do*** things than when you *read* about things. And we made the exercises challenging-yet-do-able, because that's what most people prefer.

We used ***multiple learning styles***, because *you* might prefer step-by-step procedures, while someone else wants to understand the big picture first, and someone else just wants to see an example. But regardless of your own learning preference, *everyone* benefits from seeing the same content represented in multiple ways.

We include content for ***both sides of your brain***, because the more of your brain you engage, the more likely you are to learn and remember, and the longer you can stay focused. Since working one side of the brain often means giving the other side a chance to rest, you can be more productive at learning for a longer period of time.

And we included ***stories*** and exercises that present ***more than one point of view***, because your brain is tuned to learn more deeply when it's forced to make evaluations and judgments.

We included ***challenges***, with exercises, and by asking ***questions*** that don't always have a straight answer, because your brain is tuned to learn and remember when it has to *work* at something. Think about it—you can't get your *body* in shape just by *watching* people at the gym. But we did our best to make sure that when you're working hard, it's on the *right* things. That ***you're not spending one extra dendrite*** processing a hard-to-understand example, or parsing difficult, jargon-laden, or overly terse text.

We used ***people***. In stories, examples, pictures, etc., because, well, because *you're* a person. And your brain pays more attention to *people* than it does to *things*.

Here's what YOU can do to bend your brain into submission

So, we did our part. The rest is up to you. These tips are a starting point; listen to your brain and figure out what works for you and what doesn't. Try new things.

Cut this out and stick it on your refrigerator.

---

1 **Slow down. The more you understand, the less you have to memorize.**

Don't just *read*. Stop and think. When the book asks you a question, don't just skip to the answer. Imagine that someone really *is* asking the question. The more deeply you force your brain to think, the better chance you have of learning and remembering.

2 **Do the exercises. Write your own notes.**

We put them in, but if we did them for you, that would be like having someone else do your workouts for you. And don't just *look* at the exercises. **Use a pencil.** There's plenty of evidence that physical activity *while* learning can increase the learning.

3 **Read the "There are No Dumb Questions."**

That means all of them. They're not optional sidebars, *they're part of the core content!* Don't skip them.

4 **Make this the last thing you read before bed. Or at least the last challenging thing.**

Part of the learning (especially the transfer to long-term memory) happens *after* you put the book down. Your brain needs time on its own, to do more processing. If you put in something new during that processing time, some of what you just learned will be lost.

5 **Talk about it. Out loud.**

Speaking activates a different part of the brain. If you're trying to understand something, or increase your chance of remembering it later, say it out loud. Better still, try to explain it out loud to someone else. You'll learn more quickly, and you might uncover ideas you hadn't known were there when you were reading about it.

6 **Drink water. Lots of it.**

Your brain works best in a nice bath of fluid. Dehydration (which can happen before you ever feel thirsty) decreases cognitive function.

7 **Listen to your brain.**

Pay attention to whether your brain is getting overloaded. If you find yourself starting to skim the surface or forget what you just read, it's time for a break. Once you go past a certain point, you won't learn faster by trying to shove more in, and you might even hurt the process.

8 **Feel something.**

Your brain needs to know that this *matters*. Get involved with the stories. Make up your own captions for the photos. Groaning over a bad joke is *still* better than feeling nothing at all.

9 **Get your hands dirty!**

There's only one way to learn about Excel: get your hands dirty. And that's what you're going to do throughout this book. Excel is a skill, and the only way to get good at it is to practice. We're going to give you a lot of practice: every chapter has exercises that pose a problem for you to solve. Don't just skip over them—a lot of the learning happens when you solve the exercises. We included a solution to each exercise—don't be afraid to peek at the solution if you get stuck! (It's easy to get snagged on something small.) But try to solve the problem before you look at the solution. And definitely get it working before you move on to the next part of the book.

Read Me

This is a learning experience, not a reference book. We deliberately stripped out everything that might get in the way of learning whatever it is we're working on at that point in the book. And the first time through, you need to begin at the beginning, because the book makes assumptions about what you've already seen and learned.

Excel mastery is about rocking out with formulas.

A lot of books on Excel are little more than fancy restatements of the Help files that give as much weight to formulas as they do to all of Excel's other features. The thing is, the people who are the most skillful users of Excel are the ones who really, really know formulas. So this book was written to have you constantly using and learning new functions to make your formulas powerful.

This book uses Excel 2007 for Windows, but you can use other versions of Excel.

Excel 2007 for Windows was notable for its major user interface redesign, but it also included features like **structured references** that are really useful. So useful, in fact, that some of those features made it into *Head First Excel*, even though not everyone has upgraded yet. But even if you haven't upgraded, don't sweat it: you can just skip over those sections and not have too much trouble, because…

Most of the important stuff you need to know about Excel has been in the software for years.

There are some formulas and features that are new to Excel 2007 and 2010, but the basics of formulas are old school. So don't sweat it if you're not ready to drop the cash to upgrade (although you should eventually).

Excel 2008 for Mac doesn't have all the features of Excel 2007 for Windows.

You'd think that the 2008 software would have everything the 2007 software has and more, right? Well, not really. While **Excel 2008 for Mac** came out after Excel 2007 for Windows, there's still spotty support for some of the new Excel 2007 features. It'll all get ironed out in future versions of Excel for Mac, we're sure!

You can download data in both .xlsx and .xls format.

In this book there are a lot of situations where you'll need to download data in order to do the exercise. Suppose you're using an early version of Excel that doesn't read the newer **.xlsx** file format that's used most frequently in *Head First Excel*. It's no problem: just download the file using the **.xls** extension. Both versions of the files are on the O'Reilly website, but remember that a lot of the newer Excel features will be absent from the .xls versions.

The activities are NOT optional.

The exercises and activities are not add-ons; they're part of the core content of the book. Some of them are to help with memory, some are for understanding, and some will help you apply what you've learned. ***Don't skip the exercises.*** The crossword puzzles are the only thing you don't *have* to do, but they're good for giving your brain a chance to think about the words and terms you've been learning in a different context.

The redundancy is intentional and important.

One distinct difference in a Head First book is that we want you to *really* get it. And we want you to finish the book remembering what you've learned. Most reference books don't have retention and recall as a goal, but this book is about *learning*, so you'll see some of the same concepts come up more than once.

The book doesn't end here.

We love it when you can find fun and useful extra stuff on book companion sites. You'll find extra stuff on networking at the following URL:
http://www.headfirstlabs.com/books/hfexcel/

The Brain Power exercises don't have answers.

For some of them, there is no right answer, and for others, part of the learning experience of the Brain Power activities is for you to decide if and when your answers are right. In some of the Brain Power exercises, you will find hints to point you in the right direction.

The technical review team

Bill Mietelski

Tony Rose

Ken Bluttman

Technical reviewers:

Bill Mietelski is a software engineer and a three-time Head First technical reviewer. He can't wait to run a data analysis on his golf stats to help him win on the links.

Anthony Rose has been working in the data analysis field for nearly 10 years and is currently the president of Support Analytics, a data analysis and visualization consultancy. Anthony has an MBA concentrated in management and a finance degree, which is where his passion for data and analysis started. When he isn't working, he can normally be found on the golf course in Columbia, Maryland, lost in a good book, savoring a delightful wine, or simply enjoying time with his young girls and amazing wife.

Ken Bluttman is the author of over a dozen computer and other nonfiction titles. His "other career" is working as a web developer. Visit Ken at *www.kenbluttman.com*.

Acknowledgments

My editor:

Brian Sawyer edited *Head First Excel* and is a creative, generous, and fun guy to work with. This book and *Head First Data Analysis* benefited immeasurably from his input and guidance. Thank you for all that you do, Brian.

The O'Reilly Team:

Brett McLaughlin's vision and input have left an indelible mark on the Head First series and on my writing. His work is much appreciated. **Karen Shaner** provided logistical support for this book, most of which was invisible to me but all of which is greatly appreciated. **Roger Magoulas** provided some useful advice, along with the data set that was excerpted in Chapter 14.

The **technical review team** was a tremendous help. I am very grateful that this book has the endorsement of these supportive experts.

My family:

A very special thank you goes to my father, also known as **Michael Milton**, who introduced me to spreadsheets. He and I have passed spreadsheets back and forth over the years and have enjoyed learning Excel together.

My wife, **Julia**, is a tolerant person who has supported me through two (!) Head First books and has listened to more speeches about data analysis than any spouse should have to. Thank you, Julia.

Also indispensable has been the support of the rest of my family, **Elizabeth**, **Sara**, **Gary**, and **Marie**. Thank you all!

Brian Sawyer

Mike Sr.

Julia Burch

Safari® Books Online

 Safari Books Online is an on-demand digital library that lets you easily search over 7,500 technology and creative reference books and videos to find the answers you need quickly.

With a subscription, you can read any page and watch any video from our library online. Read books on your cell phone and mobile devices. Access new titles before they are available for print, and get exclusive access to manuscripts in development and post feedback for the authors. Copy and paste code samples, organize your favorites, download chapters, bookmark key sections, create notes, print out pages, and benefit from tons of other time-saving features.

O'Reilly Media has uploaded this book to the Safari Books Online service. To have full digital access to this book and others on similar topics from O'Reilly and other publishers, sign up for free at *http://my.safaribooksonline.com/?portal=oreilly*.

1 introduction to formulas

Excel's real power

As soon as I get out of here, I'm totally going to get a computer to solve this sort of problem.

We all use Excel to keep lists.

And when it comes to lists, Excel does a great job. But the real Excel ninjas are people who have mastered the world of formulas. Using data well is all about executing the **calculations** that will tell you what you need to know, and **formulas** do those calculations, molding your data into something useful and illuminating. If you know your formulas, you can really make your numbers *sing*.

Can you live it up on the last night of your vacation?

It's your last night in New York City on a vacation you've taken with your friends Bob and Sasha. You've had a great time and really enjoyed the city.

But you've also spent plenty of money, and now the three of you want to see if you have enough left to go to a nice restaurant on your last night.

We'd better straighten out our finances.

Finances? I hope one of you has been keeping track.

Sasha

Bob

Here's what you budgeted and what you spent

You've been handling expenses by having only one of you pay at a time. Instead of splitting up every check at every restaurant, you all figured you'd settle up later.

Now you need to settle up and decide whether you have any more money left in your **budget** for a big meal.

This is how much you decided you wanted to spend on food.

Your NYC food budget:

$400

I spent $61. Can we keep better records this time?

I spent $296.

Sharpen your pencil

1 What approach would you take to splitting up your expenses?

....

....

....

2 How would you record your calculations?

....

....

....

Sharpen your pencil
Solution

1 What approach would you take to splitting up your expenses?

You could go through each check and try to split them all up, but that would be

kind of a pain. An easier approach would be just to divide everyone's bill by three.

That way you have a good estimate of each person's share of each bill.

Here are some basic approaches... your answers might be different.

2 How would you record your calculations?

Why not try using Excel? You could do it with paper or in an email, but since you

probably want Excel to do calculations for you anyway, you can also use Excel to

keep a record.

Excel is great for keeping records...

You can keep track of this sort of stuff forever using Excel spreadsheets.

People often use Excel to keep permanent records of their data. The program is a great way to take a snapshot of your data and thinking at a certain point in time.

With your budgeting calculations set up in an Excel spreadsheet, you'll be able to show your friends exactly how you came to your conclusions about how you should split up the expenses.

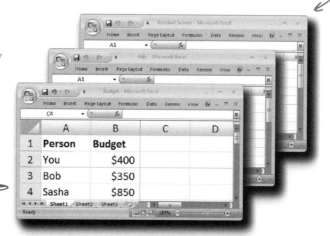

	A	B	C	D
1	**Person**	**Budget**		
2	You	$400		
3	Bob	$350		
4	Sasha	$850		

You never know when you'll need to go back and check your stats.

...but Excel is at its most powerful when you use it to crunch numbers.

Formulas work with your data

To add up and divide what you spent, you use **formulas**.

Say you want to **add together** the totals from the two bills on the right. Here's the formula you'd use.

Here are two of your restaurant bills.

This is a formula.

= 66 + 116

The plus is for addition.

Here are your bills.

The equals sign tells Excel to expect a formula.

Excel has a large variety of formulas you can use to make calculations, from basic addition to highly specialized engineering and statistical tools.

Tom's Restaurant

Coffee	$2
Coffee	$2
Coffee	$2
Big Breakfast	$14
Eggs & Bacon	$15
Pancakes	$13
Fruit cup	$6
Tip	$12
Total	**($66)**

Lupa

Salad	$7
Baccala	$20
Frutti di Mare	$19
Olives	$6
Bagna Cauda	$20
Spaghetti alla Carbonara	$15
Eggplant Parm	$8
Tip	$21
Total	**$116**

EXERCISE

Open Excel and write the formula that adds up the total you all spent together. Remember, Bob spent $61 and Sasha spent $296. *You* spent $332.

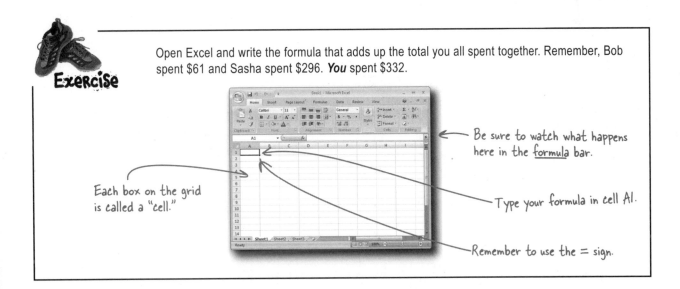

Be sure to watch what happens here in the <u>formula</u> bar.

Each box on the grid is called a "cell."

Type your formula in cell A1.

Remember to use the = sign.

Exercise Solution

You just typed a formula to calculate how much you and your friends spent in total. What did you find?

What Sasha spent

What Bob spent

What you spent

You aren't limited to adding two numbers; you can add as many numbers as you like.

When you type the formula, you can see the output both inside this cell and inside the formula bar.

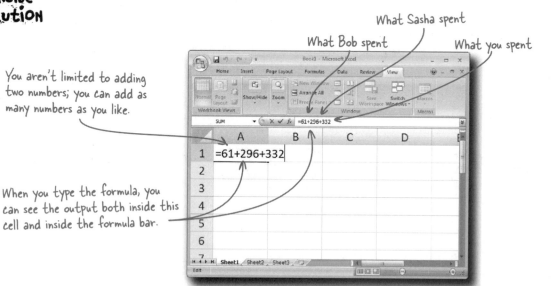

When you press Return, cell A1 shows the calculated answer...

...but if you highlight cell A1 again, the formula bar shows the formula you wrote.

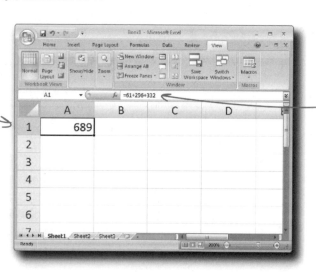

Now you just need to split up the grand total among the three of you.

And that means dividing the $689 total you spent by three. What symbol will you use to make this calculation?

WHO DOES WHAT?

Match each operation on the left with the formulas that implement the operation on the right.

Addition ——————————→ **= 66 + 116**

Subtraction **= 332 / 2**

Division **= 400 * 10**

Multiplication **= 400 – 400 * 0.2**

Exercise

Write the formula to split up the total you spent ($689) among the three of you.

Put your formula here.

	A	B	C	D	
1	689				
2					
3					
4					
5					
6					
7					

Have you spent less than your budget?

....

....

WHO DOES WHAT? SOLUTION

Match each operation on the left with the formulas that implement the operation on the right.

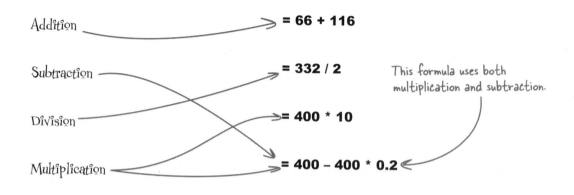

Addition

Subtraction

Division

Multiplication

= 66 + 116

= 332 / 2

= 400 * 10

= 400 – 400 * 0.2

This formula uses both multiplication and subtraction.

EXERCISE SOLUTION

You wrote a formula to calculate $689 split three ways. What value did Excel return?

Here's the formula.

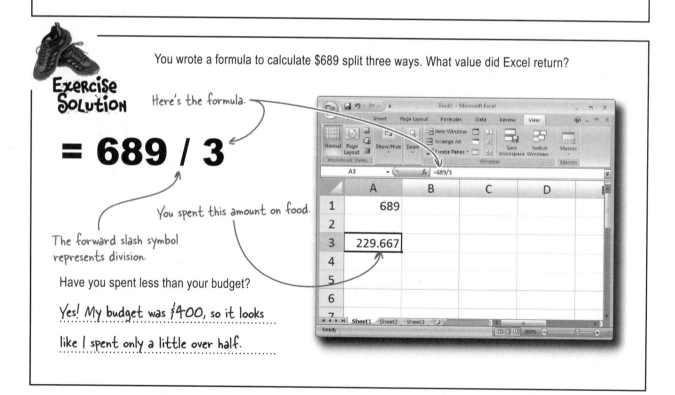

= 689 / 3

You spent this amount on food.

The forward slash symbol represents division.

Have you spent less than your budget?

Yes! My budget was $400, so it looks like I spent only a little over half.

Looks like Bob forgot a receipt...

I left a receipt in the bottom of one of my shopping bags. I have so many receipts...ugh! Do you mind running those numbers again? Maybe we should just give you all the receipts.

Nice, Bob. It looked like we had everything figured out, but now that he left out something from his total, we're going to have to go back and fix our numbers.

Maybe he's right: instead of getting totals from Bob and Sasha, we should just take a look at all the receipts. The total you find might be more accurate that way. On the other hand, that could be even *more* work....

Your friends sent you all the receipts

Bob and Sasha sent you all their receipts. Combined with your own receipts, the final list looks like this.

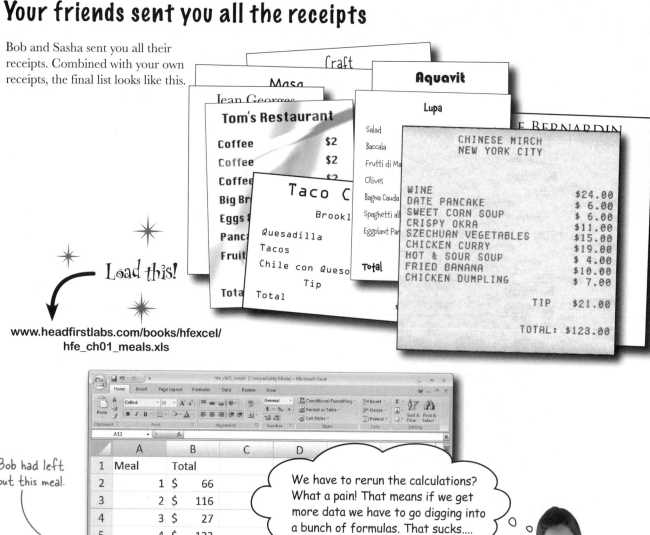

Löad this!

www.headfirstlabs.com/books/hfexcel/
hfe_ch01_meals.xls

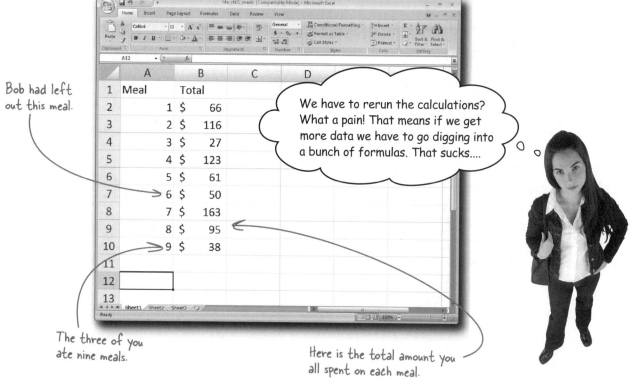

Bob had left out this meal.

The three of you ate nine meals.

We have to rerun the calculations? What a pain! That means if we get more data we have to go digging into a bunch of formulas. That sucks....

Here is the total amount you all spent on each meal.

References keep your formulas working even if your data changes

You don't have to write your formula like this:

This formula just keeps going....

=66+116+27+123+61+50

This formula is hard to read, and even more importantly, it's hard to change if a data point turns out to be wrong.

Instead of writing a long string of numbers like this, you can use **references**. References are a shorthand that Excel uses to look for values. For example, if you tell Excel to look at the reference B2, it will return the value 66, because that's what it finds at B2.

The reference for the value of the first bill is B2.

	A	B
	Meal	Total
1		
2	1	$ 66
3	2	$ 116
4	3	$ 27
5	4	$ 123
6	5	$ 61
7	6	$ 50
8	7	$ 163
9	8	$ 95
10	9	$ 38
11		

Exercise

Write the formulas you use in the blanks.

Write the formula that adds your bills together using references.

....

Then write a formula to split that value three ways.

....

Write a formula to determine whether you are still under budget and, if so, by how much.

....

....

Exercise Solution

Write the formula that adds your bills together using references.

=B2+B3+B4+B5+B6+B7+B8+B9+B10

This expression calculates the <u>corrected</u> total amount you spent, which is $739.

Did you notice how the colors in your references conveniently match the colors in column B?

Then write a formula to split that value three ways.

=E3/3

This formula takes the value you just calculated and divides it by three.

Your actual references might be different, depending on where you decided to put your formulas.

Be sure to create text labels for your formulas, so you know what they mean when you look at them later!

Write a formula to determine whether you are still under budget and, if so, by how much.

=400-E5

I'm still under my budget of $400.

This is what you have left to spend.

Um, excuse me. I'm trying to learn a little Excel myself, so I've been running the numbers along with you. And there is a problem: I didn't get $246.33!

Sasha

Sasha came up with her own formula, but when she ran it she got a different answer from yours. Here's her formula:

=(B2+B3+B4+B5+B6+B7+B9+B10)/3

And here's the answer she received from it.

$192

✏ **Sharpen your pencil**

How is Sasha's formula different from your formulas? Why do you think she got a different answer?

....

....

....

....

Sharpen your pencil
Solution

Sasha wrote a different formula from you and came up with a different answer. How do you account for the difference?

Hers is different because, instead of separating the operations into formulas, she tried to add the bills together and then split them into three in the same formula. And it looks like her formula would have worked, except that she forgot to add cell B8 to the mix.

Check your formulas carefully

One really important skill for Excel users is the ability to go back and look carefully at formulas that have been already written. Formulas might look complex and long, but that doesn't mean that they're **correct**.

Be patient when you look at formulas and pay close attention to their references. One small mistake will usually create a false result.

Here is a corrected version of Sasha's formula.

$$=(B2+B3+B4+B5+B6+B7+B8+B9+B10)/3$$

This formula's result matches yours.

If there is a mistake in the formula, everything will turn out wrong!

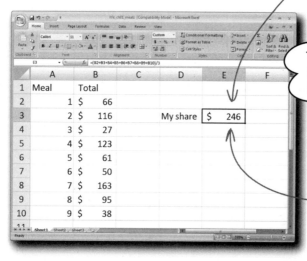

	A	B	C	D	E	F
1	Meal	Total				
2	1	$ 66				
3	2	$ 116		My share	$ 246	
4	3	$ 27				
5	4	$ 123				
6	5	$ 61				
7	6	$ 50				
8	7	$ 163				
9	8	$ 95				
10	9	$ 38				

That formula may be right, but it's still really long. It'd be nice to tighten it up.

Your result might also be $246.33, depending on your number format.

Refer to a bunch of cells using a range

You can point to a list of references in Excel using a **range**. A range is simply two references with a colon between them, and the colon tells Excel to look at every cell in between those two references.

For example, say you want your formula to do something to this list of references.

Here are a bunch of cell references you want to evaluate.

B2, B3, B4, B5, B6, B7, B8, B9, B10

Here's the range.

By placing a colon between B2 and B10, you tell Excel to look at those two cells and everything in between.

This colon tells Excel to evaluate every cell from B2 to B10.

B2:B10

Use SUM to add the elements in a range

In order to make your ranges work, you need to pass them to formulas that know what to do with them. You can use the SUM **function** to add together all the cells in your range.*

This SUM formula adds together all the cells in the range B2:B10.

=SUM(B2:B10)

Most functions consist of a word followed by parentheses that contain one or more **arguments**. They often need arguments in order to know where to look to get the data they need to evaluate.

A formula's arguments are the ranges or values you put between the parentheses.

*SUM is a "function," and the real implementation of a function (like =SUM(B2:B10) is a "formula."

Exercise

Inside your spreadsheet, rewrite the formula that calculates each person's share using a range and the SUM function.

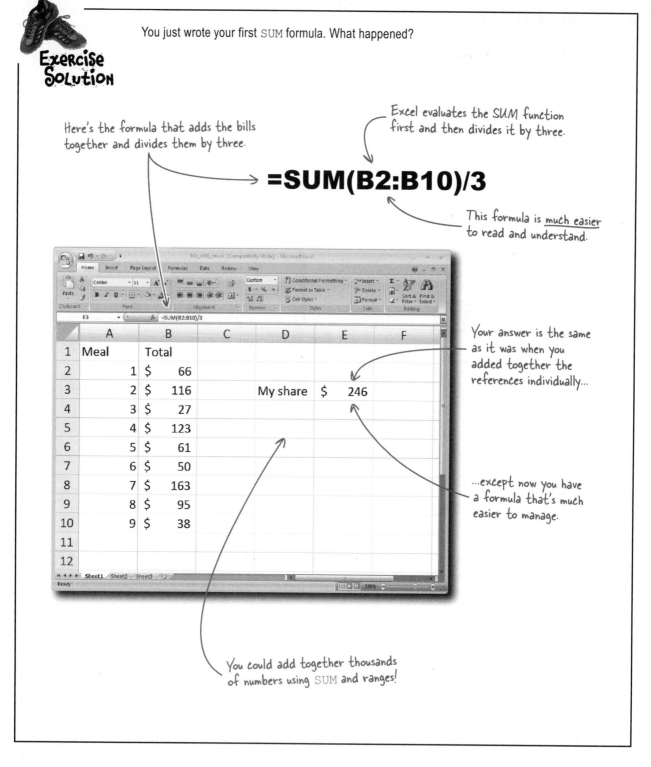

Exercise Solution

You just wrote your first SUM formula. What happened?

Here's the formula that adds the bills together and divides them by three.

Excel evaluates the SUM function first and then divides it by three.

=SUM(B2:B10)/3

This formula is <u>much easier</u> to read and understand.

Your answer is the same as it was when you added together the references individually...

...except now you have a formula that's much easier to manage.

You could add together thousands of numbers using SUM and ranges!

Bob and Sasha wonder whether we've been taking the right approach...

From: Sasha
To: You and Bob
Subject: A question of fairness

Hey you two,

You know, I've been thinking about how we're splitting up the checks and all.

It seems like splitting them evenly would work well only if we all spent about the same. But there are a number of times when I know I spent more than either of you, so if we split those checks three ways, you'd really be paying for me.

Since we really do want to be fair, shouldn't we split up the restaurant bills item by item, so that we each only pay for exactly what we ordered?

—S

From: Bob
To: You and Sasha
Subject: Re: A question of fairness

Amigos,

I hear what you're saying, Sasha. It does seem fair. But splitting the checks evenly three ways is certainly an easier calculation. I wouldn't be able to crunch those numbers in Excel.

But then again it appears we have some sort of spreadsheet whiz as a travelling companion. Maybe they can work some magic and sort everything out as precisely as you want. Ya think?

The Bobster

How would you go about splitting up all the bills?

Your friends agree: split the checks individually

Since you're going to the trouble to create a spreadsheet for your dining expenses, you might as well go ahead and break each check down individually. This approach will give the most equitable results.

Here are the receipts for the meals **you** bought yourself.

Tom's Restaurant

Coffee	$2
Coffee	$2
Coffee	$2
Big Breakfast	**$14**
Eggs & Bacon	**$15**
Pancakes	**$13**
Fruit cup	**$6**
Tip	**$12**
Total	**$66**

You → Big Breakfast
Bob → Eggs & Bacon
Sasha → Pancakes
Sasha → Fruit cup

Each of you had coffee.

Split each tip three ways.

Lupa

You →	Salad	$7
Sasha →	Baccala	$20
Bob →	Frutti di Mare	$19
Sasha →	Olives	$6
Sasha →	Bagna Cauda	$20
You →	Spaghetti alla Carbonara	$15
Bob →	Eggplant Parm	$8
→	Tip	$21
Total		**$116**

Taco Chulo

Brooklyn

Quesadilla	$9
Tacos	$5
Chile con Queso	$7
Tip	$6
Total	$27

Sasha → Quesadilla
You → Tacos
Bob → Chile con Queso

Split each tip three ways.

CHINESE MIRCH
NEW YORK CITY

Bob →	WINE	$24.00
Sasha →	DATE PANCAKE	$ 6.00
Bob →	SWEET CORN SOUP	$ 6.00
You →	CRISPY OKRA	$11.00
Sasha →	SZECHUAN VEGETABLES	$15.00
Sasha →	CHICKEN CURRY	$19.00
You →	HOT & SOUR SOUP	$ 4.00
Sasha →	FRIED BANANA	$10.00
Bob →	CHICKEN DUMPLING	$ 7.00
	TIP	$21.00
	TOTAL:	$123.00

Split this wine order three ways.

Split each tip three ways.

formulas

Exercise

Here is a spreadsheet to help you split up the expenses for the restaurant bills you paid for.

1. Fill in the blanks for **Bob** and **Sasha** using the values on the facing page.

Load this!

www.headfirstlabs.com/books/hfexcel/
hfe_ch01_your_tab.xls

First, sum only the amounts for each meal for Bob and Sasha.

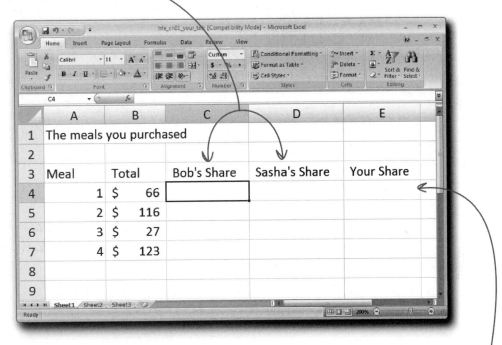

Put your subtraction formula here.

2. Now, write a formula to calculate your share of meal #1. Instead of adding elements from the facing page, just subtract what Bob and Sasha spent from the total.

3. Select the formula you just wrote in cell E4 and copy/paste it for meals 2–4. What happens? Look at the references for each result.

you are here ▸ **19**

You just calculated the breakdown for each bill you paid. What did you find?

1 Fill in the blanks for **Bob** and **Sasha** using the values on the facing page.

Here's one of the formulas you just wrote, which is for Bob's bill at Tom's Restaurant.

Coffee

Eggs & Bacon

This is the value for the tip, which needs to be split into three.

Here is the result.

=2+15+12/3

	A	B	C	D	E
1	The meals you purchased				
2					
3	Meal	Total	Bob's Share	Sasha's Share	Your Share
4	1	$ 66	$ 21	$ 25	$ 20
5	2	$ 116	$ 34	$ 53	$ 29
6	3	$ 27	$ 9	$ 11	$ 7
7	4	$ 123	$ 39	$ 50	$ 34
8					
9					

E7 =B7-C7-D7

2 Now, write a formula to calculate your share of meal #1. Instead of adding elements from the facing page, just subtract what Bob and Sasha spent from the total.

Use this formula.

=B4–C4–D4

The formula goes here.

3 Select the formula you just wrote in cell E4 and copy/paste it for meals 2–4. What happens? Look at the references for each result.

When you copied and pasted the formula, Excel updated the references for each position.

=B7–C7–D7

=B6–C6–D6

=B5–C5–D5

When you copy and paste a formula, the references shift

This feature of formulas is really useful because you can write **just one formula** to do a whole lot of different stuff.

You wrote just one formula here...

	A	B	C	D	E
1	The meals you purchased				
2					
3	Meal	Total	Bob's Share	Sasha's Share	Your Share
4	1	$ 66	$ 21	$ 25	$ 20
5	2	$ 116	$ 34	$ 53	$ 29
6	3	$ 27	$ 9	$ 11	$ 7
7	4	$ 123	$ 39	$ 50	$ 34
8					
9					

Sheet1 / Sheet2 / Sheet3

...but Excel was able to transform it into similar formulas by shifting the references.

It actually would not have taken you long to write three more similar formulas to calculate your share of the meals you bought. But what if, instead of four meals, you'd bought **a hundred or a thousand** meals? In that case, being able to copy formulas with automatic reference shifting would be a big help.

So how are we going to figure out who owes what to whom?

LONG EXERCISE

Here are summaries of what each of you spent.

Load this!

www.headfirstlabs.com/
books/hfexcel/
hfe_ch01_all_tabs.xls

Write your new
values down here.

	A	B	C	D	E	F
1	**The meals you purchased**					
2	Meal	Total	Bob's Share	Sasha's Share	Your Share	
3	1	$ 66	$ 21	$ 25	$ 20	
4	2	$ 116	$ 34	$ 53	$ 29	
5	3	$ 27	$ 9	$ 11	$ 7	
6	4	$ 123	$ 39	$ 50	$ 34	
7						
8	**The meals Bob purchased**					
9	Meal	Total	Bob's Share	Sasha's Share	Your Share	
10	5	$ 61	$ 19	$ 18	$ 24	
11	6	$ 50	$ 17	$ 16	$ 17	
12						
13	**The meals Sasha purchased**					
14	Meal	Total	Bob's Share	Sasha's Share	Your Share	
15	7	$ 163	$ 75	$ 51	$ 37	
16	8	$ 95	$ 47	$ 20	$ 28	
17	9	$ 38	$ 19	$ 12	$ 7	
18						
19						
20						

Sheet1 Sheet2 Sheet3

Below these three tables on your spreadsheet, write the formulas to answer these questions. Be sure to put text labels in the cells next to each formula to remind you what they mean.

1 Write the formula that shows what you spent on Bob.

2 Write the formula that shows what Bob spent on you.

3 Using the above two formulas, write a formula that shows what Bob owes you.

4 Write the formulas to show what Sasha owes you.

5 Write the formulas to show what Sasha owes Bob.

6 Now how are you doing relative to your budget of $400?

....

Long Exercise Solution

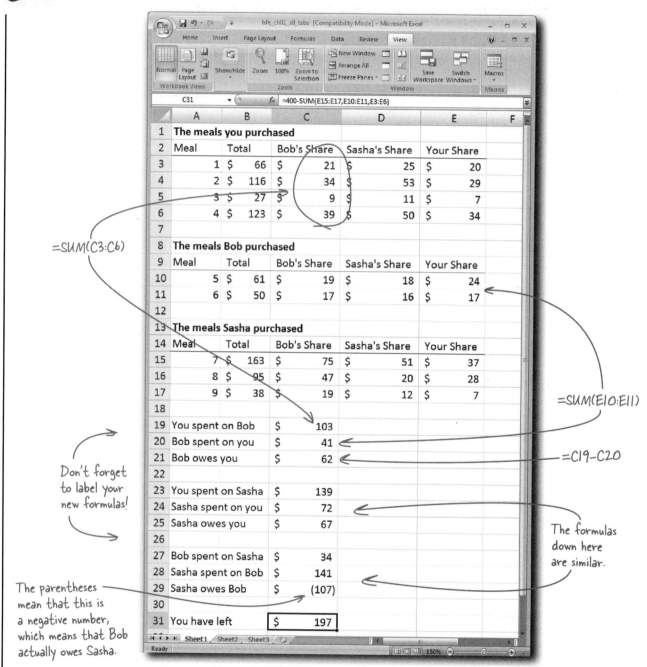

C31   =400-SUM(E15:E17,E10:E11,E3:E6)

	A	B	C	D	E	F
1	The meals you purchased					
2	Meal	Total	Bob's Share	Sasha's Share	Your Share	
3	1	$ 66	$ 21	$ 25	$ 20	
4	2	$ 116	$ 34	$ 53	$ 29	
5	3	$ 27	$ 9	$ 11	$ 7	
6	4	$ 123	$ 39	$ 50	$ 34	
7						
8	The meals Bob purchased					
9	Meal	Total	Bob's Share	Sasha's Share	Your Share	
10	5	$ 61	$ 19	$ 18	$ 24	
11	6	$ 50	$ 17	$ 16	$ 17	
12						
13	The meals Sasha purchased					
14	Meal	Total	Bob's Share	Sasha's Share	Your Share	
15	7	$ 163	$ 75	$ 51	$ 37	
16	8	$ 95	$ 47	$ 20	$ 28	
17	9	$ 38	$ 19	$ 12	$ 7	
18						
19	You spent on Bob	$ 103				
20	Bob spent on you	$ 41				
21	Bob owes you	$ 62				
22						
23	You spent on Sasha	$ 139				
24	Sasha spent on you	$ 72				
25	Sasha owes you	$ 67				
26						
27	Bob spent on Sasha	$ 34				
28	Sasha spent on Bob	$ 141				
29	Sasha owes Bob	$ (107)				
30						
31	You have left	$ 197				

Sheet1   Sheet2   Sheet3

Ready   150%

=SUM(C3:C6)

=SUM(E10:E11)

=C19-C20

Don't forget to label your new formulas!

The formulas down here are similar.

The parentheses mean that this is a negative number, which means that Bob actually owes Sasha.

Below these three tables on your spreadsheet, write the formulas to answer these questions.
Be sure to put text labels in the cells next to each formula to remind you what they mean.

1 Write the formula that shows what you spent on Bob.

=SUM(C3:C6) ⟵

These are pretty straightforward SUM formulas.

2 Write the formula that shows what Bob spent on you.

=SUM(E10:E11) ⟵

3 Using the above two formulas, write a formula that shows what Bob owes you.

=C19–C20 ⟵

This formula just subtracts what Bob spent on you from what you spent on Bob.

4 Write the formulas to show what Sasha owes you.

=SUM(D3:D6)

=SUM(E15:E17) ⟵

=C23–C24

5 Write the formulas to show what Sasha owes Bob.

=SUM(D10:D11)

=SUM(C15:C17) ⟵

=C27–C28

These groups of formulas go through the same motions with different combinations of people.

6 Now how are you doing relative to your budget of $400?

Subtract the total amount you spent from your budget.

=400–SUM(E15:E17)–SUM(E10:E11)–SUM(E3:E6)

=400–SUM(E15:E17,E10:E11,E3:E6) ⟵

Alternatively, you can place commas between ranges for a more concise SUM formula.

Looks like you're in good shape!

I have $197 left!

Excel formulas let you drill deep into your data

You can use spreadsheets as a hugely powerful tool with formulas. You might want to run a simple calculation, or you might need to build a really elaborate system of formulas to help you find the answers you need.

Simple

You started off here with a simple formula.

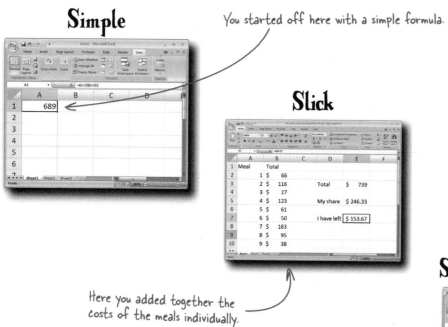

Slick

Here you added together the costs of the meals individually.

Super-sophisticated!

No matter which approach you choose to take, Excel is ready with the formulas you need to get the job done.

In this spreadsheet you broke everything down to a really fine level.

Everyone has plenty of cash left for a food-filled night in New York City!

Your friends loved your spreadsheet and used it to figure out how they are doing relative to their own budgets. The verdict: everyone has plenty of money left.

With $197 burning a hole in **your** pocket, you are ready for a crazy night out with your friends in one of the most exciting cities in the world!

2 visual design

Spreadsheets as art

The calculations work, but the spreadsheet just doesn't have <u>the look</u>. I'd better call Louis Vuitton....

You know, Excel has some pretty solid formatting tools built in!

Most people usually use Excel for page layout.

A lot of formula-writing masters, who are familiar with just how powerful Excel can be, are shocked that people "just" use the software for showing information with a grid. But Excel, especially in its more recent versions, has become quite handy as a page layout tool. You're about to get comfortable with some important and not-so-obvious Excel tools for serious visual design.

CRMFreak needs to present their financials to analysts

Because CRMFreak is a publicly traded company and is heavily influenced by what Wall Street analysts have to say about them, it's really important that they do a good job with their public financial statements.

The CEO needs you to format CRMFreak's **income statement**, using your Excel skills to make the formulas work correctly and provide an elegant presentation.

We really need you to impress our company's analysts. My money and your career depend on it.

Let's take a look at CRMFreak's data....

Exercise

Here's CRMFreak's *income statement* data for the past year. What is their net income?

① Write a formula to calculate **Total revenue** (cell B7), adding together the elements in the Revenue section.

....

Write the formulas you use in the blanks.

Load this!

www.headfirstlabs.com/books/hfexcel/
income_statement.xlsx

② Write a formula to calculate the **Total cost of revenues** (cell B12), adding together the elements in the Cost of revenues section.

....

③ Write a formula to calculate the **Gross profit** (cell B14), subtracting the Total cost of revenues from the Total revenue.

....

④ Write a formula to calculate the **Total expenses** (cell B20), adding together the elements in the Expenses section.

....

⑤ Finally, write a formula to calculate the **Net income** (cell B22), subtracting the Gross profit from the Total expenses.

....

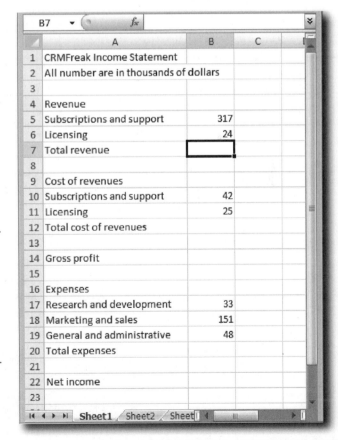

	B7	▼	fx		
	A		**B**	**C**	**D**
1	CRMFreak Income Statement				
2	All number are in thousands of dollars				
3					
4	Revenue				
5	Subscriptions and support		317		
6	Licensing		24		
7	Total revenue				
8					
9	Cost of revenues				
10	Subscriptions and support		42		
11	Licensing		25		
12	Total cost of revenues				
13					
14	Gross profit				
15					
16	Expenses				
17	Research and development		33		
18	Marketing and sales		151		
19	General and administrative		48		
20	Total expenses				
21					
22	Net income				
23					

Sheet1   Sheet2   Sheet

Exercise Solution

You just wrote a bunch of formulas to calculate CRMFreak's net income. What did you find?

1 Write a formula to calculate **Total revenue** (cell B7), adding together the elements in the Revenue section.

=SUM(B5:B6)

2 Write a formula to calculate the **Total cost of revenues** (cell B12), adding together the elements in the Cost of revenues section.

=SUM(B10:B11)

3 Write a formula to calculate the **Gross profit** (cell B14), subtracting the Total cost of revenues from the Total revenue.

=B7–B12

4 Write a formula to calculate the **Total expenses** (cell B20), adding together the elements in the Expenses section.

=SUM(B17:B19)

5 Finally, write a formula to calculate the **Net income** (cell B22), subtracting the Gross profit from the Total expenses.

=B14–B20

Here are your new formulas.

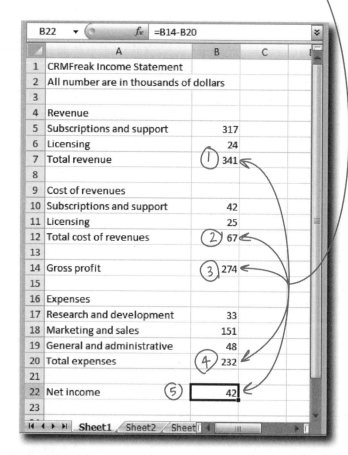

Those calculations are definitely correct. But shouldn't the income statement have dollar signs?

The income statement data points are all dollar figures.

So they should have dollar signs in front of them to let people know what they mean. Let's try adding some $s.

The numbers in the income statement need to have dollar signs.

Exercise

1 Add a dollar sign in front of the numbers in cells B5 and B6 by double-clicking each cell and then editing it. What happens? What does the formula bar say?

....

2 Add a dollar sign in front of the formula you created in B7.
What happens?

....

....

Exercise Solution

What happened when you tried to add the $ symbol to some values and formula?

1 Add dollar signs in front of the numbers in cells B5 and B6 by double-clicking each cell and then editing it. What happens? What does the formula bar say?

When I press Enter, dollar signs show up inside the cells, but the signs aren't in the formula bar.

The dollar signs are inside these cells...

...but they don't show up inside the formula bar.

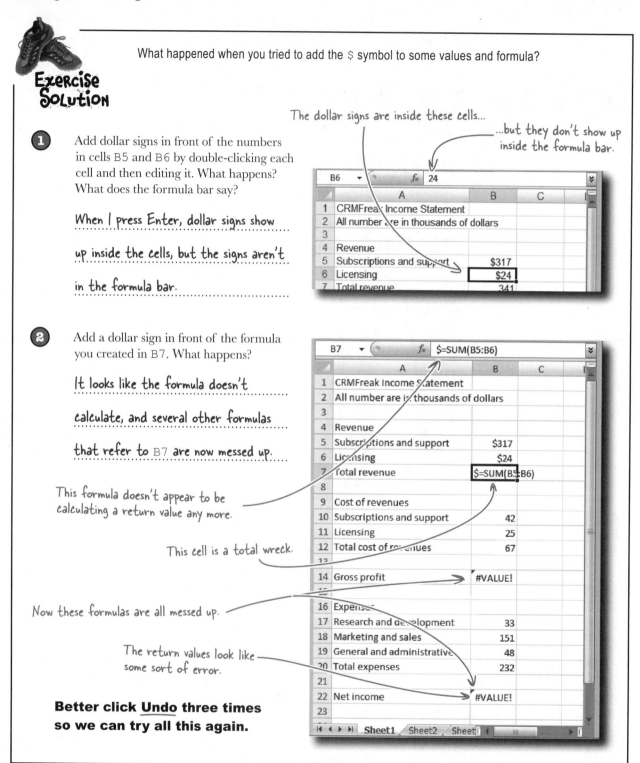

2 Add a dollar sign in front of the formula you created in B7. What happens?

It looks like the formula doesn't calculate, and several other formulas that refer to B7 are now messed up.

This formula doesn't appear to be calculating a return value any more.

This cell is a total wreck.

Now these formulas are all messed up.

The return values look like some sort of error.

Better click Undo three times so we can try all this again.

The dollar sign is part of your cell's <u>formatting</u>

When you put dollar signs in front of the numbers in cells B5 and B6, Excel **applied currency formatting** to those cells. The dollar signs did not show up inside the formula bar, because Excel continued to see the actual values of those cells as 317 and 24.

Your data is different from its formatting, and typing dollar signs in front of numbers is just one way of telling Excel to apply currency formatting to your data.

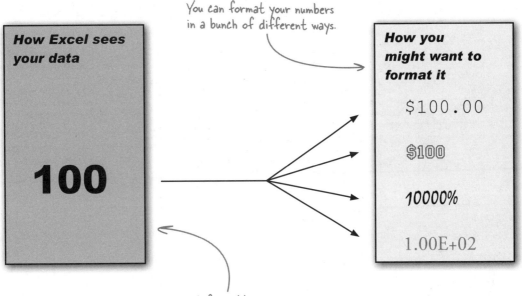

You can format your numbers in a bunch of different ways.

How Excel sees your data

100

How you might want to format it

$100.00

$100

10000%

1.00E+02

No matter what formatting you use, Excel sees the underlying data the same.

On the other hand, when you tried to type a dollar sign into the **formula** in cell B7, Excel didn't understand that you wanted to apply currency formatting. Excel thought you were changing the formula to plain text, which is why the formula stopped working.

In order to change a formula from general formatting to currency formatting, you need to do something *different* from typing the dollar sign into the cell itself.

BRAIN POWER

How would you go about applying currency formatting to your cells, aside from typing dollar signs into the cells themselves?

How to format your data

In order to format your cells the way you want, select those cells and then choose formatting options on the Home tab of the Ribbon.

This up here is called the "Ribbon."

Tip: Double-click on one of these tabs to hide the Ribbon for more screen space.

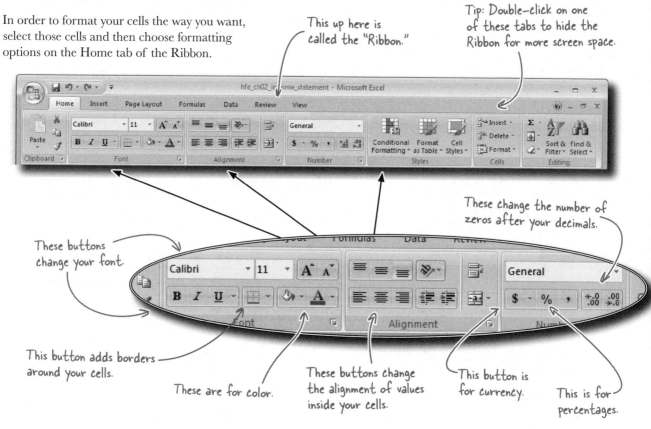

These buttons change your font.

These change the number of zeros after your decimals.

This button adds borders around your cells.

These are for color.

These buttons change the alignment of values inside your cells.

This button is for currency.

This is for percentages.

there are no Dumb Questions

Q: So the formulas you write completely ignore the formatting choices you make?

A: Not entirely. Excel does try to figure out how to format your formula's cells by looking at the arguments in your function. If, for example, you wanted to use the SUM function to add a bunch of numbers that were already formatted as currency, Excel would automatically apply that formatting to the cell where you put your formula.

Q: What if I wanted to use SUM to add a number that was formatted as currency with a number that didn't have any formatting?

A: In that case, Excel would have no way of knowing what the calculation meant and would have the formula output display without any formatting.

Q: That's kind of confusing. It's like Excel has different rules for formatting things automatically depending on the context.

A: You could say that, but what's important is that you take control of your spreadsheet's formatting early. When Excel's automatic formatting works for you automatically, that's great, but it's important to remember that formatting is a **design choice** you make to create a more readable and useful spreadsheet.

Using the buttons on the Ribbon, make all the cells in column B have currency formatting. Be sure to press the button to eliminate the zeros after the decimal point (and press Undo if you make a mistake!).

Select all the cells in column B by clicking the letter B here.

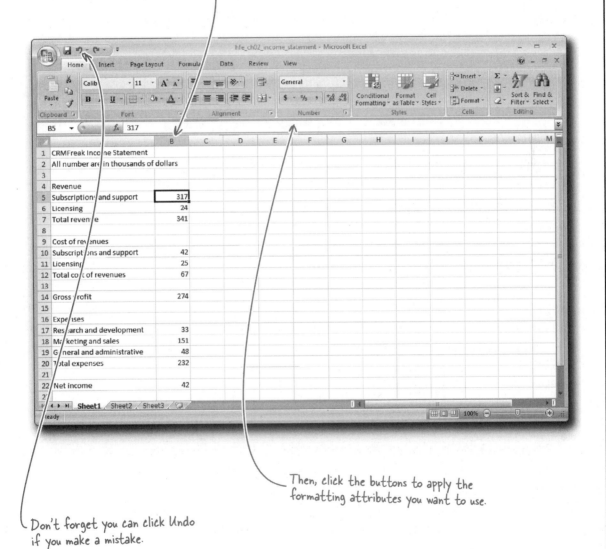

Then, click the buttons to apply the formatting attributes you want to use.

Don't forget you can click Undo if you make a mistake.

Exercise Solution

Were you able to apply currency formatting to the values in column B?

You pressed the $ button to apply currency formatting.

Then, you pressed this button twice to remove the zeros after the decimal place.

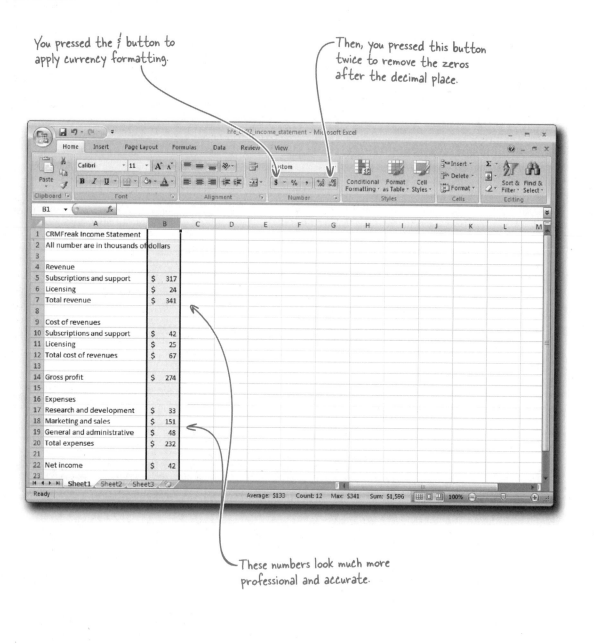

These numbers look much more professional and accurate.

The boss approves!

Great job! I made a few formatting tweaks of my own, and now we're ready to go!

He's smiling...that's good!

But this spreadsheet looks out of control!

CRM Freak Income Statement

All number are in thousands of dollars

	A	B	C
1			
2			
3			
4	Revenue		
5	Subscriptions and support	$ 317	
6	Licensing	$ 24	
7	Total revenue	$ 341	
8			
9	Cost of revenues		
10	Subscriptions and support	$ 42	
11	Licensing	$ 25	
12	Total cost of revenues	$ 67	
13			
14	Gross profit	$ 274	
15			
16	Expenses		
17	Research and development	$ 33	
18	Marketing and sales	$ 151	
19	General and administrative	$ 48	
20	Total expenses	$ 252	
21			
22	NET INCOME	$ 42	
23			

Wait a second. That spreadsheet is hideous! It appears that he wrecked your work, visually speaking. Worst of all, **gaudy design undermines your credibility with your audience**. You need some serious design principles to guide you away from a mess like this....

Design principle: keep it simple

The analysts who are trying to assess the health of CRMFreak are **not interested in being dazzled**. What they want to do is to be able to make the best decisions about CRMFreak's data as they can.

Which of these spreadsheets do you think will do the best job of facilitating that sort of thinking?

This one is plain and unadorned.

	A	B	C
1	CRMFreak Income Statement		
2	All number are in thousands of dollars		
3			
4	Revenue		
5	Subscriptions and support	$ 317	
6	Licensing	$ 24	
7	Total revenue	$ 341	
8			
9	Cost of revenues		
10	Subscriptions and support	$ 42	
11	Licensing	$ 25	
12	Total cost of revenues	$ 67	
13			
14	Gross profit	$ 274	
15			
16	Expenses		
17	Research and development	$ 33	
18	Marketing and sales	$ 151	
19	General and administrative	$ 48	
20	Total expenses	$ 232	
21			
22	Net income	$ 42	
23			
24			
25			
26			
27			

Here is the one that the CEO did.

	A	B	C
1	**CRMFreak Income Statement**		
2	***All number are in thousands of dollars***		
3			
4	**Revenue**		
5	**Subscriptions and support**	$ 317	
6	**Licensing**	$ 24	
7	**Total revenue**	$ 341	
8			
9	**Cost of revenues**		
10	**Subscriptions and support**	$ 42	
11	**Licensing**	$ 25	
12	**Total cost of revenues**	$ 67	
13			
14	**Gross profit**	$ 274	
15			
16	**Expenses**		
17	**Research and development**	$ 33	
18	**Marketing and sales**	$ 151	
19	**General and administrative**	$ 48	
20	**Total expenses**	$ 232	
21			
22	**NET INCOME**	$ 42	
23			
24			
25			

Both spreadsheets have the same data.

The spreadsheet on the right has excessive formatting that *gets in the way* of your ability to understand the data. The spreadsheet on the left is very simple, but perfectly ***clear***.

Keeping it simple makes for better thinking about data.

Clash of the design titans...

Jim: No, no, no! You have to have colors in a spreadsheet like that. Maybe the boss didn't get it exactly right, but people expect something more than the plain Jane stuff that has no formatting.

Joe: Fool! There can be no distraction. When someone is looking at a spreadsheet, they need to have the utmost concentration and never be seduced by silly formatting.

Frank: Guys, isn't there a middle ground here? Maybe a little formatting can help, but one should take it easy and not go overboard?

Jim: Joe's just off his rocker here. I know that when *I* use spreadsheets, I need to use colors and fonts and boxes to help me keep track of what I'm looking at. Using color is part of the way I think about data.

Joe: Nonsense. You just *think* you're using the colors to help you think about data. You're really just pretending to do good thinking. If you knew better you'd see that numbers have no color.

Frank: Now, Joe, that's out of line. If Jim wants to use colors to help him think through his spreadsheet, that's totally fine. Everyone thinks differently.

Joe: There is no reason Jim should torment us with his "colorful" ideas.

Frank: You have a point there. Just because you feel the need to highlight a bunch of stuff on your spreadsheets, Jim, doesn't mean that you should assume that everyone else thinks that way, too.

Jim: [Mumbling something unkind about Joe....] I like colors. Colors are nice.

Frank: Well maybe if we find a way to use fonts and colors with taste and restraint we can get a result that all of us can appreciate....

***How* do you use fonts and colors with taste and restraint?**

Use fonts to draw the eye to what is most important

The font panel is the first place many people look to set the formatting for their document. Let's see how the font panel works.

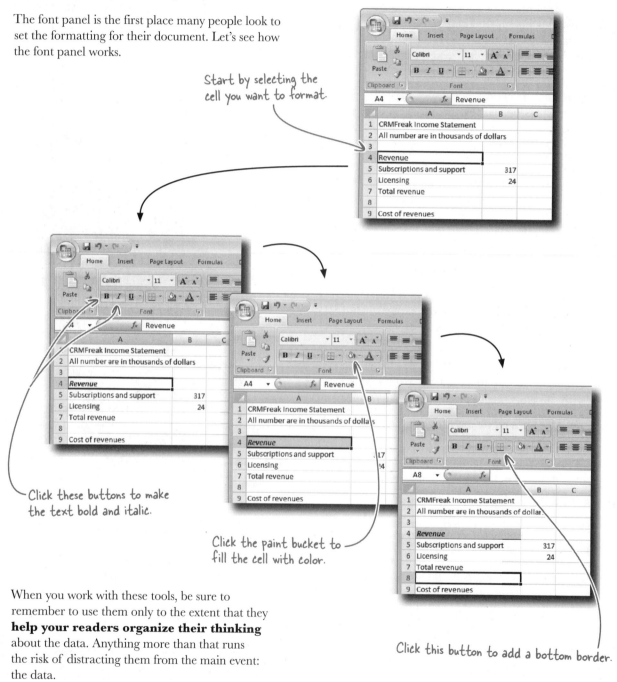

Start by selecting the cell you want to format.

Click these buttons to make the text bold and italic.

Click the paint bucket to fill the cell with color.

Click this button to add a bottom border.

When you work with these tools, be sure to remember to use them only to the extent that they **help your readers organize their thinking** about the data. Anything more than that runs the risk of distracting them from the main event: the data.

Exercise

Using one or more of the elements on the left, change your spreadsheet's formatting to draw the eye to key elements. Remember, less is more.

Select cells and use these design elements to draw the eye to what's most important.

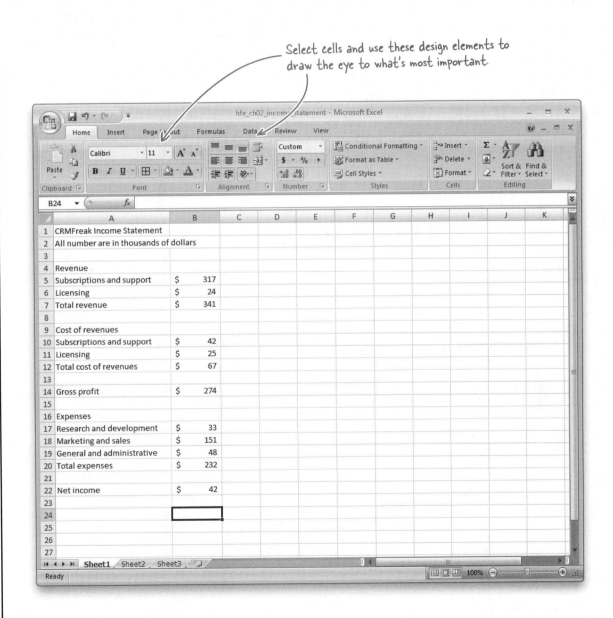

EXERCISE SOLUTION

You just applied some formatting to your CRMFreak income statement. Were you successful?

You might have come up with slightly different results, which is fine.

This title is a little larger than the rest of the text.

It's also bold and italic.

These little headings can just be bold.

Here are some borders that separate the totals.

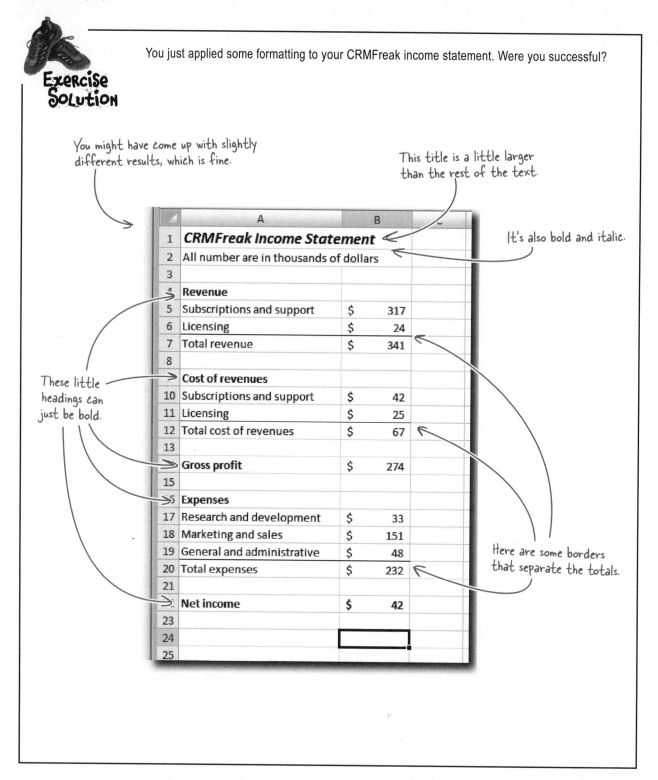

	A	B
1	*CRMFreak Income Statement*	
2	All number are in thousands of dollars	
3		
4	**Revenue**	
5	Subscriptions and support	$ 317
6	Licensing	$ 24
7	Total revenue	$ 341
8		
9	**Cost of revenues**	
10	Subscriptions and support	$ 42
11	Licensing	$ 25
12	Total cost of revenues	$ 67
13		
14	**Gross profit**	$ 274
15		
16	**Expenses**	
17	Research and development	$ 33
18	Marketing and sales	$ 151
19	General and administrative	$ 48
20	Total expenses	$ 232
21		
22	**Net income**	$ 42
23		
24		
25		

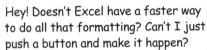

Hey! Doesn't Excel have a faster way to do all that formatting? Can't I just push a button and make it happen?

You're only just getting started with Excel's formatting features.

And when it comes to simple, push-button formatting, Excel has a much more powerful feature that ties together everything you've been doing so far into a single, elegant interface.

This feature gives you more speed and flexibility along with access to the visual acumen of a professional designer. It's called **cell styles**.*

---

* Cell styles are fully supported in Excel 2007 for Windows and later, but as of this writing, their support in Mac versions of Excel is spotty. Go figure.

Cell styles keep formatting consistent for elements that repeat

You'll usually have several headings in your spreadsheets, and you'll want those headings to look the same. Styles let you tell Excel which cells are headings and *then* what you want the **formatting** of those headings to be.

And styles aren't just for headings: you can use them for **any elements that repeat**. They're especially handy if you want, say, to change the look of all your Totals. Instead of finding each one, you can just change the style, and all the cells with that style will incorporate that change.

To take styles for a spin, select the cells you want to affect and then select a style with the Cell Styles button under the Home tab.

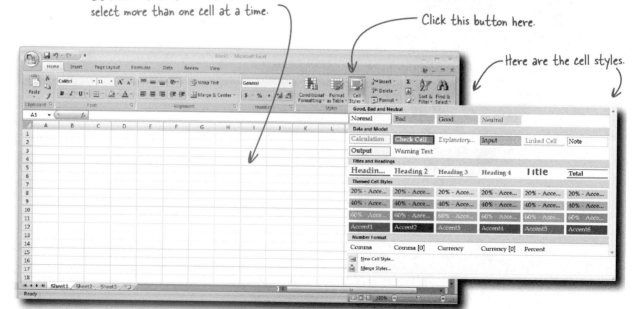

This is the Title.

This is Explanatory Text.

These are Headings.

These are Totals.

	A	B	C
1	CRMFreak Income Statement		
2	All number are in thousands of dollars		
3			
4	Revenue		
5	Subscriptions and support	$ 317	
6	Licensing	$ 24	
7	Total revenue	$ 341	
8			
9	Cost of revenues		
10	Subscriptions and support	$ 42	
11	Licensing	$ 25	
12	Total cost of revenues	$ 67	
13			
14	Gross profit	$ 274	
15			
16	Expenses		
17	Research and development	$ 33	
18	Marketing and sales	$ 151	
19	General and administrative	$ 48	
20	Total expenses	$ 232	
21			
22	Net income	$ 42	
23			

Ctrl-click and ctrl-shift-click to select more than one cell at a time.

Click this button here.

Here are the cell styles.

With your cell styles selected, use Themes to change your look

Once you've told Excel which cell styles match up with your data, then the fun can really begin. Head on over to the Themes button group under the Page Layout tab and play around with the prepackaged themes and font/color configurations. Which looks appeal to you?

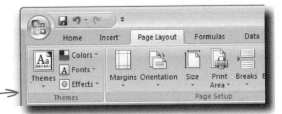

These buttons read your cell styles and can change your formatting in a bunch of quick and easy ways.

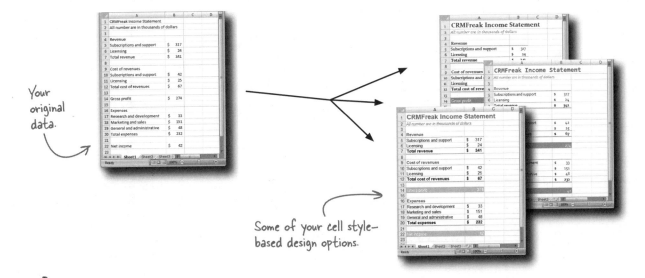

Your original data.

Some of your cell style-based design options.

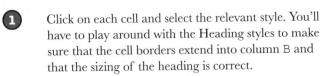

Exercise

Assign the cell styles listed on the facing page to your CRMFreak income statement data.

Load this!

www.headfirstlabs.com/books/hfexcel/ hfe_ch02_income_statement_styles.xlsx

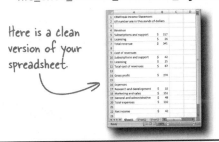

Here is a clean version of your spreadsheet.

① Click on each cell and select the relevant style. You'll have to play around with the Heading styles to make sure that the cell borders extend into column B and that the sizing of the heading is correct.

② Go to Page Layout > Themes and try out a few of the configurations. Which is your favorite?

EXERCISE SOLUTION

You assigned cell styles and themes to your income statement data. Do you like how it looks now?

Here's an example spreadsheet...your own probably looks different, depending on what you chose.

This is the Title.

This is Explanatory Text.

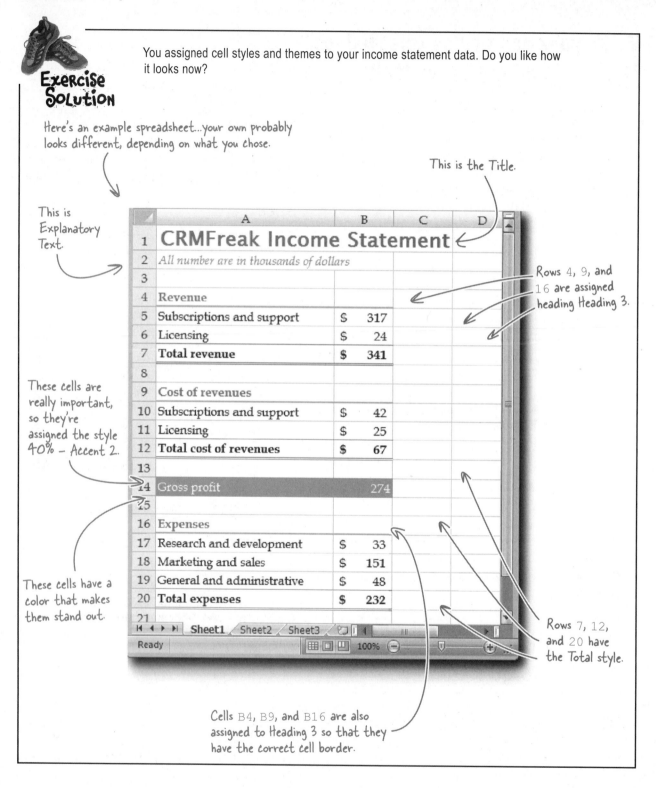

	A	B	C	D
1	**CRMFreak Income Statement**			
2	*All number are in thousands of dollars*			
3				
4	Revenue			
5	Subscriptions and support	$ 317		
6	Licensing	$ 24		
7	**Total revenue**	**$ 341**		
8				
9	Cost of revenues			
10	Subscriptions and support	$ 42		
11	Licensing	$ 25		
12	**Total cost of revenues**	**$ 67**		
13				
14	Gross profit	274		
15				
16	Expenses			
17	Research and development	$ 33		
18	Marketing and sales	$ 151		
19	General and administrative	$ 48		
20	**Total expenses**	**$ 232**		
21				

Sheet1 / Sheet2 / Sheet3

Ready   100%

Rows 4, 9, and 16 are assigned heading Heading 3.

These cells are really important, so they're assigned the style 40% – Accent 2.

These cells have a color that makes them stand out.

Rows 7, 12, and 20 have the Total style.

Cells B4, B9, and B16 are also assigned to Heading 3 so that they have the correct cell border.

there are no
Dumb Questions

Q: **A while back, you said something about the design elements in the themes being "professional." What did you mean?**

A: The prepackaged themes have been carefully selected so that the colors and fonts all complement each other. The choice of font (or "type") and color in documents is a really big deal for people who take visual design seriously, and it's convenient that Excel has built-in design options that are likely to look good.

Q: **I've heard a lot of people complain about how ugly writing and spreadsheets and slide shows look when they're made in Microsoft Office, but this looks like Microsoft has made it pretty easy to employ good visual design.**

A: While it's always been *possible* to create visually well-designed documents in Microsoft Office programs, it's not always been easy. Some of the templates in previous versions of the software are indeed ugly, and sometimes you've really had to work hard to make your documents look good. But Microsoft has become progressively more sensitive to people's need to have good design, and recent versions of Office show it.

Q: **So are some of the same themes that I've been seeing in Excel available in other Office programs, like Word or PowerPoint?**

A: Yes! And integration throughout Office is precisely the idea. If you make use of styles everywhere you can, you'll have no trouble having consistent visual integration across all your documents.

Q: **Are there limitations to what I can do in Excel in terms of visual design?**

A: There are loads of features you'll find in graphic design programs that you won't find in Excel. But even when it comes to making drawings, Excel is surprisingly powerful for a number-crunching program. If you have a specialized design objective, you should still poke around under the Page Layout tab before reaching for your graphic design program.

Q: **What if I don't like any of the color configurations that Excel offers? Can I make up my own themes?**

A: Absolutely. Making your own theme would be a great idea if your business already has its own design standards—official corporate fonts and colors. Under these circumstances, the benefits of using styles and themes in Excel would be immense.

Let's see what the boss thinks about your work....

He likes it, but there's something else...

Love it! It's just what we needed. Oh, by the way, I want you to do the balance sheet, too. And fit them both on the same page. Can you do that?

The boss wants more than just a pretty income statement. He wants you to add a balance sheet to your spreadsheet, integrate the new elements visually, and make sure it all fits on a *single page*. Better start thinking about how you're going to accomplish all that!

Sharpen your pencil

Here are small versions of the CRMFreak income statement and balance sheet. How would you lay them out?

Draw your answer here.

Here's the income statement you've been working on.

	A	B	C	D
1	**CRMFreak Income Statement**			
2	*All number are in thousands of dollars*			
3				
4	Revenue			
5	Subscriptions and support	$	317	
6	Licensing	$	24	
7	**Total revenue**	$	341	
8				
9	Cost of revenues			
10	Subscriptions and support	$	42	
11	Licensing	$	25	
12	**Total cost of revenues**	$	67	
13				
14	Gross profit		274	
15				
16	Expenses			
17	Research and development	$	33	
18	Marketing and sales	$	151	
19	General and administrative	$	48	
20	**Total expenses**	$	232	
21				

Sheet1 Sheet2 Sheet3
Ready   100%

Here is your new balance sheet data.

	A	B	C
1	CRMFreak Balance Sheet		
2	All number are in thousands of dollars		
3			
4	Assets		
5	Cash and cash equivalents	532	
6	Marketable securities	439	
7	Accounts receivable	293	
8	Deferred commissions	63	
9	Deferred income taxes	64	
10	Prepaids	36	
11	Fixed assets	85	
12	Goodwill	49	
13	Other	66	
14	Total		
15			
16	Liabilities		
17	Accounts payable	202	
18	Deferred revenue	653	
19	Long-term liabilities	22	
20	Total		
21			
22	Stockholder's equities		
23	Controlling interest	739	
24	Noncontrolling interest	11	
25	Total		
26			

Sheet1 Sheet2 Shi
Select destinati..   100%

Sharpen your pencil
Solution

What do your CRMFreak draft financial statements look like?

Here's one way it might look.

Income statement

   Revenue

   Cost of revenue

   Expenses

Balance sheet

   Assets

   Liabilities

   Stockholder equity

Here are your financial statements.

	A	B	C	D
1	**CRMFreak Income Statement**			
2	*All number are in thousands of dollars*			
3				
4	Revenue			
5	Subscriptions and support	$	317	
6	Licensing	$	24	
7	**Total revenue**	$	**341**	
8				
9	Cost of revenues			
10	Subscriptions and support	$	42	
11	Licensing	$	25	
12	**Total cost of revenues**	$	**67**	
13				
14	Gross profit		274	
15				
16	Expenses			
17	Research and development	$	33	
18	Marketing and sales	$	151	
19	General and administrative	$	48	
20	**Total expenses**	$	**232**	
21				

Sheet1 Sheet2 Sheet3
Ready   100%

	A	B	C
1	CRMFreak Balance Sheet		
2	All number are in thousands of dollars		
3			
4	Assets		
5	Cash and cash equivalents	532	
6	Marketable securities	439	
7	Accounts receivable	293	
8	Deferred commissions	63	
9	Deferred income taxes	64	
10	Prepaids	36	
11	Fixed assets	85	
12	Goodwill	49	
13	Other	66	
14	Total		
15			
16	Liabilities		
17	Accounts payable	202	
18	Deferred revenue	653	
19	Long-term liabilities	22	
20	Total		
21			
22	Stockholder's equities		
23	Controlling interest	739	
24	Noncontrolling interest	11	
25	Total		
26			

Sheet1 Sheet2 Sh
Select destinati...   100%

Use proximity and alignment to group like things together

Why doesn't your drawing look like one of these spreadsheets?

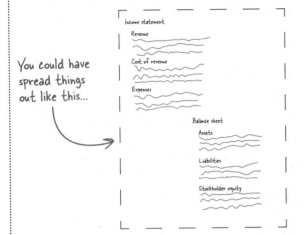

You could have spread things out like this...

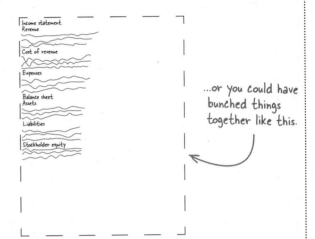

...or you could have bunched things together like this.

You probably didn't draw your spreadsheet that way because you intuitively grasp the fundamental visual design principles of **proximity** and **alignment**. By bunching like elements together and keeping all your elements in alignment with each other, you make your document more readable and usable.

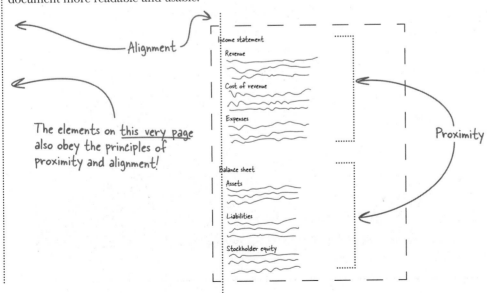

Alignment

The elements on this very page also obey the principles of proximity and alignment!

Proximity

Proximity

Now let's incorporate that balance sheet into your spreadsheet....

Long Exercise

1. Copy the data in **hfe_ch02_balance_sheet.xlsx** and paste it below your income statement. Save it all to a file called `financials.xlsx`.

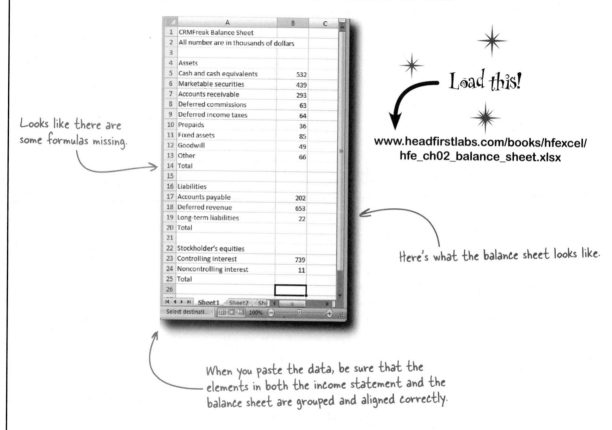

Looks like there are some formulas missing.

	A	B	C
1	CRMFreak Balance Sheet		
2	All number are in thousands of dollars		
3			
4	Assets		
5	Cash and cash equivalents	532	
6	Marketable securities	439	
7	Accounts receivable	293	
8	Deferred commissions	63	
9	Deferred income taxes	64	
10	Prepaids	36	
11	Fixed assets	85	
12	Goodwill	49	
13	Other	66	
14	Total		
15			
16	Liabilities		
17	Accounts payable	202	
18	Deferred revenue	653	
19	Long-term liabilities	22	
20	Total		
21			
22	Stockholder's equities		
23	Controlling interest	739	
24	Noncontrolling interest	11	
25	Total		
26			

Load this!

www.headfirstlabs.com/books/hfexcel/
hfe_ch02_balance_sheet.xlsx

Here's what the balance sheet looks like.

When you paste the data, be sure that the elements in both the income statement and the balance sheet are grouped and aligned correctly.

2. Write formulas to total the Assets, Liabilities, and Stockholder's equity, and then apply the cell styles to the balance sheet.

Use this button to apply the cell styles.

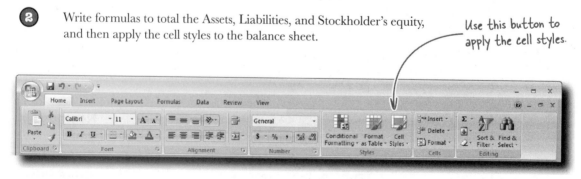

3 Switch to page layout mode to see how your spreadsheet will look on the printed page.

This is the bottom of your Excel window.

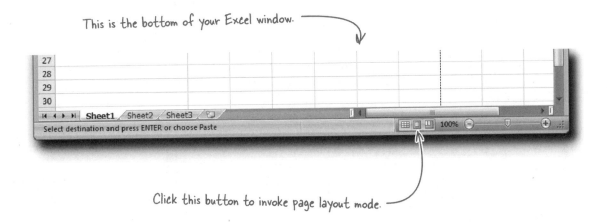

Click this button to invoke page layout mode.

4 Does it fit on one page? If not, scale it down on the page layout bar.

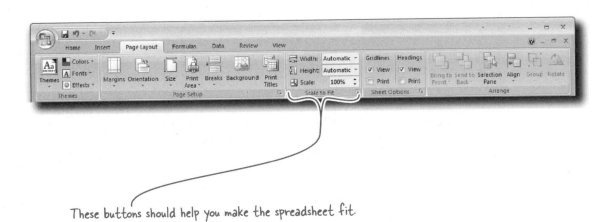

These buttons should help you make the spreadsheet fit.

Long Exercise Solution

You just incorporated a balance sheet into your spreadsheet, added some formulas, and formatted the whole thing. What was the result?

Be sure to add some spacing to separate the balance sheet and income statement.

The cell styles make incorporating new information into your visual design a snap.

You need to bring the scale down on your spreadsheet a little to get it all to fit on the page.

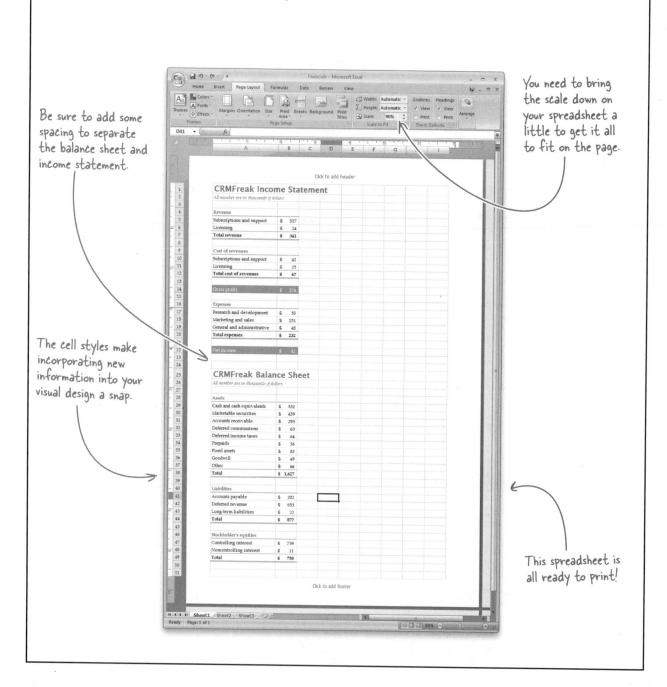

This spreadsheet is all ready to print!

Your spreadsheet is a hit!

CRMFreak used your spreadsheet as part of the materials they made available to stock analysts, and the critical consensus has been overwhelmingly positive.

Important Wall Street analyst

That's an exquisitely professional presentation. The spreadsheet is well designed and makes my job as an interpreter much easier.

Here's what your boss had to say....

From: CEO, CRMFreak
To: You
Subject: Your work product

Dear Head First,

I was delighted but not the least bit surprised by your excellent work with our financial statements. You handled the formula work with grace and crafted a sophisticated yet crystal-clear presentation.

It was truly a *tour de force* and I am confident it played a large role in the favorable reviews we received from the analysts this season.

The only thing to do with talent like yours is to give it more responsibility with bigger jobs. Expect to see bigger challenges with bigger rewards very soon!

—CEO

3 references

Point in the right direction

Well, on paper your application looks fantastic, but I have to say that when I checked your references a rather different picture emerged....

A formula is only as good as its references.

No matter how creative and brilliant your formula is, it won't do you much good if it does not point to the correct data. It's easy to get references right for short, individual formulas, but once those formulas get long and need to be copied, the chance of reference mistakes increases dramatically. In this chapter, you'll exploit **absolute and relative references** as well as Excel's advanced new **structured reference** feature, ensuring that no matter how big and numerous your references are, your formulas will stay tight and accurate.

Your computer business is in disarray

As the boss of Ace Computer Manufacturing, you know how critical it is to maintain your profit margins in the volatile and competitive business of selling computers.

You need to get on top of your supply chain: **are you marking up your computers enough to make a profit?** You need to take control of your data to figure it out.

You've got a lot of satisfied customers in your computer business.

What would I do without your computers?

Finally, Mom got me a 64 bit!

This box was a great deal!

But how profitable are you?

Exercise

Here are last quarter's costs and sales for low-end computers. The figures below list the cost and revenue for a single computer. Calculate the profit margin on this configuration. How profitable is a single sale of this model?

Load this!

www.headfirstlabs.com/books/hfexcel/
hfe_ch03_low_end_computer.xlsx

To calculate the **Total cost**, add the cost of the components.

To calculate the **Gross profit margin**, subtract the total cost by the sale price and divide the whole thing by the sale price.

Fill in this formula...

Sale price is the amount you charge for your computers at retail.

...and this formula!

This is what a customer would pay for your computer.

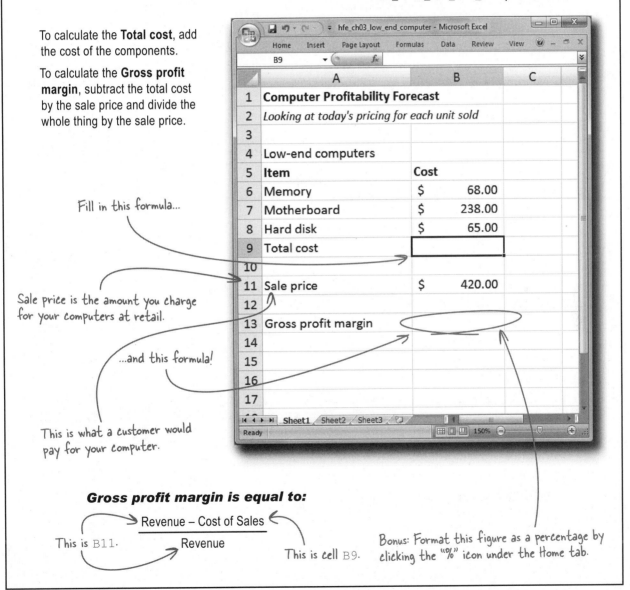

	A	B	C
1	**Computer Profitability Forecast**		
2	*Looking at today's pricing for each unit sold*		
3			
4	Low-end computers		
5	**Item**	**Cost**	
6	Memory	$ 68.00	
7	Motherboard	$ 238.00	
8	Hard disk	$ 65.00	
9	Total cost		
10			
11	Sale price	$ 420.00	
12			
13	Gross profit margin		
14			
15			
16			
17			

Gross profit margin is equal to:

$$\frac{\text{Revenue} - \text{Cost of Sales}}{\text{Revenue}}$$

This is B11.

This is cell B9.

Bonus: Format this figure as a percentage by clicking the "%" icon under the Home tab.

Exercise Solution

You created the formulas to calculate the total cost and the gross profit margin. What did you find?

This formula calculates the cost of sale to produce one low-end computer.

This one's pretty straightforward.

=SUM(B6:B8)

It's just a basic SUM.

Here's the gross profit margin.

This one is a little more complicated.

=(B11–B9)/B11

Use parentheses to keep the difference between total cost and sale price in the numerator.

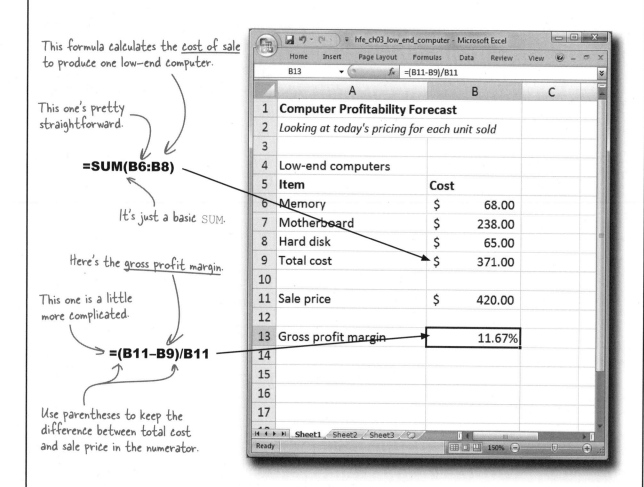

hfe_ch03_low_end_computer - Microsoft Excel

Home | Insert | Page Layout | Formulas | Data | Review | View

B13 f_x =(B11-B9)/B11

	A	B	C
1	**Computer Profitability Forecast**		
2	*Looking at today's pricing for each unit sold*		
3			
4	Low-end computers		
5	**Item**	**Cost**	
6	Memory	$ 68.00	
7	Motherboard	$ 238.00	
8	Hard disk	$ 65.00	
9	Total cost	$ 371.00	
10			
11	Sale price	$ 420.00	
12			
13	Gross profit margin	11.67%	
14			
15			
16			
17			

Sheet1 / Sheet2 / Sheet3

Ready   150%

Your gross profit margin for low-end computers is 11.67%. That's not bad at all nowadays! So far, so good.

Your production manager has a spreadsheet with costs

In the computer industry, component prices are always changing, so in order to ensure that you're getting a healthy margin on the computers you sell, you need to make sure you're getting the best deal you can.

If you bought the **least expensive acceptable parts**, how much would the resulting configuration cost?

> Here is this quarter's data. We haven't ordered the parts and need to find the cheapest configuration.

Product manager

✳ Load this! ✳

There are multiple <u>worksheets</u> in this file.

www.headfirstlabs.com/books/hfexcel/
hfe_ch03_low_end_forecast.xlsx

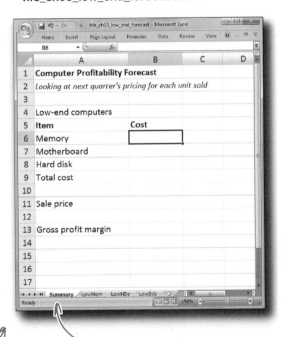

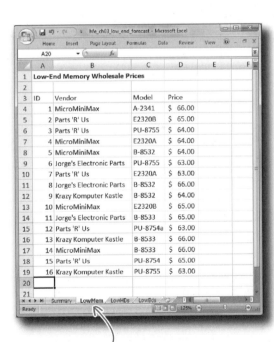

Use these tabs to select different worksheets.

Spreadsheet files are also called "workbooks."

You need a function to find the lowest price on the memory worksheet.

MIN returns the lowest number in a series

When you have a range of numbers and want
to figure out what is the smallest number in that
range, use the MIN function.

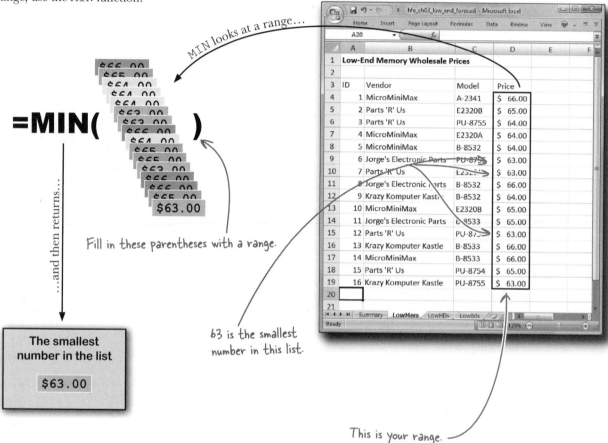

MIN looks at a range…

=MIN(   )

…and then returns…

Fill in these parentheses with a range.

**The smallest
number in the list**

$63.00

63 is the smallest
number in this list.

This is your range.

And, in case you hadn't guessed it already, the
function that tells you the *largest* number in a list
is MAX.

What you need to do now is write MIN formulas
to find **the lowest cost for each of these
components** and see how much your low-end
computer configuration will cost this quarter.
Using that information, you'll be able to forecast
your profitability.

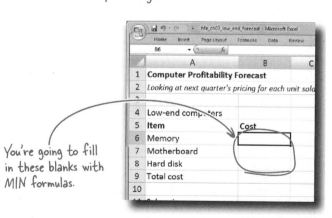

You're going to fill
in these blanks with
MIN formulas.

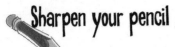

Sharpen your pencil

Let's start by looking at memory. We need a formula that will return the lowest amount we can pay for memory.

Here's the memory data we want to refer to.

1 If you write your formula the way you've been writing formulas, how will your formula know which sheet to refer to for the data?

....

....

....

....

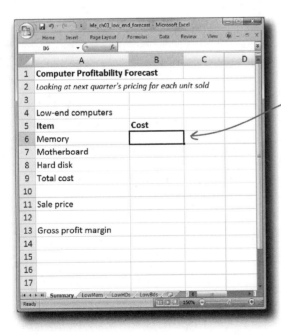

Here's where we want the formula.

2 How would you design a reference to ensure that the correct sheet is being pointed to?

....

....

....

....

Sharpen your pencil
Solution

You just grappled with the question of how to refer to cells across worksheets. What did you conclude?

1 If you write your formula the way you've been writing formulas, how will your formula know which sheet to refer to for the data?

The formula wouldn't know where to find the data. The range we want is D4:D19, but it has to be on the LowMem sheet. We don't want data from that range on other sheets.

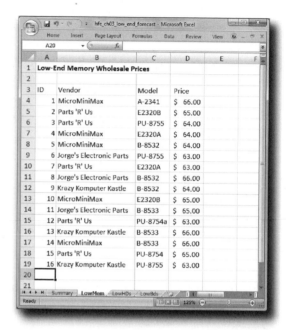

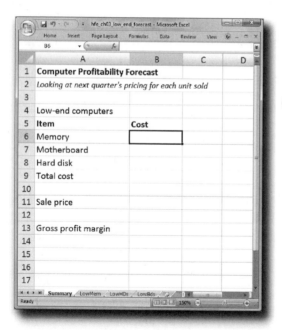

2 How would you design a reference to ensure that the correct sheet is being pointed to?

The reference would definitely have to have the name of the worksheet baked into it.

Something like this: LowMem-D4:D19.

Let's see if Excel can help figure out these ranges....

Let Excel fill in ranges by starting your formula and using your mouse

Excel does indeed have a syntax for pointing to ranges that exist on worksheets *other* than the worksheet where your function resides. And you're about to learn that syntax. But not from this book.

Instead, Excel's going to show you. One **handy trick** in writing formulas with arguments that involve cell ranges is to start writing a formula, getting to the argument of your function where you want to put the range but *not typing anything*:

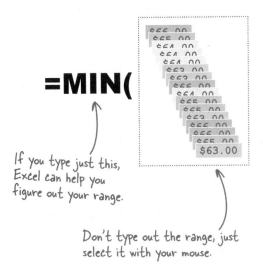

=MIN(

If you type just this, Excel can help you figure out your range.

Don't type out the range, just select it with your mouse.

Do this!

Start typing this formula on your summary sheet.

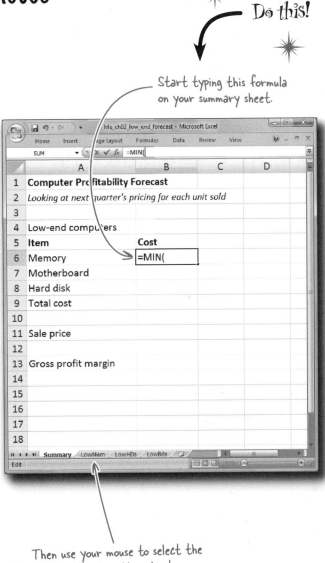

Then use your mouse to select the data on the LowMem sheet.

Now, instead of typing the reference, just **use your mouse to select the data you want**. Go ahead and click on a different worksheet (or even a different workbook) and select your data with the mouse. Excel will fill in the range for you.

Finally, type a comma for your next argument or a) symbol to end your formula and press Enter.

What happens?

Excel got the right answer using a more sophisticated reference

When you use the mouse to select the data you want your MIN formula to evaluate, Excel automatically fills in the range for that data, even if the data is on a different worksheet.

Here's Excel building your reference for you as you select it.

Here's how Excel describes the range for memory prices you want to evaluate.

=MIN(LowMem!D4:D19)

Excel added this element.

The range does look a little similar to the first one you tried…

No word on which sheet this range refers to.

=MIN(D4:D19)

Here's your selection of the memory price data.

…except that in this case it adds the LowMem! element, which tells Excel to evaluate the range D4:D19 on the LowMem worksheet. So far, we haven't included an element to describe which worksheet we want to reference, and Excel has taken that to mean that we want to reference the same worksheet where we've put our formula.

This is the lowest price for memory.

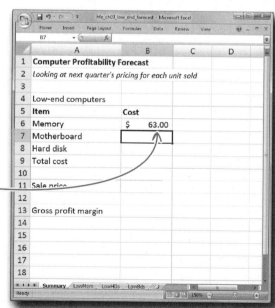

Now filling in the lowest prices for the rest of the components will be a snap!

Exercise

You know everything you need to know to complete the rest of this spreadsheet and forecast the profitability of low-end computers for next quarter.

Use the MIN function to calculate these two cells.

1 Using the MIN function and pointing to the hard disk (LowHDs) and motherboard (LowBds) pricing worksheets, calculate what is the lowest price you can get for these components.

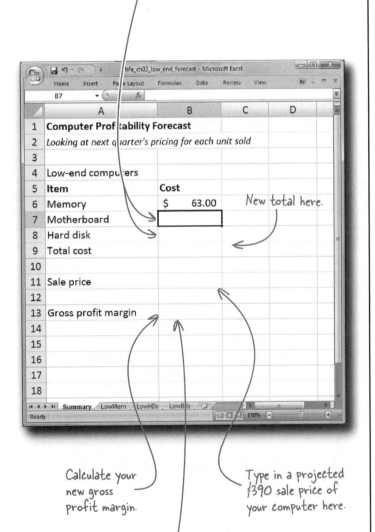

New total here.

2 Type in the formula to calculate your new cost total in B9.

3 Your sales team has determined that the highest competitive price you can charge your customers is $390. Fill that value into cell B11.

4 Calculate your new gross profit margin.

Calculate your new gross profit margin.

Type in a projected $390 sale price of your computer here.

Make sure it's formatted correctly by pressing the "%" button under the Home tab.

Exercise Solution

You just projected your profitability for low-end computers, given your component costs, for the next quarter. Do you expect a profit?

Here are the formulas that calculate your spreadsheet.

=MIN(LowBds!D4:D10)

=MIN(LowHDs!D4:D14)

=SUM(B6:B8)

=(B11–B9)/B11

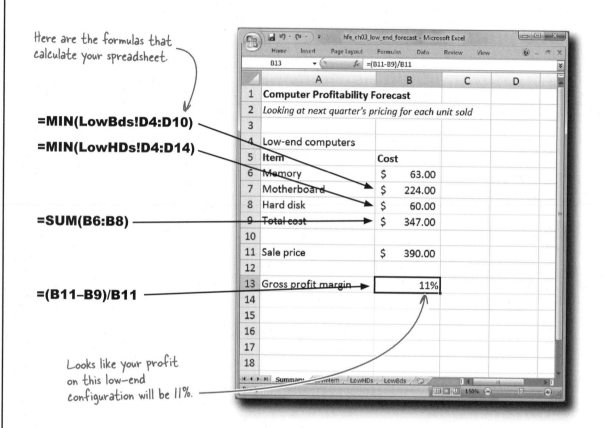

Looks like your profit on this low-end configuration will be 11%.

Geek Bits

A quick way to select *all* the numbers in column D for your MIN formula: you can type MIN(LowBds!D:D). If there are other elements in the column, such as text or blank spaces, Excel will just ignore them.

Nice work.

Looks like you'll have a handy profit per unit this quarter. Now all we have to do is sell them....

Things just got even better...

This email just came across the wire.

> **From: Purchasing**
> **To: The Boss**
> **Subject: Just scored a sweet discount!**
>
> **Hey Boss,**
>
> **One of the new guys has just persuaded all our vendors to give us a 5% discount for this quarter. You might want to incorporate the good news into your projections.**
>
> **—Purchasing**

Sweet! That definitely means that the computers you sell will earn a higher profit margin. Better calculate to see how much.

ExeRcise

Load this!

www.headfirstlabs.com/books/hfexcel/
hfe_ch03_low_end_discounted.xlsx

The 5% discount is typed into this cell.

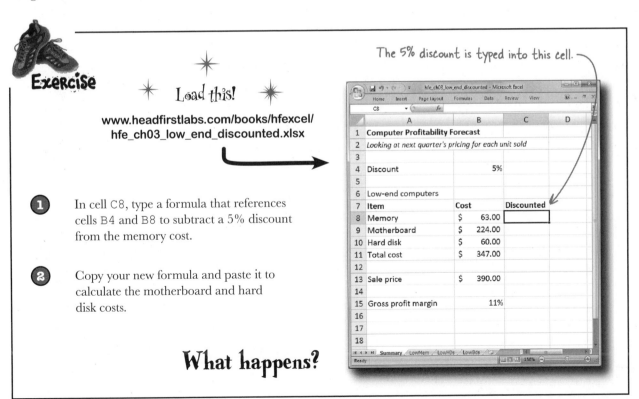

1. In cell C8, type a formula that references cells B4 and B8 to subtract a 5% discount from the memory cost.

2. Copy your new formula and paste it to calculate the motherboard and hard disk costs.

What happens?

Exercise Solution

You just tried to write formulas to calculate a discounted cost of memory, hard disks, and motherboards. Let's see how it went....

1 Refine your spreadsheet to incorporate the discount to memory.

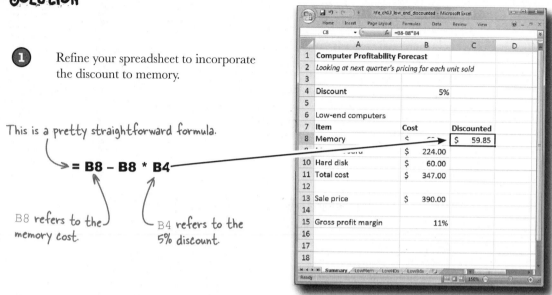

This is a pretty straightforward formula.

$$= B8 - B8 * B4$$

B8 refers to the memory cost.

B4 refers to the 5% discount.

2 Copy your new discount formula for the hard disk.

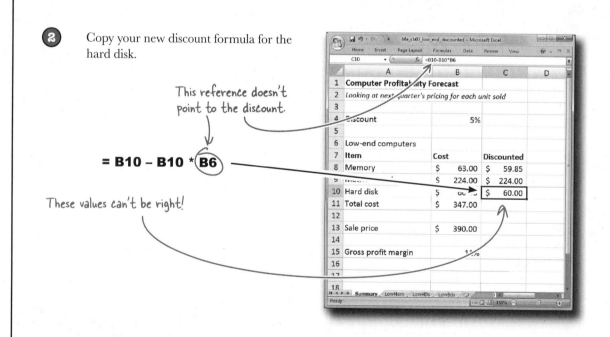

This reference doesn't point to the discount.

$$= B10 - B10 * \boxed{B6}$$

These values can't be right!

Use absolute references to prevent shifting on copy/paste

You've thus far been using **relative references** in your formulas…

…and when you copy and paste them, relative references shift in proportion to the original formula.

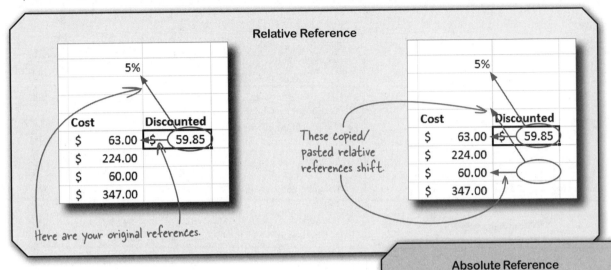

Relative Reference

5%

Cost	Discounted
$ 63.00	$ 59.85
$ 224.00	
$ 60.00	
$ 347.00	

These copied/ pasted relative references shift.

Here are your original references.

Absolute Reference

5%

Cost	Discounted
$ 63.00	$ 59.85
$ 224.00	
$ 60.00	
$ 347.00	

This <u>absolute reference</u> remains fixed to the original cell.

This relative reference shifts.

But sometimes you want a reference to stay *fixed* no matter where you copy and paste it. In that case, you need to use an **absolute reference**.

To tell Excel to make a reference absolute, the syntax is to add dollar signs. If you put a dollar sign before the column, the row can shift, and if you put one before the row, the column can shift, and if you use two dollar signs, the reference will stay totally fixed.

Hold the row.

$B$2

Hold the column.

If you wanted to hold the column but not the row, you'd <u>only</u> put a dollar sign in front of the B.

Exercise

Rewrite your memory discount formula to include an absolute reference to cell B4. Copy that formula and paste it for the motherboard and hard disk costs.

Your profit margin is now even higher...

With your corrected formula using absolute references, you were able to copy and paste to your motherboard and hard disk fields, showing your discounted component costs.

Here is your absolute reference.

=B11-B11*B$4

You could also have written $B$4.

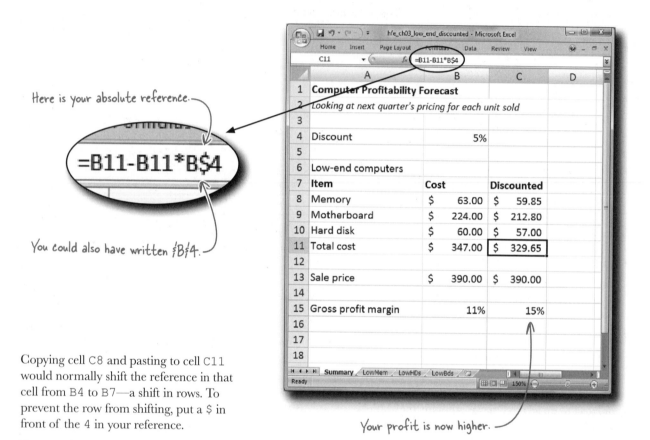

Copying cell C8 and pasting to cell C11 would normally shift the reference in that cell from B4 to B7—a shift in rows. To prevent the row from shifting, put a $ in front of the 4 in your reference.

You can also put a $ in front of the B in your reference, but it won't make a difference, because copying cell C8 to cell C11 wouldn't cause a shift in column references anyway.

Your profit is now higher.

Looks like you're going to get to pay yourself a **big dividend** this quarter, assuming that sales go well....

Absolute references give you a lot of options

Depending on where you think you might need to copy your references, you should always consider using absolute references to make sure your formulas point where you want them to.

Relative

C2:D3

C2

Ranges

B1:C2

B1

$B$1:$C$2

Single References

B$1

Original references.

$B$1:$C$2

Absolute

C$1

How the reference would look if you copied/pasted it to the cell below and to the right.

> Those dollar signs are starting to make the reference hard to read. Can't the formula just say in plain language what you want to evaluate?

It can indeed. As important as references are, they can become unwieldy once your formulas get long and numerous. If your references start to confuse you, you can turn to a powerful feature of Excel called **named ranges....**

Named ranges simplify your formulas

This reference takes a moment to understand.

$B$2

You will often have to go back and check where references are pointing, just to jog your memory.

Even if you wrote it yourself, chances are, in the future you'll forget its meaning and have to go back and forth to make sure you know where the reference is pointing. This formula takes a **long** time to understand.

A formula like this can be a real bear to check.

=SUM($B2,C4:D8)*M75

You can actually use words like these as references in your formulas.

When you used **named ranges**, you can replace those references with a plain-language name of your choosing.

Assign names to your ranges...

$B$2 ⟶ discount
$C1 ⟶ cost

And once you name your ranges, which by the way are **by definition absolute references**, you can drop them right into your formulas.

This could be a real formula using named ranges.

...and simplify your formulas.

= cost – cost * discount

Isn't this easier to read and understand?

Let's try out named ranges by incorporating one into your discount calculation formula. Instead of making the discount value reference B$4, let's make it just discount.

1 Give your discount value the name discount. To do this, select cell B4 and then highlight and delete the reference at the top left. In that blank, type discount.

Highlight this blank here, replace the reference text with the word Discount, and then press Enter.

Rewrite your memory formula.

Then copy/paste it to these cells.

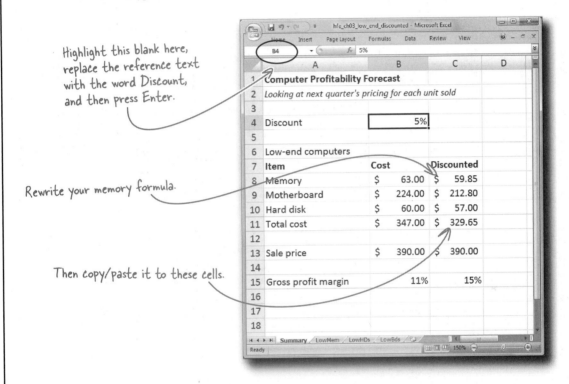

2 Rewrite the memory formula using your new named range.

3 Copy and paste your new formula to overwrite the old motherboard and hard disk discount formulas.

Exercise Solution

You just took named ranges for a spin for the first time. Did you find that they simplified your formula?

=B10–B10*discount

Here's your new formula.

This is your named range.

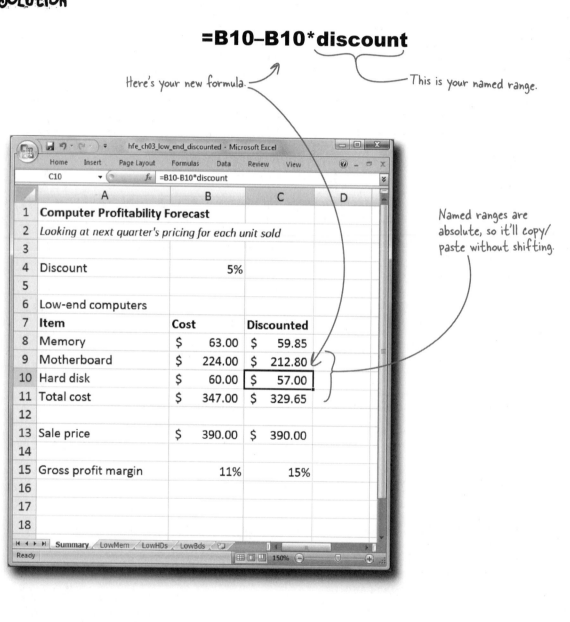

Named ranges are absolute, so it'll copy/paste without shifting.

Great, we figured out low-end computers. But we need to cover medium- and high-end computers as well. Can you do that?

No problem. Let's take a look at the data for the other computer lines and see what we can do.

This is a big workbook.

Product manager

Load this!

www.headfirstlabs.com/books/hfexcel/
hfe_ch03_all_pcs.xlsx

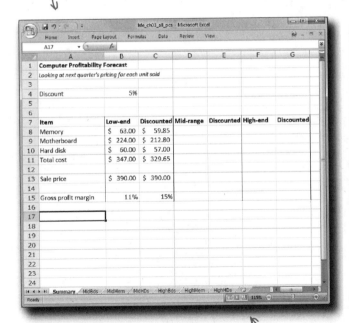

There are seven different worksheets here!

Lots of data, lots of formulas to write.

With all this data, you'd have to write a ton of formulas

It could take you quite a while to come up with this.

Here are all the formulas you'd need if you did it the long way.

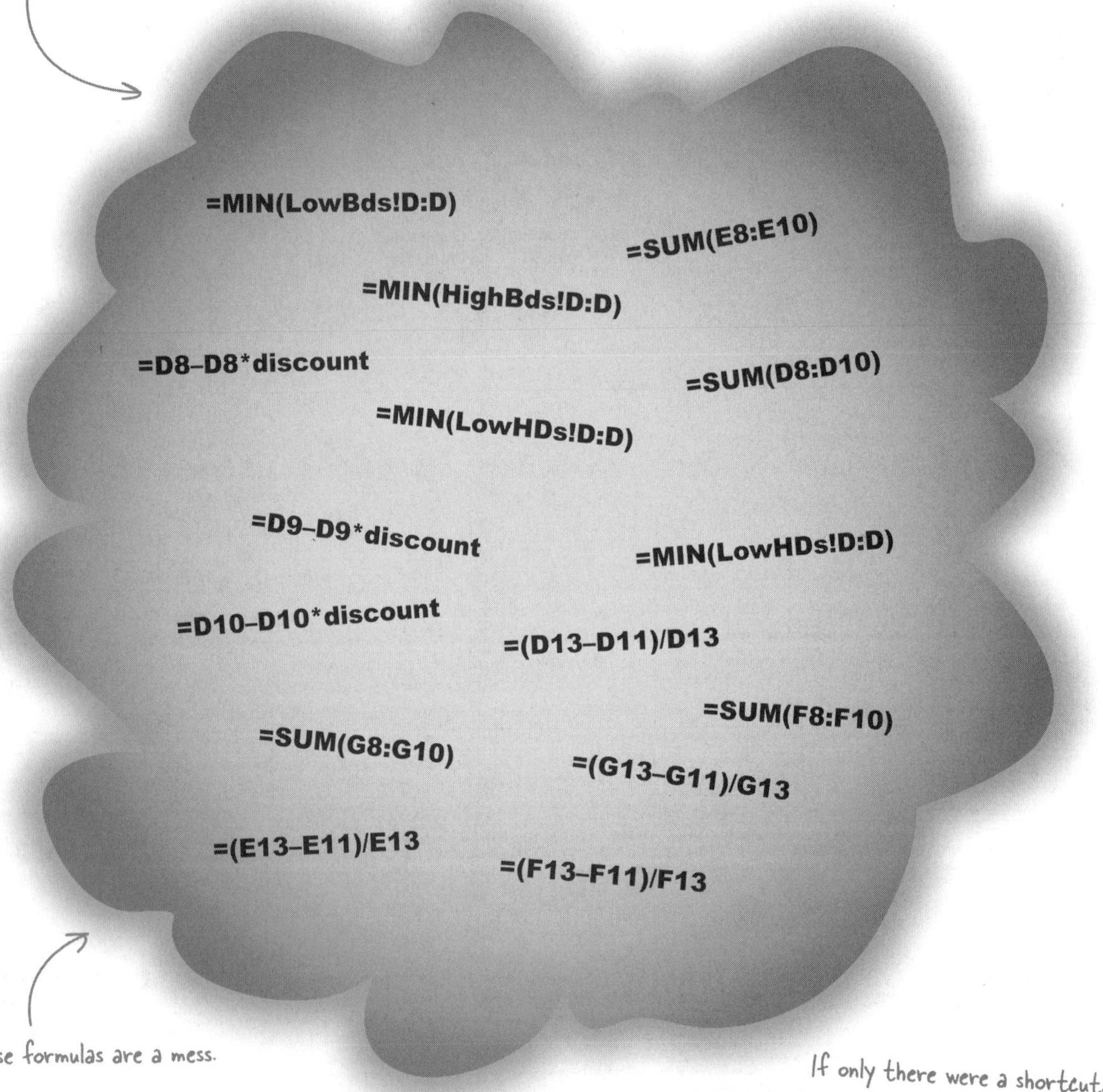

=MIN(LowBds!D:D)

=SUM(E8:E10)

=MIN(HighBds!D:D)

=D8–D8*discount

=SUM(D8:D10)

=MIN(LowHDs!D:D)

=D9–D9*discount

=MIN(LowHDs!D:D)

=D10–D10*discount

=(D13–D11)/D13

=SUM(F8:F10)

=SUM(G8:G10)

=(G13–G11)/G13

=(E13–E11)/E13

=(F13–F11)/F13

All these formulas are a mess.

If only there were a shortcut....

You could name some of the ranges. That would make things easier.

Having more named ranges would be a help.

Your formulas would certainly be easier to read. But going through a whole bunch of cells and ranges and naming them individually takes a lot of time, too!

Wouldn't it be dreamy if Excel would just name your ranges for you? But I know it's just a fantasy....

Excel's Tables make your references quick and easy

When you click inside your data and click **Table** under the Insert tab, Excel gives you all sorts of options, including *automatically generated range names*. Once you've created your table, you can use a special syntax called **structured references** to simplify your range names.* Here's how you make a table.

This is a <u>structured reference</u>.

=MIN(MidBds[Price])

The column is in brackets.

Here's where the structured reference points.

1 Select your data, then head over to the Insert tab and click **Table**.

Click here

2 Change your table name from Table1 to something more meaningful.

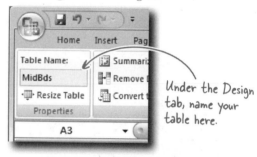

Under the Design tab, name your table here.

3 Now you have a table! Go ahead and start using it for structured references.

This new formatting shows you that your data is now a recognized table.

Easy, right? And you don't have to worry about making your references point to sheets anymore, since Excel knows how to find your table in a workbook using the structured reference.

If you don't like the formatting of the table, you can select a different style under the Design tab.

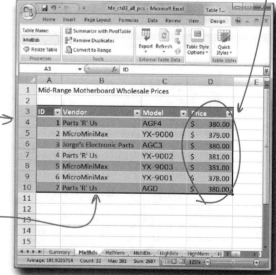

* Structured references are another one of those Excel 2007 and later–only features. It'll come to Mac eventually.

Structured references are a different dimension of absolute reference

Between the $A$1 style of references that you've learned and the references that you can name, you've spanned a broad universe of possibilities for referring to your data inside of formulas.

We're only going to scratch the surface of the power of structured references.

Simple
Named Ranges

Versatile
Structured References

If your data isn't in a tabular form, named ranges are the way to go.

Absolute ranges to the max!

See the Help files in Excel for more information about their full capabilities.

The type of reference you'll use will depend on your specific problem.

Remember, references to named ranges and structured references never shift.

Relative

C2:D3

C2

B1:C2

Ranges

B1

$B$1:$C$2

B$1

Original references.

$B$1:$C$2

Single References

Absolute

How each would look if you copied and pasted to C2

C$1

Let's finish off our computer spreadsheet with some structured references....

LONG EXERCISE

Finalize your profitability projections. Using tables and structured references, calculate the profitability forecast of your mid-range and high-end computer models.

1 Assign your new price sheets as tables. For each table that describes a component, create a table using the button under the Insert tab. Make sure you give them each a name!

Create a table for your mid-range memory.

2 Using the same approach as for evaluating low-end PCs, calculate the minimum costs for each component. This time, use **structured references** in your formula.

Here's one already completed for you.

3 Calculate expected profit margins for the other products. Use the sale prices below, and fill in the necessary formulas in row 15.

Your sale prices

Mid-range: $600

High-end: $4,000

Put your sale prices on this row.

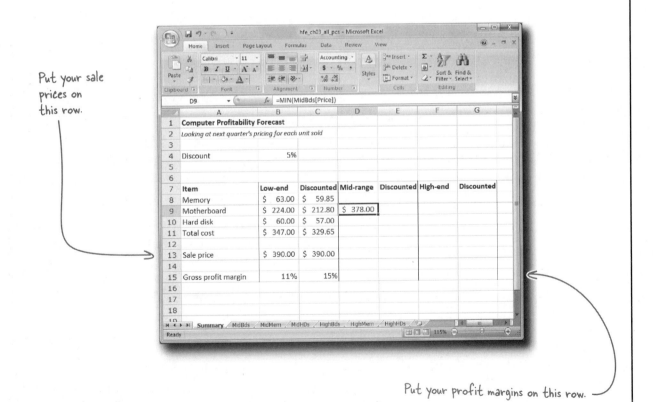

Put your profit margins on this row.

LONG EXERCISE SOLUTION

How profitable are your mid-range and high-end computers?

① Assign your new price sheets as tables. For each table that describes a component, create a table using the button under the Insert tab. Make sure you give them each a name!

② Using the same approach you had for evaluating low-end PCs, calculate the minimum costs for each component. This time, use **structured references** in your formula.

③ Calculate expected profit margins for the other products. Use the sale prices below, and fill in the necessary formulas in row 15.

Once your structured references are set up, writing formulas is a snap.

Did you notice that Excel tries to help you figure out which structured reference you're looking for?

Just press down-arrow and tab if Excel correctly starts to fill out your reference name.

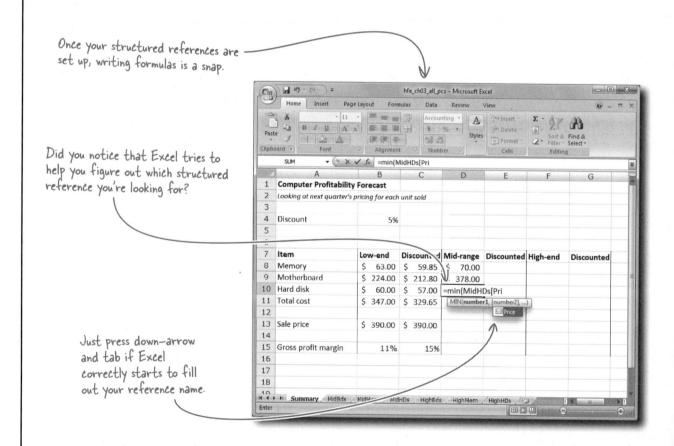

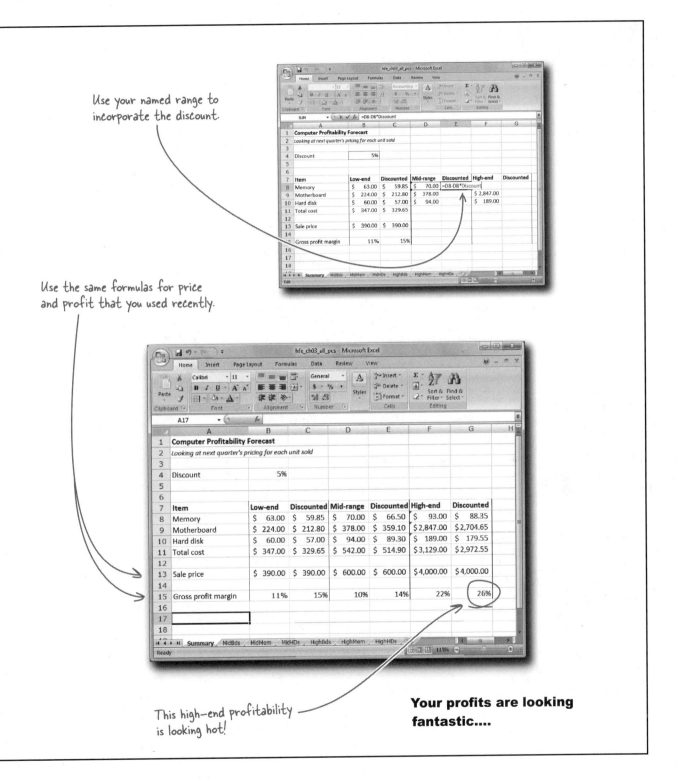

Use your named range to incorporate the discount.

Use the same formulas for price and profit that you used recently.

This high-end profitability is looking hot!

Your profits are looking fantastic....

Your profitability forecasts proved accurate

Business is great, and your sales guys are happier than ever!

4 change your point of view

Sort, zoom, and filter

The details of your data are tantalizing.

But only if you know *how* to look at them. In this chapter, you'll forget about formatting and functions and just focus on how to change your perspective on your data. When you are exploring your data, looking for issues to investigate, the **sort, zoom, and filter** tools offer surprising versatility to help you get a grip on what your data contains.

Political consultants need help decoding their fundraising database

The Main Campaign is working for the Dataville mayor and wants to solicit his supporters for money.

Your client is a super-intense, super-demanding politico. But the good news is that the data is pretty clean (that's always a relief!), and if you can help this group **organize their contributor list,** you'll have scored a huge account.

We heard you have serious data skills!

Here is their data.

The data is a list of their contributors' donations from the past year. And while the data is of a high quality, at over 4,000 rows, there's quite a lot of it!

4,100 is a lot of records!

Find the names of the big contributors

Getting in touch with their most passionate (that is, most generous!) contributors is a big deal. The small fries are important, but before anything else, the Main Campaign needs to get in touch with the big contributors.

We've got to separate the fat cats...

...from the small fries.

Sharpen your pencil

Take a look at your data. How could you change your perspective on it to show you the top donors?

....

....

....

....

Here's your data from the previous page.

✦ Load this! ✦

www.headfirstlabs.com/books/hfexcel/ hfe_ch04_data.xlsx

Sharpen your pencil
Solution

How did you decide you might change perspective on this data to show you the top donors?

If you had the data ordered by donation

amount, you could see the big donors at the

top.

....

...and put the little donors down here.

That way, you'd be able to group the big contributors together.

Maybe you could put all the big donors up here...

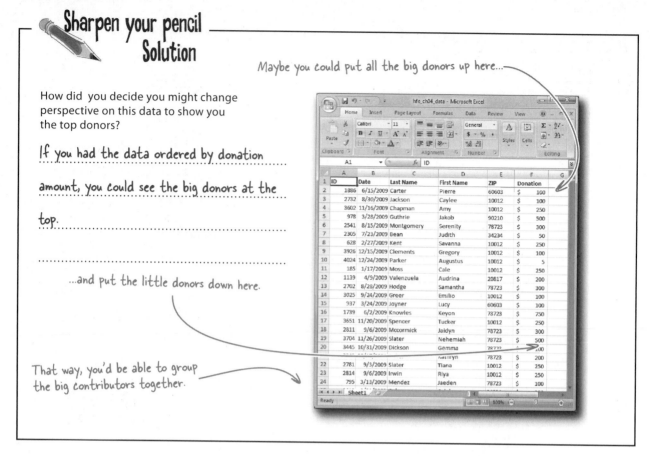

Sort changes the order of rows in your data

The **Sort** buttons are a useful tool that enables you to reshuffle the order of the rows in your data. The Sort buttons can be found under the Data tab of the Ribbon.

Here is the Ascending Sort button.

Here is the Descending Sort button.

To *sort ascending* means to order your data from first to last or smallest to largest, and to *sort descending* means to do the opposite.

There are many occasions where you'll want to use Sort to change the order of your data, but Sort is especially useful when you're looking at data for the first time and trying to get a feel for what's in it.

The plain ol' Sort button lets you do more sophisticated sorting.

Exercise

Let's sort your data to group all the big contributors together.

1 Select any cell in the column you want to sort by. Since you want to sort by donation here, you'd pick the Donation column.

You want to sort by donation, so put your cursor in this column.

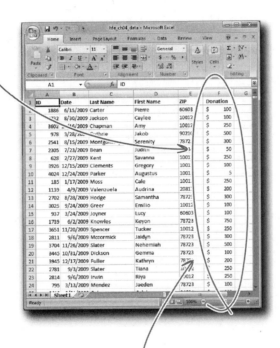

Sort by this field in a way that will send the larger donors up to the top of the list.

2 Click one of the Sort buttons to sort your data. Which button should you press to get big donors up top: Ascending or Descending?

Were you able to bring all the big contributors to the top of your list through sorting?

Exercise Solution

You can also select the whole column, and Excel will ask you whether you want it to sort just that column or the entire table.

1 Select a cell in the column you want to sort by.

Any old cell will do.

Press the Sort Descending button.

2 Sort the data. Which button should you press to get big donors up top?

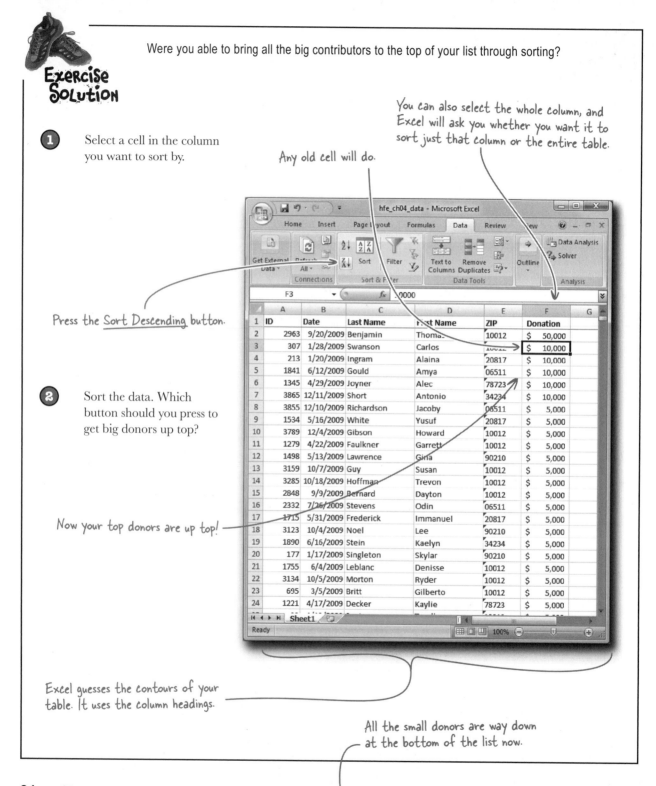

	A	B	C	D	E	F	G
1	ID	Date	Last Name	First Name	ZIP	Donation	
2	2963	9/20/2009	Benjamin	Thomas	10012	$ 50,000	
3	307	1/28/2009	Swanson	Carlos	10012	$ 10,000	
4	213	1/20/2009	Ingram	Alaina	20817	$ 10,000	
5	1841	6/12/2009	Gould	Amya	06511	$ 10,000	
6	1345	4/29/2009	Joyner	Alec	78723	$ 10,000	
7	3865	12/11/2009	Short	Antonio	34234	$ 10,000	
8	3855	12/10/2009	Richardson	Jacoby	06511	$ 5,000	
9	1534	5/16/2009	White	Yusuf	20817	$ 5,000	
10	3789	12/4/2009	Gibson	Howard	10012	$ 5,000	
11	1279	4/22/2009	Faulkner	Garrett	10012	$ 5,000	
12	1498	5/13/2009	Lawrence	Gina	90210	$ 5,000	
13	3159	10/7/2009	Guy	Susan	10012	$ 5,000	
14	3285	10/18/2009	Hoffman	Trevon	10012	$ 5,000	
15	2848	9/9/2009	Bernard	Dayton	10012	$ 5,000	
16	2332	7/26/2009	Stevens	Odin	06511	$ 5,000	
17	1715	5/31/2009	Frederick	Immanuel	20817	$ 5,000	
18	3123	10/4/2009	Noel	Lee	90210	$ 5,000	
19	1890	6/16/2009	Stein	Kaelyn	34234	$ 5,000	
20	177	1/17/2009	Singleton	Skylar	90210	$ 5,000	
21	1755	6/4/2009	Leblanc	Denisse	10012	$ 5,000	
22	3134	10/5/2009	Morton	Ryder	10012	$ 5,000	
23	695	3/5/2009	Britt	Gilberto	10012	$ 5,000	
24	1221	4/17/2009	Decker	Kaylie	78723	$ 5,000	

Now your top donors are up top!

Excel guesses the contours of your table. It uses the column headings.

All the small donors are way down at the bottom of the list now.

Sorting shows you different perspectives on a large data set

When you look at data for the first time, it's a good idea to sort by different columns to look for visible patterns.

When exploring your data, it never hurts to try sorting by a bunch of columns.

Sort by donation

	E	F	G
	ZIP	Donation	
	10012	$ 50,000	
	10012	$ 10,000	
	20817	$ 10,000	
	06511	$ 10,000	
	78723	$ 10,000	
	34234	$ 10,000	
	06511	$ 5,000	
	20817	$ 5,000	
	10012	$ 5,000	
	10012	$ 5,000	
	90210	$ 5,000	
	10012	$ 5,000	
	10012	$ 5,000	
	06511	$ 5,000	
	20817	$ 5,000	
	90210	$ 5,000	
	34234	$ 5,000	
	90210	$ 5,000	
	10012	$ 5,000	
	10012	$ 5,000	
	10012	$ 5,000	
	78723	$ 5,000	
	10012	$ 5,000	
	06511	$ 5,000	
	10012	$ 5,000	
	10012	$ 5,000	
	10012	$ 5,000	
	10012	$ 5,000	

Sort by zip

D	E	F
t Name	ZIP	Donation
ya	06511	$ 10,000
iby	06511	$ 5,000
n	06511	$ 5,000
ey	06511	$ 5,000
1son	06511	$ 5,000
na	06511	$ 3,000
ib	06511	$ 3,000
bine	06511	$ 2,500
lee	06511	$ 2,500
lisyn	06511	$ 2,500
rad	06511	$ 2,500
an	06511	$ 2,500
o	06511	$ 2,000
an	06511	$ 2,000
iyah	06511	$ 1,000
ie	06511	$ 1,000
a	06511	$ 1,000
a	06511	$ 1,000
as	06511	$ 1,000
y	06511	$ 1,000
iur	06511	$ 1,000
	06511	$ 1,000
hael	06511	$ 1,000
juin	06511	$ 1,000
son	06511	$ 1,000
a	06511	$ 1,000
:lynn	06511	$ 1,000
	06511	$ 1,000
	06511	$ 750

Sort by name

C	D
Last Name	First Name
Abbott	Corinne
Abbott	Ingrid
Abbott	Kaylie
Abbott	Rashad
Acevedo	Alma
Acevedo	Dante
Acevedo	Jeremiah
Acevedo	Natalie
Acosta	Alan
Acosta	Dayami
Acosta	Jaylin
Adams	Diamond
Adams	Hana
Adams	Jayce
Adams	Jaylan
Adams	Lewis
Adkins	Alvin
Adkins	Braxton
Adkins	Coby
Adkins	Danny
Adkins	Hanna
Aguilar	Dax
Aguilar	Isabelle
Aguilar	Mary
Aguilar	Meghan
Aguilar	Owen
Aguirre	Carlo
Aguirre	Sergio
Aguirre	Sloane

You never know what you might see when you look at your data from different perspectives.

Watch it!

Excel can figure out which columns are in your table... usually.

*If Excel doesn't sort **all** your columns together, it can wreck your database. Always save your data first and check it after sorting to make sure you and Excel got it right.*

Let's see what the Main Campaign has to say about this newly organized data....

That shows me who the big donors are, but not where they are. Could you sort by zip code and then by donation size? That way, I could look at donation-sorted sublists grouped by zip.

Here's what even more organized data would look like.

All the records are sorted by zip...

	A	B	C	D	E	F	G
1	ID	Date	Last Name	First Name	ZIP	Donation	
95	3986	12/20/2009	Boyer	Raven	06511	$ 20	
96	2549	8/15/2009	Harrington	Annie	06511	$ 20	
97	2255	7/18/2009	Gray	Jamarcus	06511	$ 20	
98	3634	11/18/2009	Hale	Kaydence	06511	$ 10	
99	111	1/11/2009	Washington	Jeremy	06511	$ 10	
100	1020	3/31/2009	Terrell	Josh	06511	$ 5	
101	11	1/1/2009	Albert	Charlie	06511	$ 5	
102	2963	9/20/2009	Benjamin	Thomas	10012	$ 50,000	
103	307	1/28/2009	Swanson	Carlos	10012	$ 10,000	
104	3789	12/4/2009	Gibson	Howard	10012	$ 5,000	
105	1279	4/22/2009	Faulkner	Garrett	10012	$ 5,000	
106	3159	10/7/2009	Guy	Susan	10012	$ 5,000	
107	3285	10/18/2009	Hoffman	Trevon	10012	$ 5,000	
108	2848	9/9/2009	Bernard	Dayton	10012	$ 5,000	
109	1755	6/4/2009	Leblanc	Denisse	10012	$ 5,000	
110	3134	10/5/2009	Morton	Ryder	10012	$ 5,000	
111	695	3/5/2009	Britt	Gilberto	10012	$ 5,000	
112	99	1/10/2009	Santos	Tyrell	10012	$ 5,000	
113	3434	10/31/2009	Holland	Kody	10012	$ 5,000	
114	1772	6/6/2009	Dominguez	Jakayla	10012	$ 5,000	

...and then they're sorted again, but this time by donation.

Your client from the Main Campaign

Exercise

Let's see if we can fulfill the client's request: first to sort the data by zip code, and *then* to sort it by donation. This sort will enable us to look at the biggest givers by grouping them by geography.

1 To execute this new and more complex sort, start by clicking the big Sort button. (Be sure your cursor is inside your data table first.)

Click this button here.

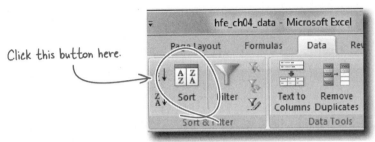

2 In the dialog that pops up, start by telling Excel to sort your data by zip.

First, you want to sort by zip.

That will group all the records together by region.

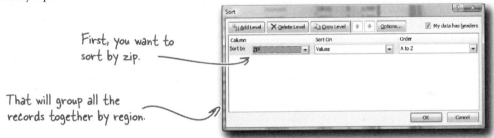

3 Now click **Add Level** and add a new level to sort by donation. You may receive a warning dialog box...just do what you think is best.

Next, you want to sort the data by donation.

Should you sort ascending or descending?

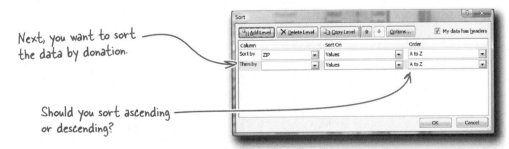

Exercise Solution

Were you able to sort the data by zip and then donation?

① To execute this new and more complex sort, start by clicking the big Sort button. (Be sure your cursor is inside your data table first.)

② In the dialog that pops up, start by telling Excel to sort your data by zip.

③ Now click **Add Level** and add a new level to sort by donation. You may receive a warning dialog box…just do what you think is best.

Here is your newly sorted data!

It's sorted by zip, and then it's sorted by donation.

Now you can look at the top donors from each zip code.

You probably received this warning dialog box.

Excel needs to store zips as text, because if zips were numbers, Excel would get rid of the 0 in 06511.

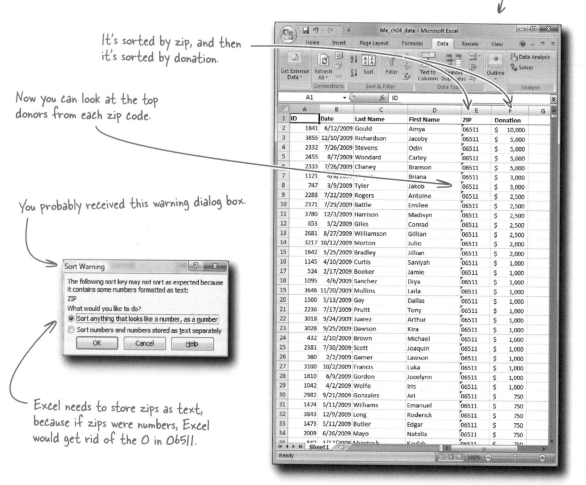

there are no
Dumb Questions

Q: What do some of those other options mean inside of the Sort dialog box?

A: There are lots of different ways you can sort besides alphabetizing text and sorting numbers from smallest to largest or vice versa. For example, you can sort by color.

Q: Why would I want to sort by color?

A: Very often people will highlight cells in their spreadsheet to be different colors, and you'll see long spreadsheets that have various elements highlighted. If you'd like to group those elements together, you can sort by color.

Q: Is it good formatting practice to highlight cells by color? It seems like that would be an alternative to sorting in terms of drawing your eye to various parts of the spreadsheet.

A: Generally there are better ways to tag data than highlighting cells. You can sort by color, but most formulas can't read your cells' formatting. So if you want to tag interesting cells, it's better to add a column and insert your own text or Boolean functions (which you'll learn about later on).

Q: So we can sort by color. What else?

A: Under the Order drop box, you can set up a Custom List. Custom lists enable you to create any arbitrary sorting you want. So if Excel doesn't automatically sort your data in exactly the way you need it to, you can create a custom list that shows exactly how you need that data sorted.

Q: How big of a problem is it when Excel sorts one column but not another?

A: It can be terrible. Think about what would happen with this data: each donation amount is tied to a specific person, so if you changed the order of the donations but kept the order of people the same, you wouldn't know who gave what anymore.

Q: That sounds awful.

A: It happens. And it's indeed awful.

Q: How do I avoid it?

A: This is a reminder of a very important principle of dealing with data: always keep copies of your original data. Once you've done an analysis of the data, it's always a good idea to check your data against the original to make sure that nothing weird happened.

Q: That sounds true, but it's not very reassuring. How do I *avoid* a screwed-up sort?

A: Sorting is another place where the Tables feature you learned about in Chapter 2 comes in handy. If you define your data set as a table, then you are being really explicit with Excel about the dimensions of your data.

Q: So then Excel always knows what data is in my table, and it won't accidentally just sort a single column.

A: Exactly. You don't *have* to define your data as a table in order to sort it correctly, but for the uber-paranoid the Table feature is the way to go.

Nice work on sorting that data.

Now you can see how many large donations fall into each zip. Let's see what the client thinks....

Yeah, that's OK, but I'm still having a hard time <u>seeing</u> it all. Scrolling up and down takes forever. I just need a way to look at more of the data at once.

Looking at the data is a good thing.
It's a nonobvious but important part of data analysis, and your client is right to want to be able to see the data better, not just group it correctly. What should you do?

← Your client

Scrolling all the way from the top to the bottom can take a long time...

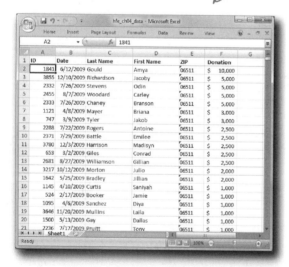

...and a long scroll is a great way to lose track of the big picture about your data.

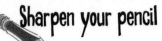
Sharpen your pencil

What do you think of each of these solutions? Is it a good idea? Is one of them the best?

1 Use formulas to create summaries of the data.

....

....

....

2 Get a really big monitor.

....

....

....

3 Delete records you don't need.

....

....

....

4 Zoom out.

....

....

....

Sharpen your pencil
Solution

What can you do to help your client get a better perspective on the big picture of the data?

1   Use formulas to create summaries of the data.

I can do this, but it isn't really what the client is asking for. Formulas and their results might be illuminating, but they take you away from actually looking at the data.

2   Get a really big monitor.

This is a great idea! It would be great to be able to see a few thousand legible spreadsheet cells on the screen at once. Problem is, big monitors can get expensive, and that's probably not a reasonable response to the client.

3   Delete records you don't need.

No way. This is just asking for trouble. If I really can't find a way to get the right visualization of your data, I can use summaries based on formulas. Deleting records is the fastest way to lose all perspective on the data.

4   Zoom out.

Zooming in and out on data is something that spreadsheet ninjas do all the time.

Zooming out is a great idea. Sometimes you need to look at the forest, and sometimes you need to look at the trees. Zooming will let us do it.

See a lot more of your data with Zoom

Sometimes you need to focus on a small part of your data. Why not zoom **way** in?

Here's your spreadsheet at 400% zoom.

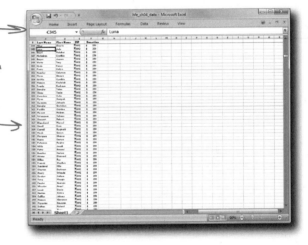

Maybe you need to think really hard about Jada Luna!

Sometimes you need to focus on the big picture. In that case, zoom way out.

This is your spreadsheet zoomed out to 25%.

If you look closely, you can see quite a lot.

Getting the big picture through zooming out is **not about straining your eyes** (if you feel your eyes strain, you should be zooming in!). It's about looking at as much of the whole picture of your data as you can see at once. To zoom, click the View tab to get to the Zoom button.

Click this button for all your zoom options.

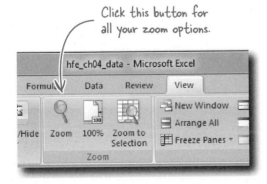

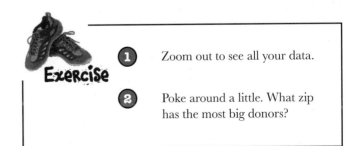

Exercise

1. Zoom out to see all your data.

2. Poke around a little. What zip has the most big donors?

Exercise Solution

Were you able to get a better perspective on the data after zooming way out?

A93 f_x 2398

	ID	Date	Last Name	First Name	ZIP	Donation
92	2406	8/14/2009	Berry	Reid	06511	$ 100
93	2393	7/31/2009	Hiner	Madeleine	06511	$ 50
94	3447	10/31/2009	Erter	Tristian	06511	$ 20
95	3986	12/20/2009	Bayer	Raven	06511	$ 20
96	2549	8/15/2009	Harrington	Annie	06511	$ 20
97	2255	7/18/2009	Gray	Jamarcus	06511	$ 20
98	3634	11/18/2009	Hale	Kaydence	06511	$ 10
99	111	1/11/2009	Washington	Jeremy	06511	$ 10
100	1020	3/31/2009	Terrell	Josh	06511	$ 5
101	11	1/11/2009	Albert	Charlie	06511	$ 5
102	2963	9/20/2009	Benjamin	Thamar	10012	$ 50,000
103	307	1/28/2009	Swanson	Carlar	10012	$ 10,000
104	3789	12/14/2009	Gibran	Howard	10012	$ 5,000
105	1279	4/22/2009	Faulkner	Garrett	10012	$ 5,000
106	3159	10/7/2009	Guy	Swan	10012	$ 5,000
107	3285	10/18/2009	Hoffman	Trevon	10012	$ 5,000
108	2848	9/4/2009	Bernard	Dayton	10012	$ 5,000
109	1755	6/4/2009	Leblanc	Deniere	10012	$ 5,000
110	3134	10/5/2009	Martan	Ryder	10012	$ 5,000
111	695	3/5/2009	Britt	Gilberto	10012	$ 5,000
112	99	1/10/2009	Santar	Tyrell	10012	$ 5,000
113	3434	10/31/2009	Holland	Kady	10012	$ 5,000
114	1772	6/6/2009	Dominguez	Jakayla	10012	$ 5,000
115	2712	8/29/2009	Walker	Izabella	10012	$ 5,000
116	3833	12/8/2009	Knapp	Guadalupe	10012	$ 5,000
117	3027	9/25/2009	Cooper	Cristina	10012	$ 5,000
118	610	2/26/2009	Kramer	Camryn	10012	$ 5,000
119	2835	9/8/2009	Cochran	Shirley	10012	$ 5,000
120	2380	7/30/2009	Waodard	Calten	10012	$ 5,000
121	709	3/6/2009	Workman	Haylie	10012	$ 5,000
122	567	2/21/2009	Aguirre	Valentina	10012	$ 5,000
123	3286	10/18/2009	Webb	Hailey	10012	$ 3,000
124	1738	6/2/2009	Abbott	Farhad	10012	$ 3,000
125	1611	5/23/2009	Ruiz	Motiar	10012	$ 3,000
126	486	2/14/2009	Berg	Ezequiel	10012	$ 3,000
127	1499	5/13/2009	Pugh	Zechariah	10012	$ 3,000
128	1652	5/26/2009	Cohen	Ainsley	10012	$ 3,000
129	1547	5/17/2009	Stanley	Amiah	10012	$ 3,000

hfe_ch04_data - Microsoft Excel

Home   Insert   Page Layout   Formulas   Data   Review   View

Zip 10012 appears to have the most large donors!

135	3744	11/30/2009	Baker	Izayah	10012	$	3,000
136	3268	10/17/2009	Mccarty	Baran	10012	$	2,500
137	3150	10/16/2009	Shepard	Marquez	10012	$	2,500
138	1132	4/9/2009	Berry	Alanna	10012	$	2,500
139	811	3/15/2009	Dillard	Nick	10012	$	2,500
140	732	3/8/2009	Watts	Heidi	10012	$	2,500
141	55	1/6/2009	Madden	Cullen	10012	$	2,500
142	3814	12/6/2009	Wells	Sonny	10012	$	2,500
143	2721	8/30/2009	Bender	Conor	10012	$	2,500
144	1788	6/7/2009	Kinney	Jazlene	10012	$	2,500
145	3881	12/12/2009	Cortez	Campbell	10012	$	2,500
146	3336	10/22/2009	Obrien	Rory	10012	$	2,500
147	3596	11/15/2009	Dunlap	Tristan	10012	$	2,500
148	679	3/14/2009	Mendez	Katelyn	10012	$	2,500
149	1640	5/25/2009	Daniels	Jaqueline	10012	$	2,000
150	298	1/27/2009	Bird	Pranav	10012	$	2,000
151	749	3/9/2009	Watkins	Maroli	10012	$	2,000
152	1653	5/26/2009	Delacruz	Kendra	10012	$	2,000
153	3191	10/10/2009	Harrington	Gina	10012	$	2,000
154	1267	4/21/2009	Noble	Brian	10012	$	2,000
155	34	1/4/2009	Knight	Darnell	10012	$	2,000
156	286	1/26/2009	Ray	Amiya	10012	$	2,000
157	2550	8/16/2009	Roberts	Jardin	10012	$	2,000
158	1641	5/25/2009	Marsh	Karter	10012	$	2,000
159	2067	7/2/2009	Lynch	Vincent	10012	$	2,000
160	2316	7/25/2009	Fleming	Kareem	10012	$	2,000
161	3269	10/17/2009	Callahan	Mohammed	10012	$	2,000
162	2317	7/25/2009	Snider	Alfreda	10012	$	2,000
163	4086	12/31/2009	Marshall	Karran	10012	$	2,000
164	2439	8/6/2009	Daugherty	Autumn	10012	$	2,000
165	3866	12/11/2009	Dickerson	Jadan	10012	$	2,000
166	1192	4/15/2009	Townsend	Ariana	10012	$	2,000
167	598	2/25/2009	Moody	Sophie	10012	$	2,000
168	3288	10/18/2009	Zimmerman	Edith	10012	$	2,000
169	925	3/24/2009	Mayer	Kendrick	10012	$	2,000
170	1094	4/6/2009	Schmidt	Howard	10012	$	2,000
171	913	3/23/2009	Wilkins	Kadence	10012	$	1,500
172	3113	10/3/2009	Sweeney	Alina	10012	$	1,500
173	2432	8/5/2009	Mcmillan	Haley	10012	$	1,500
174	1193	4/15/2009	Preston	Theresa	10012	$	1,500
175	3597	11/16/2009	Santiago	Abbie	10012	$	1,500
176	3734	11/29/2009	Suarez	Addisyn	10012	$	1,500
177	3907	12/14/2009	Zimmerman	Jazmine	10012	$	1,500
178	2311	7/24/2009	Maynard	Kareem	10012	$	1,500
179	3519	11/18/2009	Johnston	Cassidy	10012	$	1,500
180	324	1/30/2009	Bates	Bailey	10012	$	1,500
181	1418	5/6/2009	Bates	Daniela	10012	$	1,500

Sheet1

Ready

This spreadsheet is zoomed out to 50%, but you can zoom at whatever feels best for your eyes given the size of your monitor.

This slider down here is a great way to zoom in and out.

50%

Your client is impressed!

That is just what we're looking for. Good job. I believed in your abilities and I can see that I was right. Now I have a more specific question for you. I really just want to look at the big donors (say, people who've given $1,000 or more) in zip code 78723. Let me see what you can come up with.

Looks like Mr. Demanding is impressed!
Without running any sort of function or doing any sort of formatting, you were able to sort and zoom your way to a greater clarity about his data.

But now he wants to focus on just one subset of the data. You know you can't just **delete** the data he doesn't want to focus on. How can you look at just the data he wants without changing the rest of the data?

Filters hide data you don't want to see

Sorting and zooming have given you a rich big-picture perspective, but sometimes you want to look at just a slice of data. Try clicking on the **Filter** button.

Filters are under the Data tab on the Ribbon.

This little funnel represents the Filter.

Filters are convenient because they give you a way to **hide the data you don't want to see**. It's still very much there; it's just conveniently out of the way. And just as with sorting, when you're exploring a new data set for the first time, it's a great idea to run filters to look at various subsets of the data.

Do this!

Select a cell in the column you want to filter and click Filter. What happens?

Use Filter drop boxes to tell Excel how to filter your data

When you click on the Filter button, Excel puts a drop box on every column in your data table.

Click one of these to activate the Filter drop box for that column.

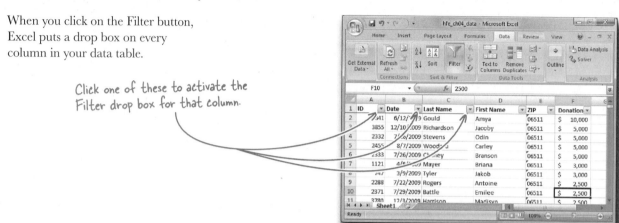

When you click on one of the drop boxes, Excel gives you a bunch of options for filtering the data based on the data in that column.

You tell Excel to sort from inside the Filter drop box.

These values are a complete list of all the different pieces of data in the ZIP column.

Uncheck "Select All" to reset the filter so that nothing is selected.

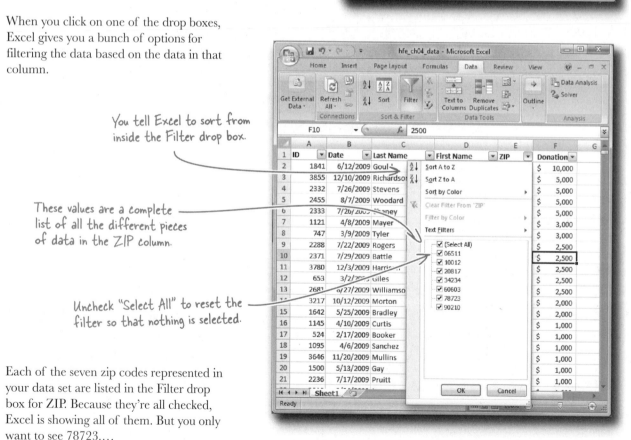

Each of the seven zip codes represented in your data set are listed in the Filter drop box for ZIP. Because they're all checked, Excel is showing all of them. But you only want to see 78723....

An unexpected note from the Main Campaign...

From: Main Campaign
To: Head First
Subject: 78723

Dear Head First,

Something you should know about political campaigns: we move fast. Everything we do is due yesterday.

What I'm saying is, we need that 78723 data subset now. For real, *right now*.

—M.C.

Better get that database back to them right away....

Yikes...they're cracking the whip!

Exercise

Your client wants to see a list that contains only people who live in the 78723 zip code and who gave $1,000 or more. Use filters to create that list.

1 Tell Excel to filter by zip 78723. With the Filter drop box activated for the ZIP field, uncheck the Select All box so that none of the zips are selected. Then select the 78723 zip and press OK.

This one is easy.

2 Apply *another* filter that shows only people with donations of $1,000 or more. Select the Donation filter drop box and then the options that you believe will show you only the individuals you want to see.

This one's a little trickier. —

Exercise Solution

Were you able to apply the filters that show only people from zip 78723 who gave $1,000 or more?

1 Tell Excel to filter by zip 78723. With the Filter drop box activated for the ZIP field, uncheck the Select All box so that none of the zips is selected. Then select the 78723 zip and press OK.

Here's what your filter should look like to make the screen show only 78723.

Your data has now gone from showing everything to showing only 78723.

You can see your filter is working by looking at the blue row numbers.

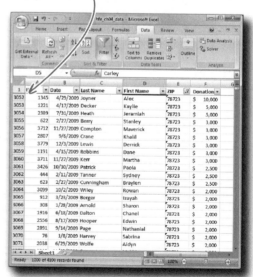

2 Apply ***another*** filter that shows only people with donations of $1,000 or more. Select the Donation filter drop box and then the options that you believe will show you only the individual you want to see.

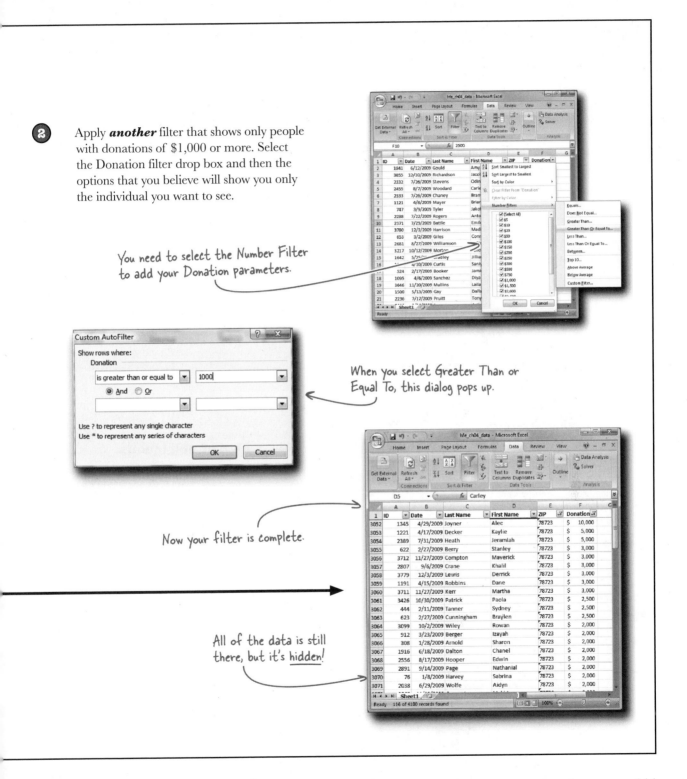

You need to select the Number Filter to add your Donation parameters.

When you select Greater Than or Equal To, this dialog pops up.

Now your filter is complete.

All of the data is still there, but it's *hidden!*

The Main Campaign is delighted with your work

Great data work! We'll raise a lot of money for the mayor with this. One more thing...I met this guy the other day named Alex (I think). He was a big donor, but I'd never heard of him, and now I can't figure out who he is. Maybe you could do one of your fancy filters and help me out?

This is kind of ambiguous.

A guy named Alex who's a big giver? There could be tons of people in the database named Alex! This could be like finding a needle in a haystack. Except that we have a potent tool: filters.

there are no
Dumb Questions

Q: What ever happened to writing formulas? It seems like all this sorting, zooming, and filtering is really just a prelude to writing formulas, which is the real meat of data analysis.

A: It'd be better to say that good thinking about data is the substance of data analysis, not writing formulas or any other feature of Excel or any other software.

Q: So where do sort/zoom/filter and formulas fit into data analysis?

A: Sorting, zooming, and filtering are great tools to use to get a sense of what is inside data that you are looking at for the first time. Sometimes you just need a better perspective on your data, and the way to get at that perspective is literally to look at the data in a bunch of different ways.

Q: So once I want to start drawing conclusions about data, I'm probably not going to need sort/zoom/filter so much, right?

A: Your mileage may vary. It may be that your specific problem really needs nothing besides the perspective that these visualization tools give you. Or it may be that you need to create a model that summarizes and manipulates the data once you've gotten the perspective you need.

Q: So that is where formulas come in?

A: Yes. Formulas, in their most general sense, take data as arguments and return new data. If your analytic goals aren't met by simply changing your point of view on the data, chances are you'll need to hit the data with some formulas to achieve the manipulation or summary that you need.

Q: Still, it's kind of cool just how much you can do with these visualization tools.

A: Definitely. Don't just accept without question the default zoom amount of Excel or the ordering of the data for analysis you receive. You can use sorting, zooming, and filtering to change up your perspective in a big way, enabling you to understand your data better.

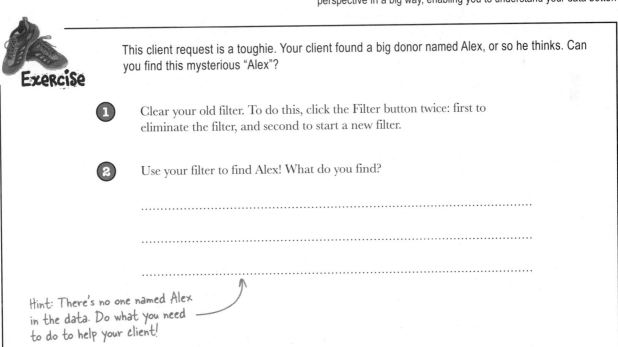

Exercise

This client request is a toughie. Your client found a big donor named Alex, or so he thinks. Can you find this mysterious "Alex"?

1 Clear your old filter. To do this, click the Filter button twice: first to eliminate the filter, and second to start a new filter.

2 Use your filter to find Alex! What do you find?

....

....

....

Hint: There's no one named Alex in the data. Do what you need to do to help your client!

Exercise Solution

Were you able to dig up this mysterious donor?

1 Clear your old filter. To do this, click the Filter button twice: first to eliminate the filter, and second to start a new filter.

2 Use your filter to find Alex!

There's no Alex, but there's Alec, Alejandro, and Alessandro. All of
them are small givers, except for one of them. There's an Alec who's a
$10,000 donor. He must be the one!

What you see here depends on the specific filter you created.

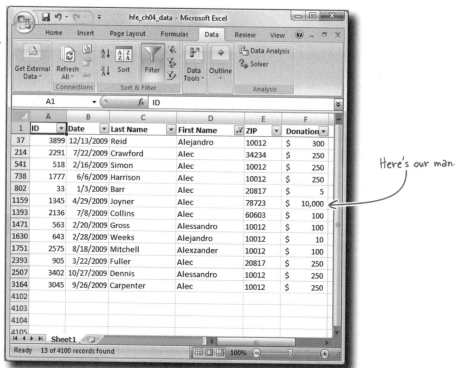

Here's our man.

Your own screen may look different.

Donations are pouring in!

The Main Campaign was able to
get in touch with Alec, and the lists
you isolated have proven to be really
valuable for the Dataville mayor's
fundraising efforts!

From: Dataville Mayor
To: Head First
Subject: Nice job with the data

Dear Head First,

As I kicked off my campaign I was
frankly somewhat surprised to
discover all my top donors fully
organized and taken care of. In the
past, this has been like herding cats.

I asked the Main Campaign what they'd
done differently this year to achieve
such expedient and efficient results.
Their answer was that you'd done it.

I've suggested to the Main Campaign
that they send all my campaign's
data work to you. It's quite a lot, but
you've shown that you can handle it.
Congratulations.

—The Dataville Mayor

Great work!

This is what you had hoped for!

5 data types

Make Excel value your values

This diploma is going to triple my salary....

This thing is just words on paper.

Excel doesn't always show you what it's thinking.

Sometimes, Excel will show you a number but think of it as text. Or it might show you some text that it sees as a number. Excel will even show you data that is neither number nor text! In this chapter, you're going to **learn how to see data the way Excel sees it**, no matter how it's displayed. Not only will this knowledge give you greater control over your data (and fewer "What the #$%! is going on?" experiences), but it will also help you unlock the whole universe of formulas.

Your doctor friend is on a deadline and has broken data

He's just completed a landmark study that evaluates the effectiveness of a drug on a patient's white blood cell counts, and his results are going to be really important for clinical practice.

But there's a problem. His data is exhibiting **weird behaviors** that prevent him from using formulas. Can you fix his data for him? If you help, he'll put your name on the paper he publishes.

My data is a mess and I need to submit my paper soon! What's the etiology of these formula anomalies?

Your buddy, the doctor

Let's see what the problem is....

Exercise

Let's start off by trying to get the average white blood cell count for the pre-treatment control group. Load the data and see if you can use the AVERAGE() function to calculate the average.

Load this!

www.headfirstlabs.com/books/hfexcel/
hfe_ch05_white_blood_cells.xlsx

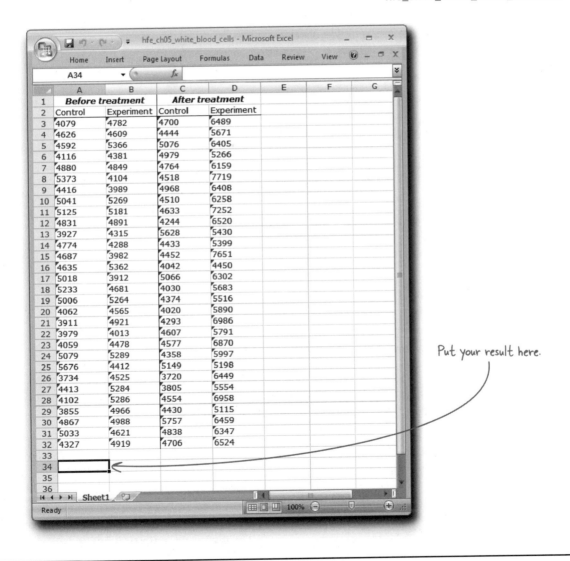

	Before treatment		After treatment	
	Control	Experiment	Control	Experiment
3	4079	4782	4700	6489
4	4626	4609	4444	5671
5	4592	5366	5076	6405
6	4116	4381	4979	5266
7	4880	4849	4764	6159
8	5373	4104	4518	7719
9	4416	3989	4968	6408
10	5041	5269	4510	6258
11	5125	5181	4633	7252
12	4831	4891	4244	6520
13	3927	4315	5628	5430
14	4774	4288	4433	5399
15	4687	3982	4452	7651
16	4635	5362	4042	4450
17	5018	3912	5066	6302
18	5233	4681	4030	5683
19	5006	5264	4374	5516
20	4062	4565	4020	5890
21	3911	4921	4293	6986
22	3979	4013	4607	5791
23	4059	4478	4577	6870
24	5079	5289	4358	5997
25	5676	4412	5149	5198
26	3734	4525	3720	6449
27	4413	5284	3805	5554
28	4102	5286	4554	6958
29	3855	4966	4430	5115
30	4867	4988	5757	6459
31	5033	4621	4838	6347
32	4327	4919	4706	6524

Put your result here.

Exercise Solution

You just attempted to use the AVERAGE() function to get the average white blood cell count of the control group before treatment. What happened?

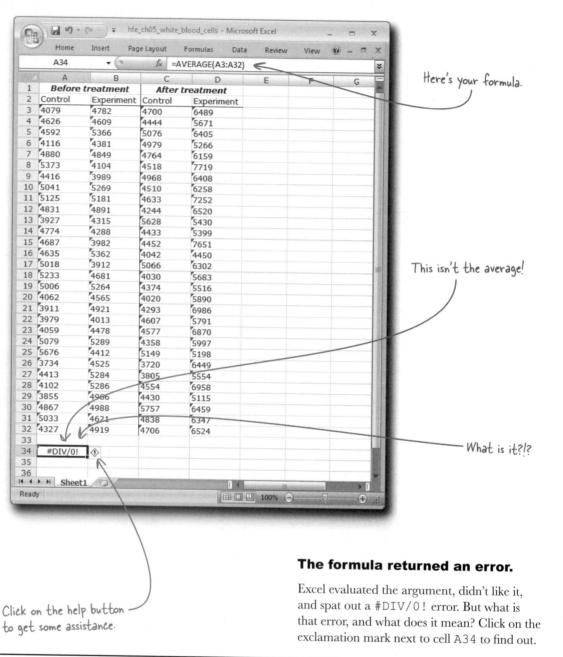

Here's your formula.

This isn't the average!

What is it?!?

Click on the help button to get some assistance.

The formula returned an error.

Excel evaluated the argument, didn't like it, and spat out a #DIV/0! error. But what is that error, and what does it mean? Click on the exclamation mark next to cell A34 to find out.

Somehow your average formula divided by zero

The help screen for the error you receive will tell you the kinds of things that are causing that error. Sometimes there are a bunch of possible reasons you're getting the error, and you need to rule some out in order to figure out which reason is in effect.

This is what `#DIV/0!` *means.*

Under the hood, Excel is using the `AVERAGE()` formula like this. For some reason, Excel sees "Count of patients" as equal to 0.

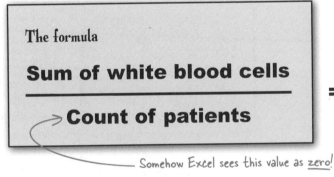

The formula

Sum of white blood cells
─────────────────────
Count of patients

=

The output

Average blood cell count

Somehow Excel sees this value as zero!

> This makes no sense! Clearly there are numbers there. Why would Excel count zero numbers?!?

See?!? Numbers!

Maybe these green triangles have something to do with this weirdness.

	A	B
1	*Before treatment*	
2	Control	Experiment
3	4079	4782
4	4626	4609
5	4592	5366
6	4116	4381
7	4880	4849

Data in Excel can be text or numbers

The problem in this case is that even though your data consists of numbers, inside the spreadsheet those numbers have the wrong **data type**. Excel uses data types to distinguish among different types of data, and sometimes Excel gets data type assignments wrong.

Here, Excel has assigned the data type **text** to your blood cell counts when it should have assigned the type **number**. This has big implications for how Excel uses the data.

These green triangles are actually the "Number stored as text" warning.

29	3855	4966	4430	5115
30	4867	4988	5757	6459
31	5033	4621	4838	6347
32	4327	4919	4706	6524

If you select a cell with a green triangle, you can click on a button that explains the warning.

The data type of your cell determines how functions can use the data in it.

These numbers are actually stored as text!

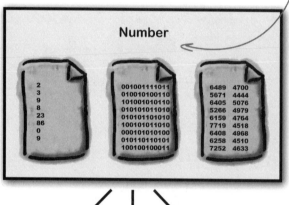

Number

Text

SUM ( )   COUNT ( )   AVERAGE ( )

LEFT ( )   MID ( )   FIND ( )

What look like numbers to you can be represented in Excel as either numbers *or text*. Usually, Excel can figure out which is which.

These only accept and return numbers.

These accept numbers and text but always return text.

When you type something like this...

1.012

...Excel will recognize it and internally represent it as a number.

Sometimes, when you load data that looks like the numbers, Excel thinks it's text.

Pŏŏl Puzzle

Your **job** is to take data types from the pool and place them into the blank lines in the Text and Number boxes. You may **not** use the same data type more than once. Your **goal** is to figure out how Excel needs to represent data internally.

Text

Number

Note: Each thing from the pool can only be used once!

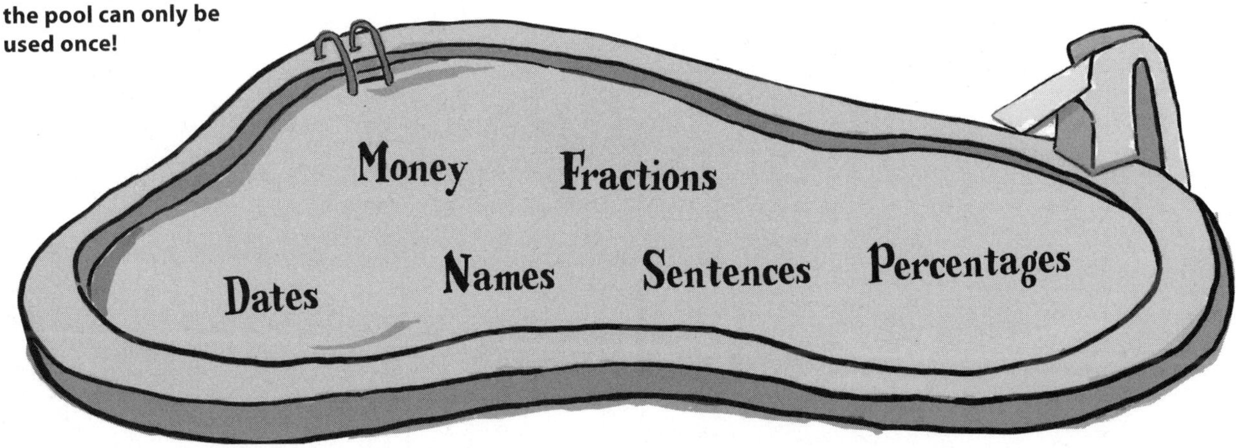

Money   Fractions

Dates   Names   Sentences   Percentages

Pool Puzzle Answers

You just classified a bunch of different
types of data as Text or Numbers.
What did you find?

Text
Sentences
Names

Number
Money
Fractions
Dates
Percentages

**Note: Each thing from
the pool can only be
used once!**

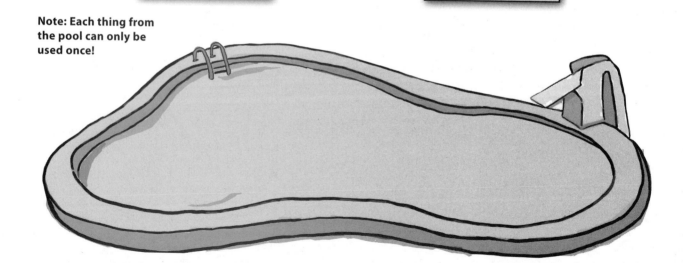

The doctor has had this problem before

I should have mentioned it...this issue can be a pain. It has to do with our proprietary database. The database exports values, but Excel reads the values as text. To fix the problem, we usually retype the data manually.

Will you have to retype the data?

Retyping the data would be a big pain. Not only would it take a lot of time, but there's a really good chance that you'll make typos. In an analysis as important as this one, it's crucial for the data to be accurate.

There's got to be a better way to get Excel to see the white blood cell counts as numbers than retyping the data....

You need a function that tells Excel to treat your text as a value

Excel has functions to do all sorts of stuff, including turning text into values. You just need to pick the right function.

You need a function that enables you to do this.

You give the function your text.

Excel reads the text value and sees that it's really a number.

=FUNCTION(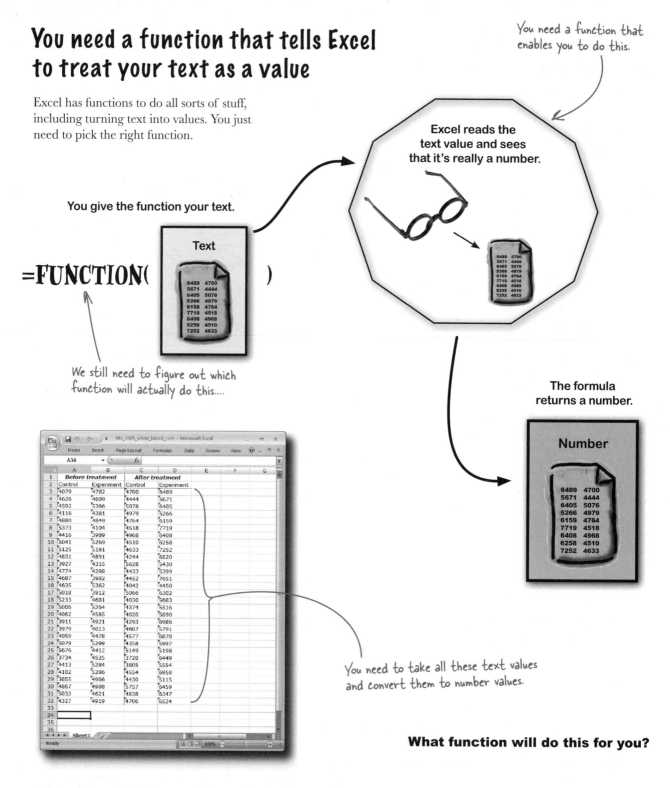)

We still need to figure out which function will actually do this....

The formula returns a number.

You need to take all these text values and convert them to number values.

What function will do this for you?

WHO DOES WHAT?

These functions are all related to data types. Some tell you about the data type of a cell, and some return values that change a cell's data type. Match each function to what it does.

VALUE   Returns a value that says whether a cell has something in it besides text.

TEXT   Tells you whether the data type of a cell is text.

ISREF   Converts a value to text.

TYPE   Tells you the data type of a cell.

ISTEXT   Returns the value of a cell regardless of whether a cell's data type is "value."

ISBLANK   Tells you whether the cell in the formulas argument is a reference.

ISNONTEXT   Tells you whether a cell is empty of data.

Which function will convert your text to numbers?   Write your answer here.

....

Each of these functions relates to data types. What did you determine that each does?

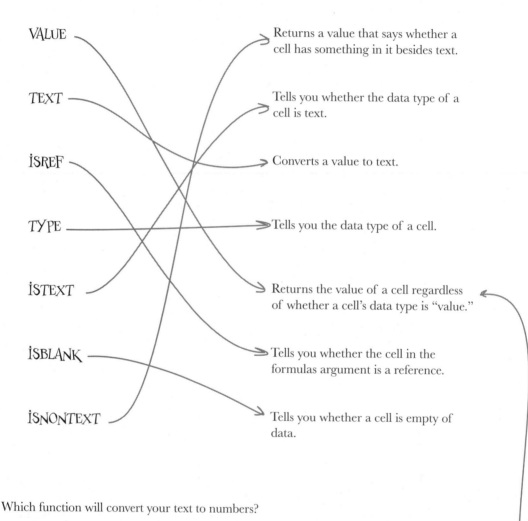

VALUE

TEXT

ISREF

TYPE

ISTEXT

ISBLANK

ISNONTEXT

Returns a value that says whether a cell has something in it besides text.

Tells you whether the data type of a cell is text.

Converts a value to text.

Tells you the data type of a cell.

Returns the value of a cell regardless of whether a cell's data type is "value."

Tells you whether the cell in the formulas argument is a reference.

Tells you whether a cell is empty of data.

Which function will convert your text to numbers?

Definitely the VALUE() function!

Let's take VALUE () for a spin.....

Exercise

Convert your text numbers to values. Get the average white blood cell count.

Fill columns F through I with VALUE() formulas that refer to A3:D32.

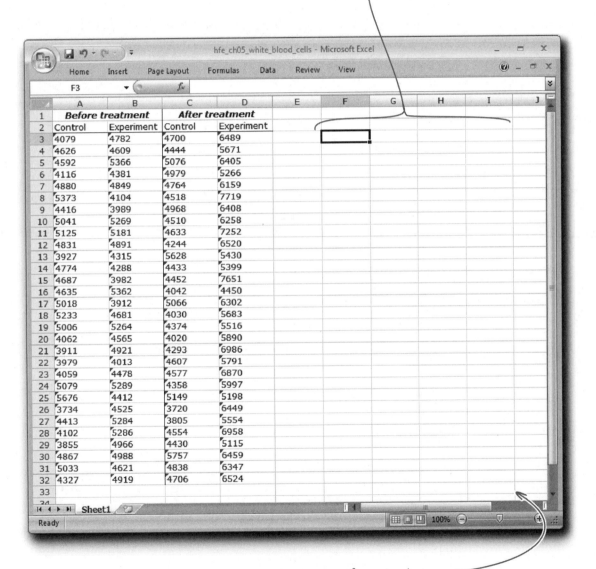

Write formulas down here to get the average for each column.

convert to values

Exercise Solution

Were you able to create formulas to tell Excel to represent the text values as numbers, and then get the average for each group?

This cell has the formula =VALUE(A3)

	A	B	C	D	E	F	G	H	I
1	*Before treatment*		*After treatment*						
2	Control	Experiment	Control	Experiment					
3	4079	4782	4700	6489		4079	4782	4700	6489
4	4626	4609	4444	5671		4626	4609	4444	5671
5	4592	5366	5076	6405		4592	5366	5076	6405
6	4116	4381	4979	5266		4116	4381	4979	5266
7	4880	4849	4764	6159		4880	4849	4764	6159
8	5373	4104	4518	7719		5373	4104	4518	7719
9	4416	3989	4968	6408		4416	3989	4968	6408
10	5041	5269	4510	6258		5041	5269	4510	6258
11	5125	5181	4633	7252		5125	5181	4633	7252
12	4831	4891	4244	6520		4831	4891	4244	6520
13	3927	4315	5628	5430		3927	4315	5628	5430
14	4774	4288	4433	5399		4774	4288	4433	5399
15	4687	3982	4452	7651		4687	3982	4452	7651
16	4635	5362	4042	4450		4635	5362	4042	4450
17	5018	3912	5066	6302		5018	3912	5066	6302
18	5233	4681	4030	5683		5233	4681	4030	5683
19	5006	5264	4374	5516		5006	5264	4374	5516
20	4062	4565	4020	5890		4062	4565	4020	5890
21	3911	4921	4293	6986		3911	4921	4293	6986
22	3979	4013	4607	5791		3979	4013	4607	5791
23	4059	4478	4577	6870		4059	4478	4577	6870
24	5079	5289	4358	5997		5079	5289	4358	5997
25	5676	4412	5149	5198		5676	4412	5149	5198
26	3734	4525	3720	6449		3734	4525	3720	6449
27	4413	5284	3805	5554		4413	5284	3805	5554
28	4102	5286	4554	6958		4102	5286	4554	6958
29	3855	4966	4430	5115		3855	4966	4430	5115
30	4867	4988	5757	6459		4867	4988	5757	6459
31	5033	4621	4838	6347		5033	4621	4838	6347
32	4327	4919	4706	6524		4327	4919	4706	6524
33									
34					Average	4581.867	4716.4	4589.167	6157.2
35									
36									

Cell I34 formula: =AVERAGE(I3:I32)

This cell has the formula =VALUE(C15).

Here you go!

These are the averages you've been looking for!

Those are exactly the figures I needed! Thank you so much. I just need to do a few more things on my side to straighten things up, and we'll be ready to submit the article. Sounds like you're going to be a published scientist! Congratulations.

there are no
Dumb Questions

Q: When is changing data types likely to be an issue for me?

A: Chances are, you're most likely to experience it when you load data into Excel that has been exported from another system, like a relational database.

Q: So Excel generally does a good job at figuring out my data types when I type data into my spreadsheet?

A: Definitely. Excel is really smart at looking at what you type and assigning the correct data type. What's really important for you to know is that the visual representation of your data—how it looks and how it's formatted—doesn't necessarily tell you how Excel is representing the data internally.

Q: Why couldn't AVERAGE() **automatically recognize my numbers as numbers even if their data type is text?**

A: For all Excel knew, you *meant* for the white blood cell counts to have the data type text. While it's not terribly common, there are cases where you need numerical values to be stored as text, and Excel doesn't want to recast those values back to numbers if you have intentionally specified that they are text.

Q: Are numbers and text the only types of data I can use?

A: There are others. For example, the Boolean data type, which you'll learn about later in this book, gives you two options: TRUE and FALSE. Some of the functions you just saw, like ISTEXT(), return values that are of data type Boolean.

Q: What about the weird-looking error that the AVERAGE() **formula returned? It certainly doesn't look like a number, or a Boolean, or text. It's like errors are their own thing entirely.**

A: That's a reasonable intuition. Do you think that error values should have their own data type? While you're chewing on that question, let's take a closer look at errors....

A grad student also ran some stats...and there's a problem

Thought you were off the hook, didn't you? Just as soon as your friend set off to do some work on his own, his grad student messed up the spreadsheet again. Oh, the agony of being an Excel guru!

Um, this is kind of embarrassing. My grad student just got a whole bunch of errors with the formulas he created. Can you get this broken-down spreadsheet running?

Let's take a look at those formulas....

Exercise

There are lots of errors in this spreadsheet. Let's take them one at a time, looking at the formulas that generated the errors. What do you think the errors mean?

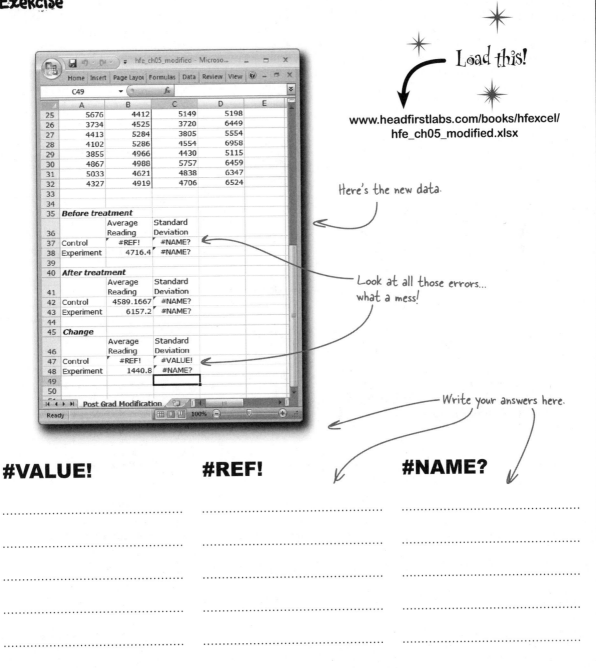

Load this!

www.headfirstlabs.com/books/hfexcel/
hfe_ch05_modified.xlsx

Here's the new data.

Look at all those errors...
what a mess!

Write your answers here.

#VALUE!

....
....
....
....
....

#REF!

....
....
....
....
....

#NAME?

....
....
....
....
....

Exercise Solution

You studied each of the errors closely. What do you think the errors mean?

	A	B	C	D	E
25	5676	4412	5149	5198	
26	3734	4525	3720	6449	
27	4413	5284	3805	5554	
28	4102	5286	4554	6958	
29	3855	4966	4430	5115	
30	4867	4988	5757	6459	
31	5033	4621	4838	6347	
32	4327	4919	4706	6524	
33					
34					
35	*Before treatment*				
36		Average Reading	Standard Deviation		
37	Control	#REF!	#NAME?		
38	Experiment	4716.4	#NAME?		
39					
40	*After treatment*				
41		Average Reading	Standard Deviation		
42	Control	4589.1667	#NAME?		
43	Experiment	6157.2	#NAME?		
44					
45	*Change*				
46		Average Reading	Standard Deviation		
47	Control	#REF!	#VALUE!		
48	Experiment	1440.8	#NAME?		
49					
50					

The formula with the #VALUE! *error points to this cell and probably is looking for a number rather than text.*

#NAME? pops up when you type a formula name that doesn't exist.

If SD() *isn't the right name for the standard deviation function, what is?*

#REF! often happens when you paste a copied formula and some of its references point outside of the spreadsheet.

This function returns #REF! *because it points to cell* B37, *which contains that error.*

#VALUE!

It looks like this formula received text when it was looking for a value. Specifically, the cell C36 is in the formula, even though it's text.

#REF!

There's something wrong with the reference here. The =AVERAGE(#REF!) formula in cell B37 is all wrong.

#NAME?

The help says #NAME? means "The formula uses a custom function that is not available." Maybe the standard deviation formula has a different name?

Errors are a special data type

The designers of Excel made errors their own special data type. And by giving errors their own data type, they made it possible to create a number of formulas that handle errors specifically.

Errors are a big deal in Excel. Understanding how they work is critical to developing tight, functional spreadsheets.

Errors have a data type all to their own.

#DIV/0!

Here's a formula that definitely won't work.

=50/0

Excel returns an error.

This in not a text, a number, or a Boolean.

A bunch of errors and functions, in full costume, are playing a party game, "Who am I?" They'll give you a clue. You try to guess who they are, based on what they say. Assume they always tell the truth about themselves. Fill in the blanks to the right to identify the attendees.

Tonight's attendees:

IFERROR()

ISERR()

#N/A!

ERROR.TYPE()

Who am I?

Name

I return different values depending on whether my argument is an error or not.

_____

I return a number to you that specifies what *sort* of error you've passed to me as an argument.

_____

You get me when you forget to enter a required argument into a function.

_____

I tell you whether my argument is an error or not.

_____

Who am I?

A bunch of errors and functions, in full costume, are playing a party game, "Who am I?" They'll give you a clue . You try to guess who they are, based on what they say. Assume they always tell the truth about themselves. Fill in the blanks to the right to identify the attendees.

Tonight's attendees:

IFERROR()　　　　**ISERR()**

#N/A!　　　　**ERROR.TYPE()**

Name

I return different values depending on whether my argument is an error or not.

IFERROR()

I return a number to you that specifies what *sort* of error you've passed to me as an argument.

ERROR.TYPE()

You get me when you forget to enter a required argument into a function.

#N/A!

I tell you whether my argument is an error or not.

ISERR()

Looks like you're getting a really up-close understanding of errors. Does that mean you can fix my data now?

LONG EXERCISE

There are a bunch of problems with this spreadsheet, but you know what you need to know to correct them all at once. For each error, look at the formula and correct it.

Go through each of these formulas and see whether you can fix the error.

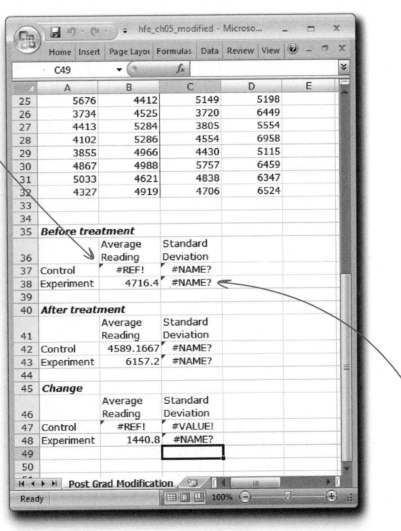

SD() is **not** the standard deviation formula...see if you can find the correct formula name in the Help files.

Long Exercise
Solution

The doctor gave you a pretty big spreadsheet project. How did it all work out?

Let's start with the formula in cell B37.

Change the argument from #REF! to a proper range.

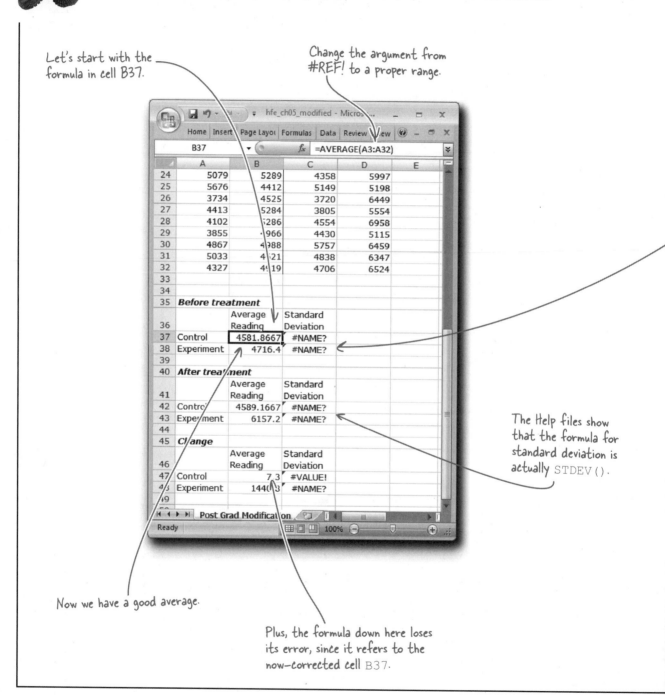

The Help files show that the formula for standard deviation is actually STDEV().

Now we have a good average.

Plus, the formula down here loses its error, since it refers to the now-corrected cell B37.

All the ranges in these formulas are correct; you just need to change the function's name.

Change this formula to refer to C37, and all is fixed!

=STDEV(A3:A32)

=STDEV(B3:B32)

=STDEV(C3:C32)

=STDEV(D3:D32)

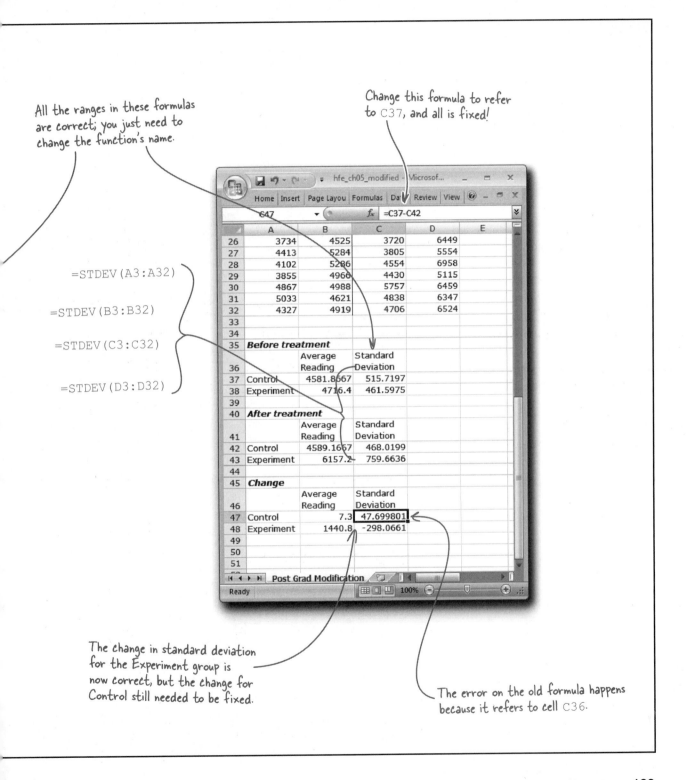

The change in standard deviation for the Experiment group is now correct, but the change for Control still needed to be fixed.

The error on the old formula happens because it refers to cell C36.

Now you're a published scientist

From: Doctor
To: Head First
Subject: Your excellent data work

Dear Head First,

I want to thank you so much for all your help with our data project.

If it had not been for you, we would have had to retype a bunch of data, probably making mistakes, and we never would have gotten to the bottom of all our formula errors.

Thank you, Head First!

—Dr.

Nice work!

Leeches like you've never seen them
They really suck... hematomas!

Music
We review Mastodon's *Blood Mountain*

Teen vampire chick flicks
An opportunity to promote healthy blood?

TODAY

DATAVILLE JOURNAL OF HISTOPATHOLOGY

Head First Finds White Blood Cell Count Increase

New drug promises to help millions of immunocompromised patients

CENTRAL AMERICA

34 7 8 3 9 999

6 dates and times

Stay on time

I think there's space on my calendar, but could you repeat that time again in "mm/dd/yyy hh:mm:ss.0"?

Dates and times in Excel are hard.

Unless you understand *how Excel represents them* internally. All of us at one point or another have had to do calculations involving these types of figures, and this chapter will give you the **keys to figuring out** how many days, months, years, and even seconds there are between two dates. The simple truth is that dates and times are a really **special case** of the data types and formatting that you already know. Once you master a couple of basic concepts, you'll be able to use Excel to *manage scheduling flawlessly*.

Do you have time to amp up your training for the Massachusetts Marathon?

You're an avid runner who is ready to make the transition to an **elite** status, pursuing more prestigious, competitive, and difficult races. Specifically, you think you're ready for the **Massachusetts Marathon**.

Or rather, you could be ready with the right training program. Elite running is all about scheduling your practices and races so that you're at the right level of fitness at the right time. Luckily, you have a trainer friend who wants to help.

Coach

I have a 10-week training program that will get you in shape for a 10K. We could then use your 10K time as a benchmark for your marathon goals.

Could this program be your ticket to an elite running status?

Better take a look at the schedules to make sure her program fits with a 10K race.

Exercise

Once you finish the training program, you'll be ready for a 10K race. Is there a 10K race you could do that takes place shortly after the training program?

Here are the dates of upcoming 10Ks. You'll use these dates to calculate whether there's a race in the right time frame. But first, let's make the dates more legible.

1. Under the Number > General drop box, reformat the dates so they look like this: 06/03/10.

2. Using the Custom Sort... dialog box, sort your dates so that they'll be in chronological order.

Load this!

www.headfirstlabs.com/books/hfexcel/
hfe_ch06_10K_races.xlsx

This data shows the upcoming races.

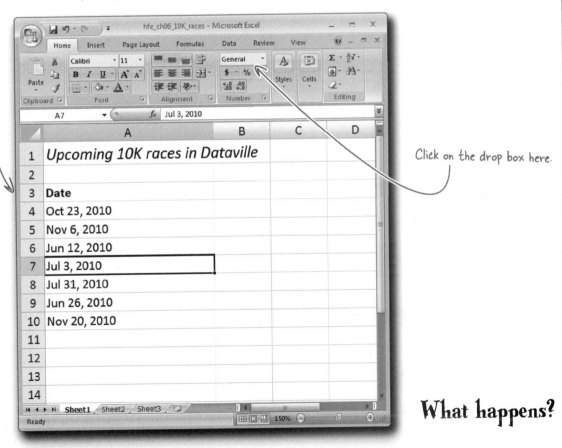

Click on the drop box here.

What happens?

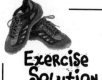

Exercise Solution

You just attempted to reformat and sort your dates. What happened?

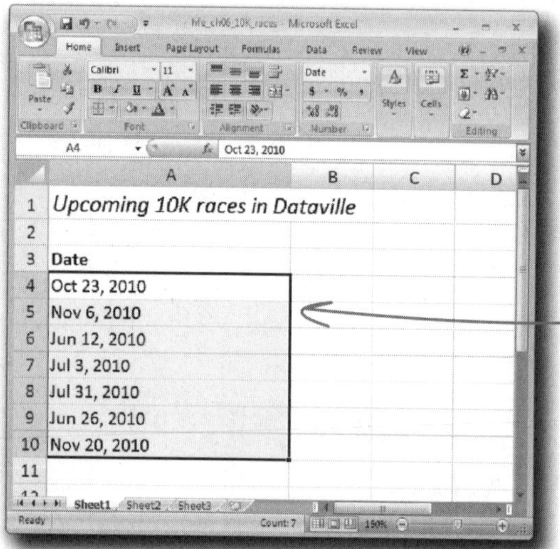

1. Under the Number > General drop box, reformat the dates so they look like this: 06/03/10.

Nothing happens when you try to change the date format.

Why might that be?

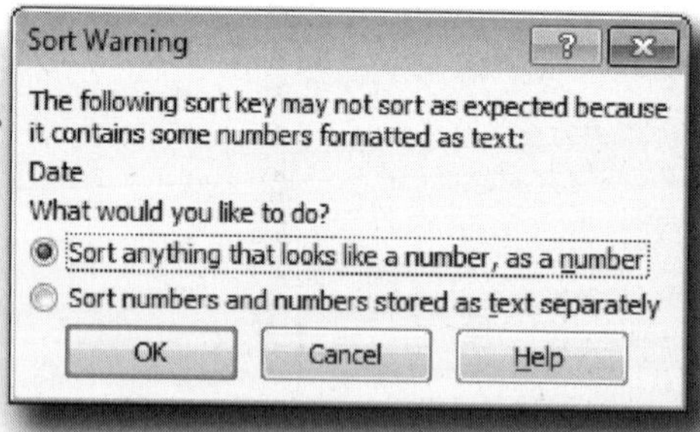

2. Using the Custom Sort... dialog box, sort your dates so that they'll be in chronological order.

Go ahead and click OK, and it'll sort correctly.

Wow...Excel sees text, but it thinks it might be a number?

Something fishy is going on here!

> Maybe Excel thinks that the dates are text. Try the ISTEXT() function to see.

If you run the ISTEXT() function on any of the cells containing your date data, the TRUE value the function returns shows that the date is indeed **text**.

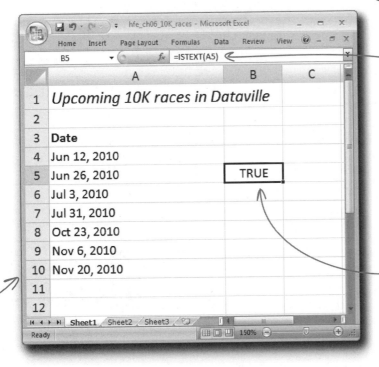

Here's the ISTEXT() formula.

The TRUE value means that the dates are text.

You know what to do when you have a numerical value that needs to be converted from text! And while the dates here aren't simple integers, they're still numbers of a sort. Why not try running the VALUE() function on them? Maybe Excel can figure out that they're dates.

Do this!

Try writing VALUE() formulas in a new column. What happens?

VALUE() returns a number on dates stored as text

The VALUE () formula takes one look at your date and returns values without any errors or warnings.

VALUE () crunches your input text with no problem at all.

Excel reads the text value and sees that it's really a number.

You give the formula your text.

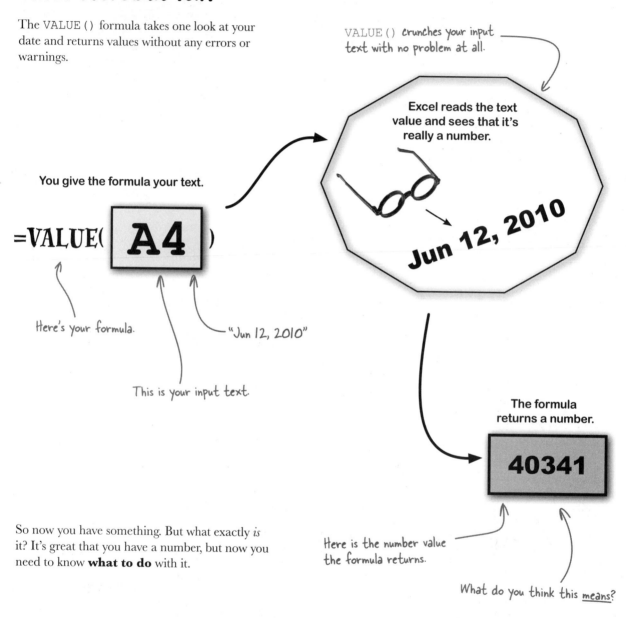

=VALUE(**A4**)

Jun 12, 2010

Here's your formula.

"Jun 12, 2010"

This is your input text.

The formula returns a number.

40341

Here is the number value the formula returns.

What do you think this <u>means</u>?

So now you have something. But what exactly *is* it? It's great that you have a number, but now you need to know **what to do** with it.

Why would Excel return a five-digit number in response to your date text?

Excel sees dates as integers

In Excel, a date is just an integer. Excel for Windows defines the integer 0 as January 1, 1900,* so the integer 1000 represents 1,000 days after January 1, 1900.

* The first date in Excel 2008 for Mac is actually 1/1/1904, but Excel can convert between the two behind the scenes.

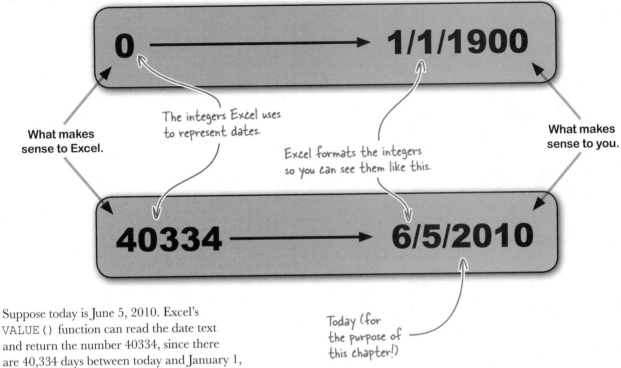

What makes sense to Excel.

The integers Excel uses to represent dates.

Excel formats the integers so you can see them like this.

What makes sense to you.

Today (for the purpose of this chapter!)

Suppose today is June 5, 2010. Excel's VALUE() function can read the date text and return the number 40334, since there are 40,334 days between today and January 1, 1900.

This is how Excel deals with dates: by converting them to integers, even though Excel applies **formatting** to the dates so that you can read them.

You usually need VALUE() only when you're importing certain data.

If you simply type in a date, Excel almost always can figure out what you mean and return the correct integer date representation while keeping your formatting straight.

If you subtract one date from another, what would the resulting number *mean*?

Subtracting one date from another tells you the number of days between the two dates

Let's say you want to find out how many days there are between today and the date of the first 10K. Here's a formula you might use:

`DATEVALUE()` converts date text to a number *inside of a formula*.

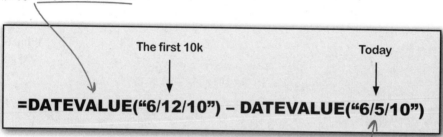

When you refer to date values already in other cells and when you use the `DATEVALUE()` formula, Excel sees your date values as simple integers. And since each number represents a count of days, subtracting one from the other shows the amount of days between the two dates.

If you already have your date values in another cell, you can use a reference rather than `DATEVALUE`.

Here are Excel's numbers.

Excel really calculates the difference between dates using integers.

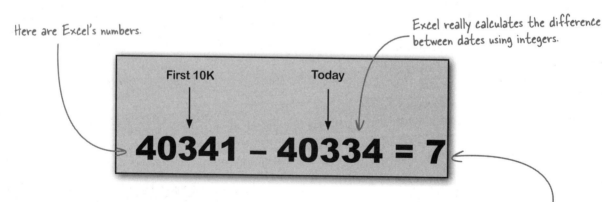

It's really not that complicated. Now that you've gotten the hang of how Excel deals with dates, you're ready to start running some calculations of your own.

There are seven days between today and 6/12/10.

Exercise

Using your knowledge about how Excel represents dates, whip your 10K spreadsheet into shape and figure out how many days each race is from today.

① Fill column B with formulas using the `VALUE()` function to make Excel return the integer representation of your dates.

② Reformat the dates in column B to *look* like dates, not integers.

③ Sort the dates so that the earliest is first.

④ Under your **Days From Now** column in cell C4, write this formula:

`=B4-DATEVALUE("6/5/10")`

`DATEVALUE()` returns the integer corresponding to date text.

You need to use this function, since Excel can't convert from text to date integers <u>inside</u> of formulas unless you tell it to.

⑤ Copy this formula and paste it to cells `C5:C10`.

Add these column headers.

Put your answers here.

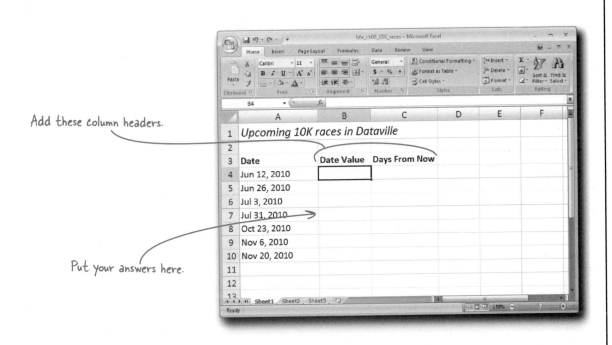

Exercise Solution

You just ran a bunch of operations to try to calculate the numbers of days between today and the 10K races you might do after training. What happened?

1 Fill column B with formulas using the VALUE() function to make Excel return the integer representation of your dates.

=VALUE(A10)

Use the VALUE() function.

No problem here.

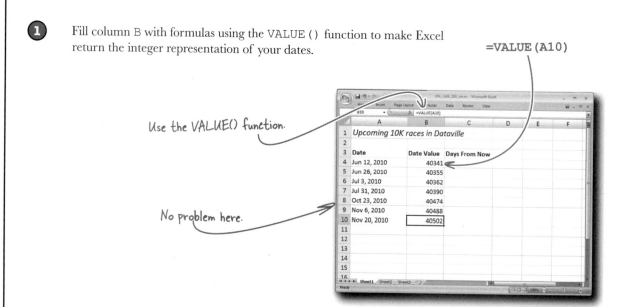

2 Reformat the dates in column B to *look* like dates, not integers.

3 Sort the dates so that the earliest is first.

Again, looking good.

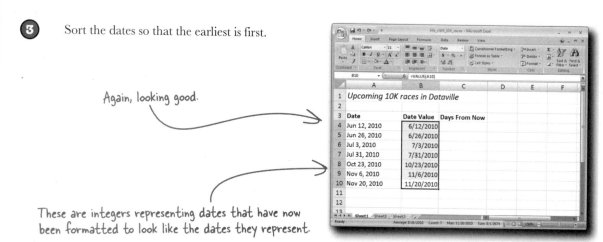

These are integers representing dates that have now been formatted to look like the dates they represent.

=B4-DATEVALUE("6/5/10")

④ Under your **Days From Now** column in cell C4, write this formula:

=B4-DATEVALUE("6/5/10")

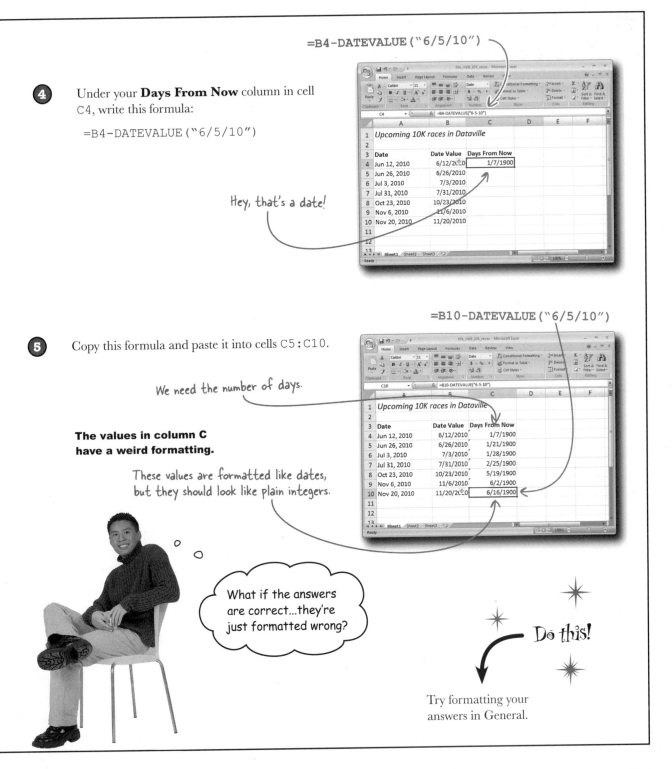

Hey, that's a date!

=B10-DATEVALUE("6/5/10")

⑤ Copy this formula and paste it into cells C5:C10.

We need the number of days.

The values in column C have a weird formatting.

These values are formatted like dates, but they should look like plain integers.

What if the answers are correct...they're just formatted wrong?

Do this!

Try formatting your answers in General.

When subtracting dates, watch your formatting

When you wrote your date subtraction formula, Excel based the format of its return value on the format of the cells that went into the arguments of the formula.

No problem, just reformat your formulas to **General**.

Just click here to put a selection into the General format.

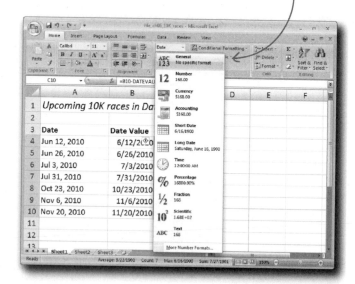

Inside your spreadsheet, these two values are in the Date format.

6/12/10 – 6/5/10 = 7

This value, on the other hand, should be in the General format.

This is exactly how you want your day calculation results to look.

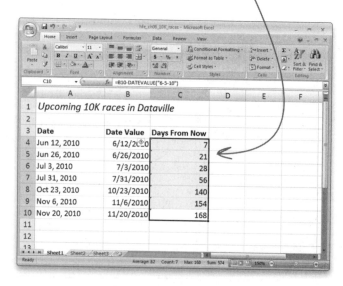

There are seven days between today and June 12, and 7 is the value that Excel returns. Once you change the formatting from Date to General, you can see your answer.

Looks like you don't have time to complete training before a 10K

Your date calculations present some discouraging news. Since the training program is 10 weeks, or 70 days, the first 10K you would be able to do *after* the program would be the one on October 23.

But that 10K is 140 days away, which is 10 **more** weeks after your training program ends!

The future...

10K
Oct 23, 2010

The first 10K after training ends is a ways off.

You want to qualify for this!

Massachusetts Marathon
Nov 6, 2010

10K
Jul 31, 2010

10K Training Ends
Aug 14, 2010

10K
Jul 3, 2010

Ideally, you'd be able to do your 10K around this point in time.

10K
Jun 26, 2010

10K
Jun 12, 2010

These are all too early.

Now
Jun 5, 2010

Coach has a better idea

You know, I bet you're ready to start training for marathons. Why not take my 4-month marathon training course? Then maybe you can do a qualifying marathon to make you eligible for Massachusetts.

Coach

Now you just need to see whether the Dataville Marathon takes place within the 4-month time frame....

Stop! First days and weeks, then months... soon it'll be years! Why can't date functions return anything besides days?

Let's see if Excel has anything else.

Most people who need to do date computations are going to need more power than counting days through simple arithmetic provides. It makes sense that Excel would have more versatile formulas....

DATEDIF() will calculate time between dates using a variety of measures

It's an old-school, little-known, strangely undocumented but very powerful function. With DATEDIF(), you specify a start date, an end date, and then a text constant that represents the unit you want to use.

This last argument is a special text constant.

You can guess how these two arguments work.

=DATEDIF(start date, end date, interval)

Choose from one of Excel's six predetermined text strings to instruct the formula to use the scale you want.

=DATEDIF(B1,B2,"y")

Here is an example of DATEDIF() in action. In this case, the "y" text constant tells Excel to ascertain the number of years between the two dates, and in the next exercise you'll look at your other options.

Here's DATEDIF()

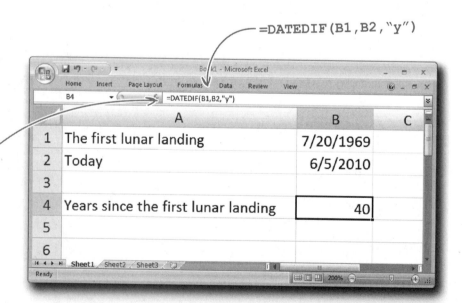

	A	B	C
1	The first lunar landing	7/20/1969	
2	Today	6/5/2010	
3			
4	Years since the first lunar landing	40	
5			
6			

WHO DOES WHAT?

Different text constants result in different measures for DATEDIF().
Which is which? Draw arrows to link the text constants with the right
behavior.

Text constant

DATEDIF() behavior

m

The number of months between the dates,
ignoring days and years.

d

The number of whole years between the dates.

y

The number of days between the dates,
ignoring months and years.

ym

The number of days between the dates,
ignoring the years.

yd

The number of whole months between the
dates.

md

The number of days between the dates.

Different text constants result in different measures for `DATEDIF()`.
Which is which?

Text constant **DATEDIF() behavior**

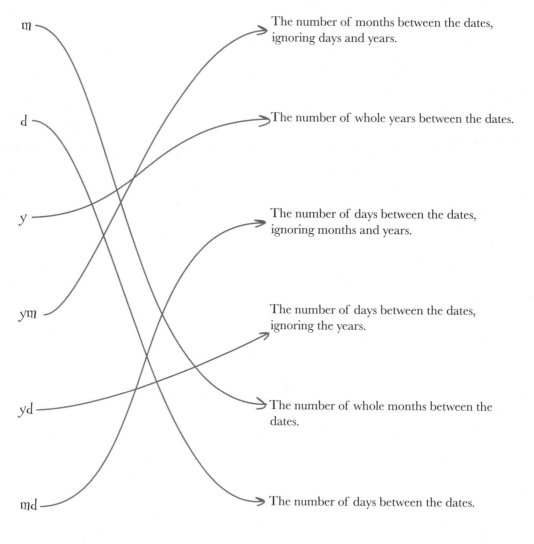

m

d

y

ym

yd

md

The number of months between the dates, ignoring days and years.

The number of whole years between the dates.

The number of days between the dates, ignoring months and years.

The number of days between the dates, ignoring the years.

The number of whole months between the dates.

The number of days between the dates.

Exercise

Now write a DATEDIF() function to see whether your class is finished in time for the two upcoming Massachusetts qualifying marathons: the Bitburg Marathon and the Dataville Marathon.

In this cell, type the date for today, 6/5/2010.

Here, type the date for the Bitburg Marathon, 9/25/2010.

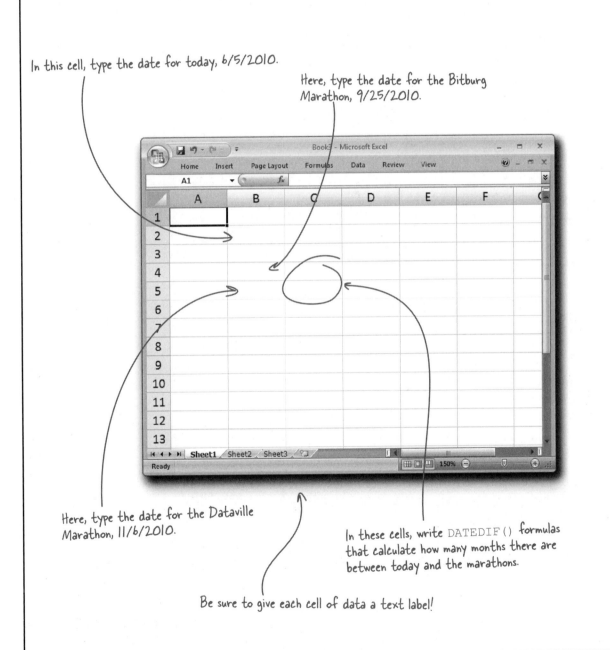

Here, type the date for the Dataville Marathon, 11/6/2010.

In these cells, write DATEDIF() formulas that calculate how many months there are between today and the marathons.

Be sure to give each cell of data a text label!

Exercise Solution

If you start a 4-month marathon training class, will you have time to do either the Bitburg or the Dataville Marathons, which are qualifiers for the Massachusetts Marathon?

Use the "m" text constant in your DATEDIF() formula.

Don't forget to use an absolute reference to point to today's date.

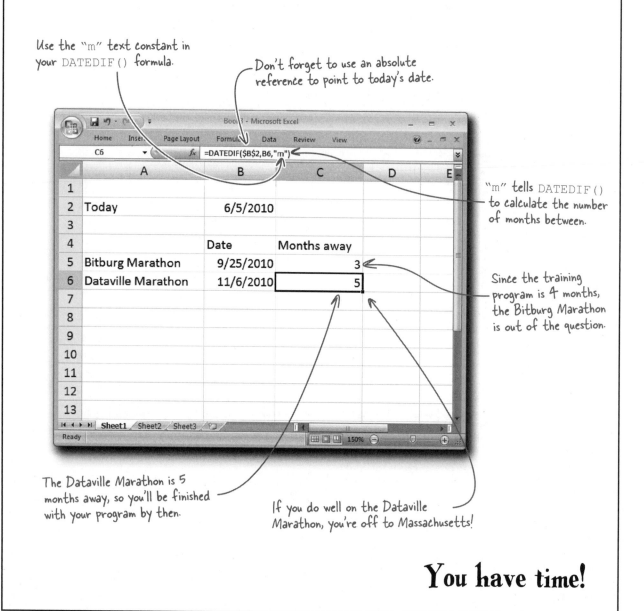

"m" tells DATEDIF() to calculate the number of months between.

Since the training program is 4 months, the Bitburg Marathon is out of the question.

The Dataville Marathon is 5 months away, so you'll be finished with your program by then.

If you do well on the Dataville Marathon, you're off to Massachusetts!

You have time!

Coach is happy to have you in her class

Great. You need to hit a 3 hour and 30 minute Dataville Marathon time to qualify. I can't remember how that breaks down for each mile, but as long as your 5K pace is no more than 10% higher than the 3:30 marathon pace, we should be able to get you where you need to be.

Your 5K pace is 8:30—eight minutes and thirty seconds per mile. What's the pace of a 3:30 marathon? If you run a marathon in three hours and thirty minutes, how long would it take you on average to run each mile? You need to do a **time calculation**.

If Excel represents days as *integers*, how do you think Excel represents hours, seconds, and minutes?

Excel represents time as decimal numbers from 0 to 1

When you type a time into your spreadsheet, Excel displays that time as a value like what you see on the left.

But what you're really looking at is a decimal number between from 0 to 1 that's ***formatted*** to look like a time.

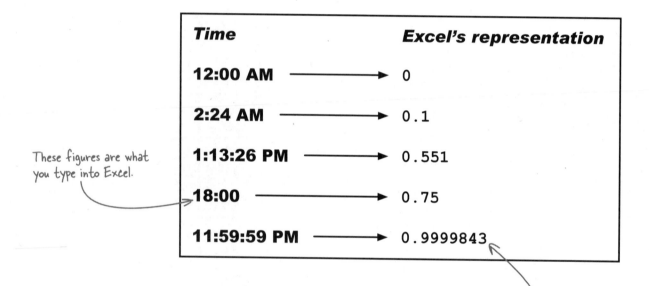

Time	Excel's representation
12:00 AM ⟶	0
2:24 AM ⟶	0.1
1:13:26 PM ⟶	0.551
18:00 ⟶	0.75
11:59:59 PM ⟶	0.9999843

These figures are what you type into Excel.

These numbers are how Excel represents your times internally.

And if you are doing really heavy time computations, you can have Excel's decimal numbers go all the way to **thousands of a second** (sorry, if you want to count nanoseconds, you'll just have to use regular decimal numbers and remember what they mean).

Let's determine our pace using time calculations in Excel.

Exercise

Your coach wants to know whether your current running pace is where it needs to be to make you a strong candidate for qualifying for Massachusetts. Are you within 10% of the 8:30 mile pace?

1 In Excel, divide the 3:30:00 marathon goal time by 26.2 to get your target pace.

2 Is your normal pace of 8:30 within 10% of your marathon target pace? Add 10% to your marathon target pace to find out.

Put your answers here.

Be sure to label your numbers with text!

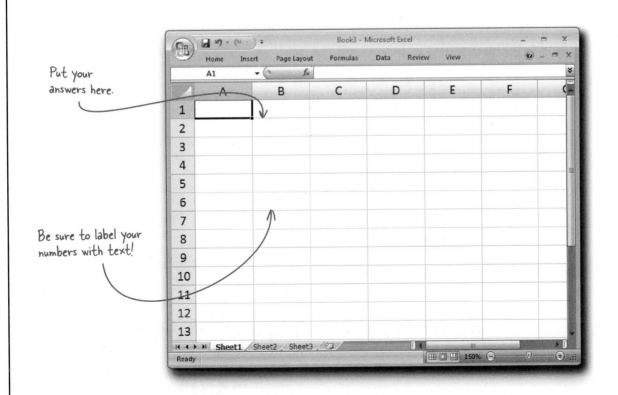

Exercise Solution

You just ran some calculations to determine whether your current pace is an adequate starting point for your marathon training. Is it?

1 In Excel, divide the 3:30:00 marathon goal time by 26.2 to get your target pace.

=B2/26.2

When you type in a time value, Excel automatically recognizes it.

Your target pace is 8:01 minutes per mile.

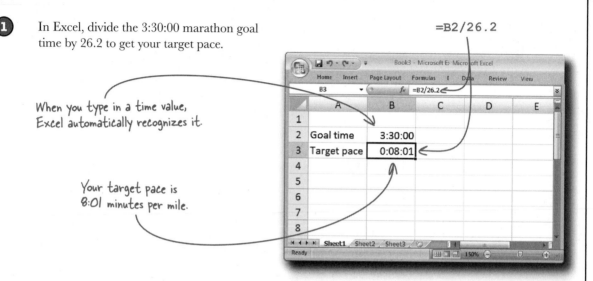

2 Is your normal pace of 8:30 within 10% of your marathon target pace? Add 10% to your marathon target pace to find out.

=B3+B3*0.1

Here's the formula you need.

B3 + B3 * 0.1

Your 8:30 pace is inside the 10% range.

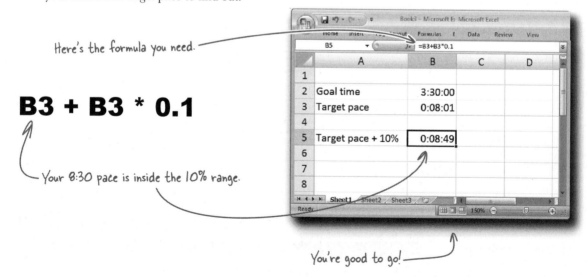

You're good to go!

Coach has an Excel challenge for you

Your coach has sent you a funny number. Dates are numbers to the left of the decimal point, and times are numbers to the right of the decimal point, so what about values with numbers on *both sides* of the decimal point?

This is a date and a time all in one value!

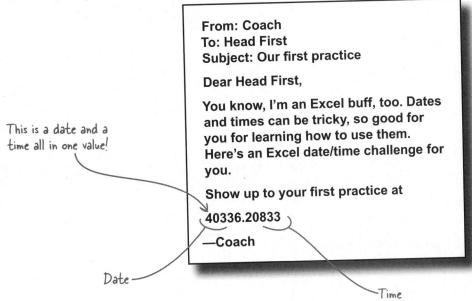

From: Coach
To: Head First
Subject: Our first practice

Dear Head First,

You know, I'm an Excel buff, too. Dates and times can be tricky, so good for you for learning how to use them. Here's an Excel date/time challenge for you.

Show up to your first practice at

40336.20833

—Coach

Date

Time

That number is a date and a time combined together into the **same value**! Better type this number into Excel and reformat it to see when you should show up for the first practice!

Combine a date and a time into the same value by having digits before and after the decimal point.

Exercise

① Open your spreadsheet and type 40336.20833 into a blank cell.

② Click on the More Number Formats area of the data formatting drop box on the Ribbon and convert your cell to a m/d/y h:mm format.

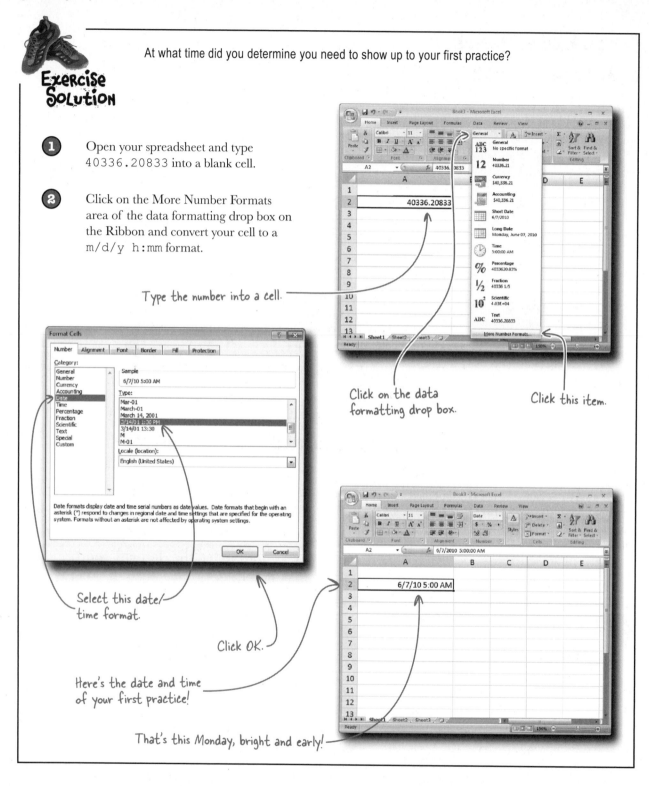

At what time did you determine you need to show up to your first practice?

Exercise Solution

1 Open your spreadsheet and type `40336.20833` into a blank cell.

2 Click on the More Number Formats area of the data formatting drop box on the Ribbon and convert your cell to a `m/d/y h:mm` format.

Type the number into a cell.

Click on the data formatting drop box.

Click this item.

Select this date/time format.

Click OK.

Here's the date and time of your first practice!

That's this Monday, bright and early!

You qualified for the Massachusetts Marathon

Elite running is all about effective planning, and with the help of your coach, not to mention your impressive Excel-savvy, you ran a 3:30 Dataville Marathon and qualified for Massachusetts!

Massachusetts, here I come!

7 finding functions

Mine Excel's features on your own

Excel has more functions than you will ever use.

Over many years and many versions, the program has accumulated specialized functions that are terribly important to the small group of people who use them. That's not a problem for you. But what *is* a problem for you is the group of functions **that you don't know** but that **are useful in your work**. Which functions are we talking about? Only you can know for sure, and you're about to learn some tips and techniques to finding quickly the formulas you need to get your work done efficiently.

Should you rent additional parking?

You're in charge of the Dataville Convention Center parking program. They do a big entertainment business in Dataville, but they have a problem. If they are expecting more than 1,000 ticket buyers to attend an event, they need to rent more parking spaces.

In the upcoming month, are they expecting more than 1,000 attendees for any of their events? Your challenge is to find out using their ticket sales data, and you'll get free box seats to your favorite shows if you can set up a workflow.

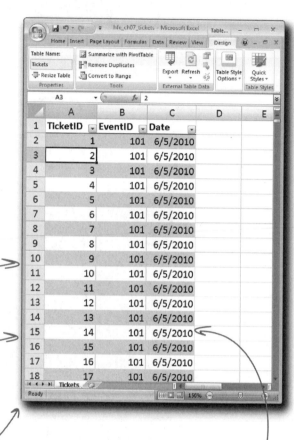

Here's their ticket sales spreadsheet for the coming month, which you'll load in a few moments.

Each line of this spreadsheet represents a single ticket sold.

It's a long spreadsheet: there are over 7,000 rows.

Let's still assume that 6/5/2010 is today.

This is important stuff!

You need formulas to count tickets sold for each day in this month's weekends.

Function Review

Here are all the functions you've learned so far. What do they do?

SUM   Tells you which in a range of numbers is smallest.

MIN   Tells you whether a cell is of data type text.

AVERAGE   Converts text into an integer that represents a date.

VALUE   Gives you the mean of a range of numbers.

ISTEXT   Returns the standard deviation of a range.

STDDEV   Converts text to numbers.

DATEVALUE   Adds numbers together.

DATEDIF   Returns the difference between dates using a metric you specify.

Write your answer here.

Can any of these formulas help you solve your parking prediction problem?

....

....

WHO DOES WHAT?
SOLUTION
Function Review

Here are all the functions you've learned so far. What do they do?

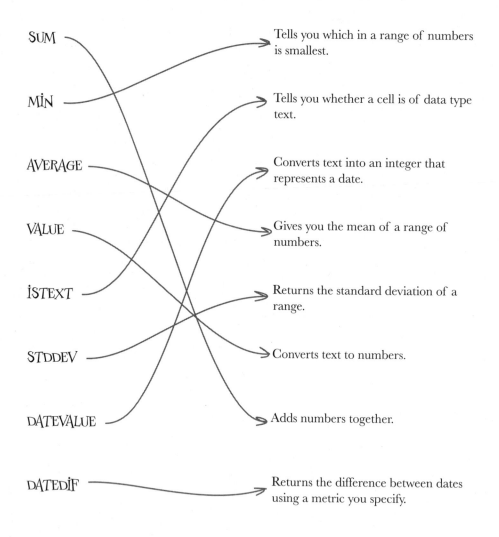

SUM

MIN

AVERAGE

VALUE

ISTEXT

STDDEV

DATEVALUE

DATEDIF

Tells you which in a range of numbers is smallest.

Tells you whether a cell is of data type text.

Converts text into an integer that represents a date.

Gives you the mean of a range of numbers.

Returns the standard deviation of a range.

Converts text to numbers.

Adds numbers together.

Returns the difference between dates using a metric you specify.

Can any of these formulas help you solve your parking prediction problem?

Unfortunately, no. None of them has the ability to count anything, much less the tickets in the data we're going to receive.

You need a plan to find more functions

Finding and learning new functions in Excel is one of the core skills you need to develop. Excel has hundreds of functions, and it would take forever for you to read through all of them every time you wanted to learn a new formula.

Here's all of 'em!

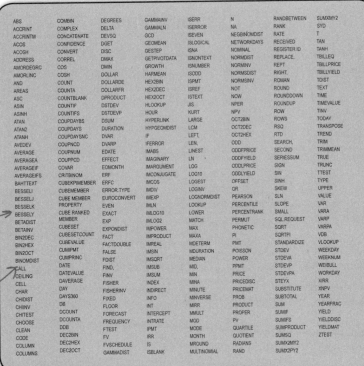

It could take a long time to learn all these.

Do this!

Click the blue button on the top right to get help on Excel functions.

Excel's help screens are loaded with tips and tricks

To get help on any of Excel's scads and scads of formulas, start by clicking the help button on the top right of the Excel screen.

Click on the help button here.

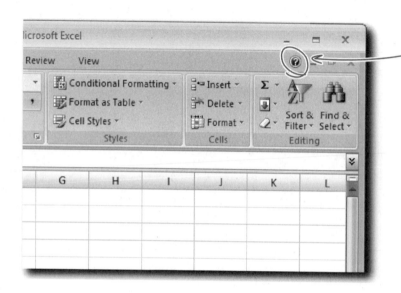

This window pops up as a result.

It used to be that you'd never look at the documentation for Excel or any other computer program. No matter whether it was on the printed page or on computer help screens, it was hard to read and poorly written.

Those days are over for Excel. The current generation of help documentation is written to be understood by **real, *live human beings*** like you. In fact, it's so useful that you should dip into the docs occasionally just to explore the new features, not just for when you're looking for a specific formula.

The evolution of Excel documentation

Then

Hard-to-read fat manual

Hard-to-read thin manual and hard-to-read help screens

Hard-to-read help screens

Well-written and useful help screens!

Now

Sharpen your pencil

Here's a closer look at Excel's main help page, the page you get when you click on the blue help button. Let's explore it.

1 Circle the topics you've already become familiar with.

2 Circle the topic that will help you find the functions you need.

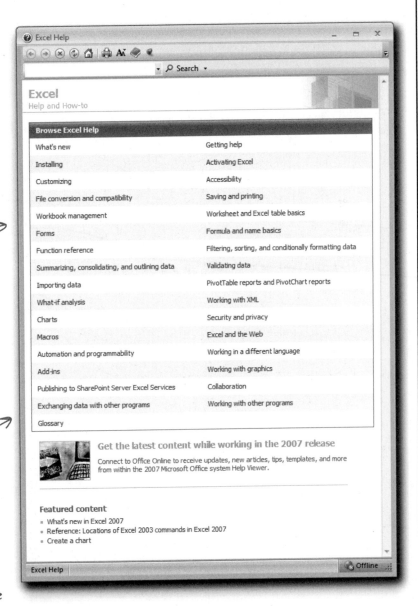

Different versions of Excel have slightly different lists, so yours might not look exactly like this.

Sharpen your pencil
Solution

Upon closer inspection, what did you learn when you looked at the main help page?

①   Circle the topics you've already become familiar with.

Probably worth checking out if you've become accustomed to a previous version of Excel.

Hopefully you've gotten past this part.

The functions we've already learned are in here.

There's a chapter on this coming up.

All over this one!

This could be useful to look up terminology.

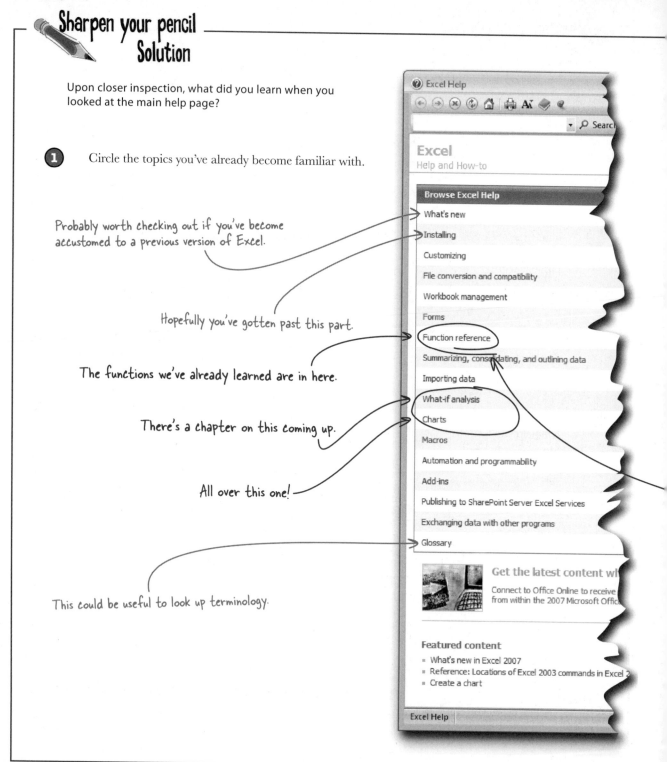

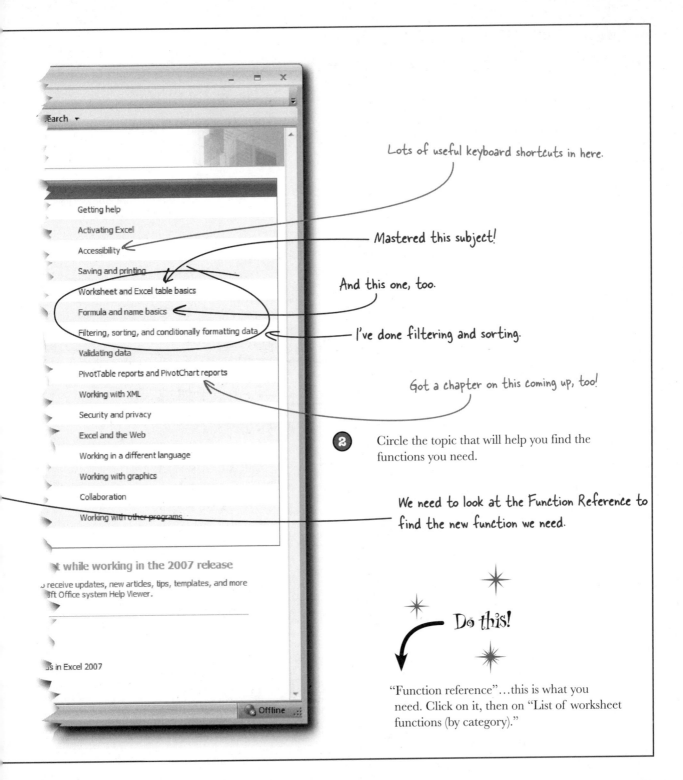

Lots of useful keyboard shortcuts in here.

Getting help

Activating Excel

Accessibility — Mastered this subject!

Saving and printing

Worksheet and Excel table basics — And this one, too.

Formula and name basics

Filtering, sorting, and conditionally formatting data — I've done filtering and sorting.

Validating data

PivotTable reports and PivotChart reports — Got a chapter on this coming up, too!

Working with XML

Security and privacy

Excel and the Web

Working in a different language

Working with graphics

Collaboration

Working with other programs

2 Circle the topic that will help you find the functions you need.

We need to look at the Function Reference to find the new function we need.

while working in the 2007 release

receive updates, new articles, tips, templates, and more
ft Office system Help Viewer.

s in Excel 2007

Offline

Do this!

"Function reference"…this is what you need. Click on it, then on "List of worksheet functions (by category)."

Here's the convention center's ticket database for the next month

Each record represents a single ticket sold for a single event on a single date. Your task is to take this ticket data and see which days will have more than 1,000 visitors to the Dataville Convention Center.

Load this!

www.headfirstlabs.com/books/hfexcel/ hfe_ch07_tickets.xlsx

This data set is already set up into a <u>table</u>, so you can use structured references.

If you scroll down, you'll see that this is a really big spreadsheet.

This data has only weekend ticket sales, because attendance never comes close to exceeding 1,000 on weekdays. What you need to do is create a list of weekend days for the remainder of the month and then count the number of tickets sold for each of those days.

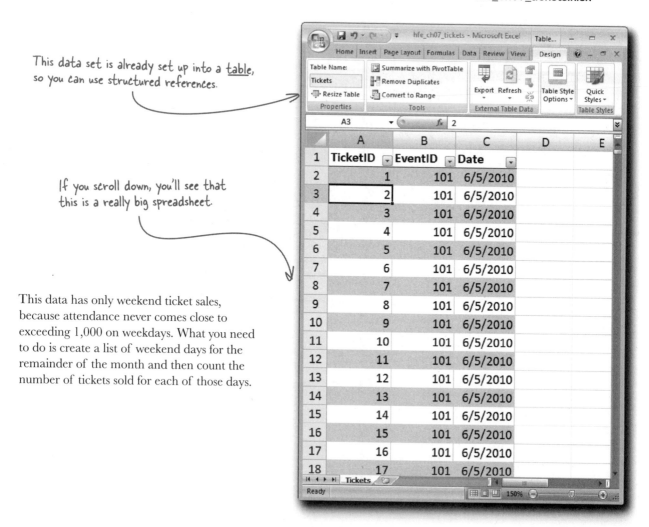

Exercise

We need to summarize ticket sales for weekend shows for the remainder of the month. First, let's create a table that lists the weekend days in this month.

① Create a new sheet in your document by clicking the "new sheet" tab. Double-click on your new sheet's tab, and rename the sheet Summary.

② Generate a series of numbers that represent the weekend days of this month. Follow the example below and the instructions in the annotations.

The number 5 represents today, a Saturday, the fifth day of June 2010.

In this cell, type a formula to add 1 day to today, creating the day for tomorrow.

In this cell, type a formula to add 7 days to today, creating the day for next Saturday.

Copy and paste the formulas you just created in these cells to represent the remaining Saturdays and Sundays of this month.

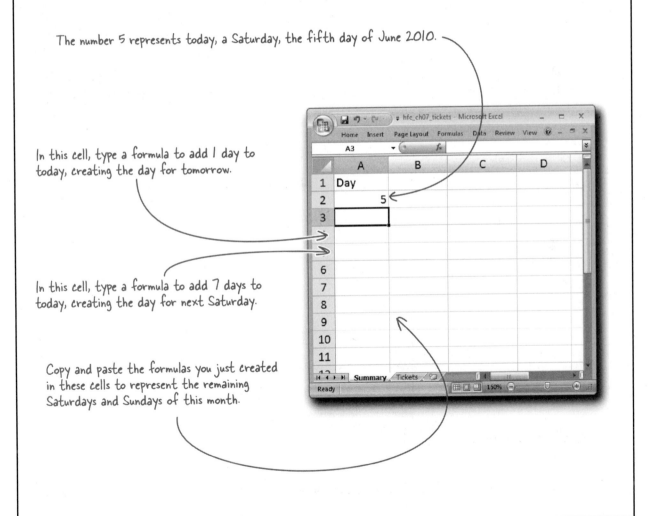

Exercise Solution

You just endeavored to create a list of numbers representing the remaining weekend days of this month. How'd it go?

1 Create a new sheet in your document by clicking the "new sheet" tab. Double-click on your new sheet's tab, and rename the sheet Summary.

2 Generate a series of numbers that represent the weekend days of this month.

Here just add 1 to cell A2.

=A2+1

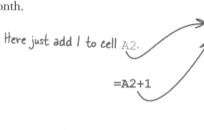

When you copy the formulas, the references shift to give you the days you need.

In this case, add 7 to cell A2.

=A2+7

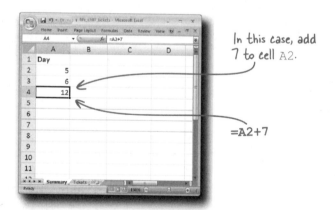

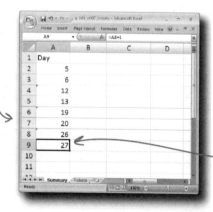

If the 27th is a Sunday, it's the last weekend day of the month.

Now let's make some proper date values out of these numbers.

Exercise

The problem is, we don't yet have the formula to do it. Under the help screen, click "Function reference," then "List of worksheet functions (by category)," then "Date and time functions."

Take a look at these functions, and click on any that seem promising. Which one do you think you can use to build proper date values out of the day integers you've created, and why?

Write your
answer here.

....

....

....

....

Here are all of Excel's
date functions.

You've already
used this one.

There are a bunch!

Excel Help

Search

Date and time functions

Function	Description
DATE	Returns the serial number of a particular date
DATEVALUE	Converts a date in the form of text to a serial number
DAY	Converts a serial number to a day of the month
DAYS360	Calculates the number of days between two dates based on a 360-day year
EDATE	Returns the serial number of the date that is the indicated number of months before or after the start date
EOMONTH	Returns the serial number of the last day of the month before or after a specified number of months
HOUR	Converts a serial number to an hour
MINUTE	Converts a serial number to a minute
MONTH	Converts a serial number to a month
NETWORKDAYS	Returns the number of whole workdays between two dates
NOW	Returns the serial number of the current date and time
SECOND	Converts a serial number to a second
TIME	Returns the serial number of a particular time
TIMEVALUE	Converts a time in the form of text to a serial number
TODAY	Returns the serial number of today's date
WEEKDAY	Converts a serial number to a day of the week
WEEKNUM	Converts a serial number to a number representing where the week falls numerically with a year
WORKDAY	Returns the serial number of the date before or after a specified number of workdays
YEAR	Converts a serial number to a year
YEARFRAC	Returns the year fraction representing the number of whole days between start_date and end_date

⬆ Top of Page

Engineering functions

Excel Help   Offline

Exercise Solution

You just inspected all of Excel's date functions at once. Did you find one that you think will enable you to create dates out of the numbers you entered to represent this month's weekend days?

The DATE formula is the one we want. If you look at the documentation, you can see that it takes three numeric values as its arguments, and we already have the numbers representing days. The numbers representing month and year are simply 6 and 2010!

This is the function we want to use.

We could use DATEVALUE() if we had text, but we already have a number.

There's lots of interesting stuff here, but none of it is useful right now.

A bunch of these functions are for converting proper date numbers to something else.

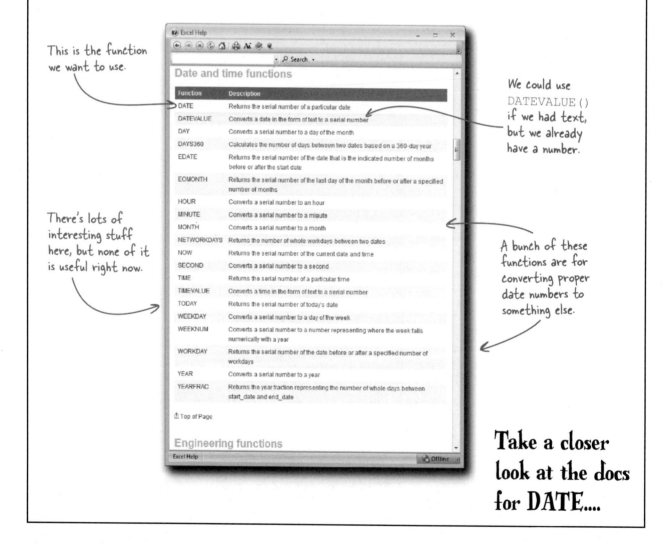

Date and time functions

Function	Description
DATE	Returns the serial number of a particular date
DATEVALUE	Converts a date in the form of text to a serial number
DAY	Converts a serial number to a day of the month
DAYS360	Calculates the number of days between two dates based on a 360-day year
EDATE	Returns the serial number of the date that is the indicated number of months before or after the start date
EOMONTH	Returns the serial number of the last day of the month before or after a specified number of months
HOUR	Converts a serial number to an hour
MINUTE	Converts a serial number to a minute
MONTH	Converts a serial number to a month
NETWORKDAYS	Returns the number of whole workdays between two dates
NOW	Returns the serial number of the current date and time
SECOND	Converts a serial number to a second
TIME	Returns the serial number of a particular time
TIMEVALUE	Converts a time in the form of text to a serial number
TODAY	Returns the serial number of today's date
WEEKDAY	Converts a serial number to a day of the week
WEEKNUM	Converts a serial number to a number representing where the week falls numerically with a year
WORKDAY	Returns the serial number of the date before or after a specified number of workdays
YEAR	Converts a serial number to a year
YEARFRAC	Returns the year fraction representing the number of whole days between start_date and end_date

⬆ Top of Page

Engineering functions

Take a closer look at the docs for DATE....

Anatomy of a function reference

Here's the help window for the DATE function. The documentation for individual functions is really interesting and useful.

Not only can you use the docs to find out what functions do, but you can also use them to learn about functions' eccentricities—all the different types of arguments they accept and all the sorts of values they return, including explanations for why different errors might result from the same formula.

This is a precise specification of what the formula does.

Here's an example that's a lot like what we need to do (except you'll use references for the days, since you've already created them).

Here's how you use the function.

There's lots more specific stuff about how the function works if you scroll down.

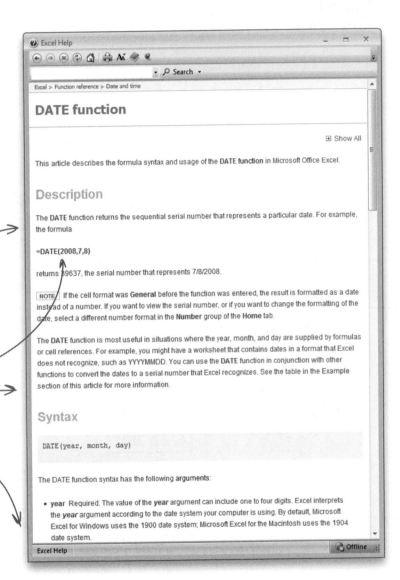

Excel Help

Excel > Function reference > Date and time

DATE function

⊞ Show All

This article describes the formula syntax and usage of the **DATE function** in Microsoft Office Excel.

Description

The **DATE** function returns the sequential serial number that represents a particular date. For example, the formula

=DATE(2008,7,8)

returns 39637, the serial number that represents 7/8/2008.

> **NOTE** If the cell format was **General** before the function was entered, the result is formatted as a date instead of a number. If you want to view the serial number, or if you want to change the formatting of the date, select a different number format in the **Number** group of the **Home** tab.

The **DATE** function is most useful in situations where the year, month, and day are supplied by formulas or cell references. For example, you might have a worksheet that contains dates in a format that Excel does not recognize, such as YYYYMMDD. You can use the **DATE** function in conjunction with other functions to convert the dates to a serial number that Excel recognizes. See the table in the Example section of this article for more information.

Syntax

    DATE(year, month, day)

The DATE function syntax has the following **arguments**:

- **year** Required. The value of the **year** argument can include one to four digits. Excel interprets the **year** argument according to the date system your computer is using. By default, Microsoft Excel for Windows uses the 1900 date system; Microsoft Excel for the Macintosh uses the 1904 date system.

Excel Help — Offline

Exercise

Use the syntax to create a list of weekends with the DATE function on your spreadsheet.

Exercise Solution

Were you able to implement the date function in your spreadsheet to get real date values out of the integers you created to represent the days?

You can just type in the year, since it's the same for every formula.

You can also just type in the month.

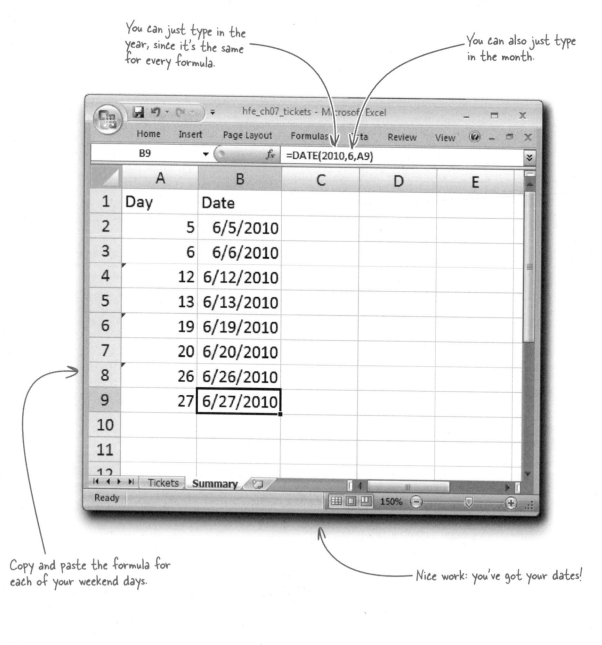

Copy and paste the formula for each of your weekend days.

Nice work: you've got your dates!

The Dataville Convention Center COO checks in...

From: Dataville Convention Ctr. COO
To: Head First
Subject:

Dear Head First,

I hope your work is coming along well.

Remember, what we're after is the dates for which we should expect more than 1,000 people. Can you write some sort of formula to tell me which dates fit this criteria?

—COO

Add this column.

Better get your spreadsheet ready for this last figure and head back to the function reference to find the formula to do this.

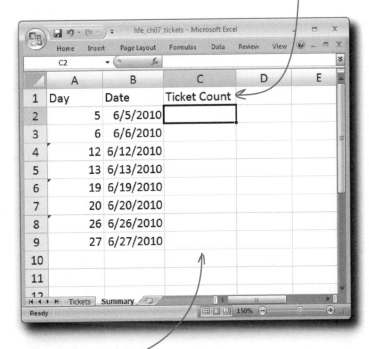

You need to fill ticket counts into this column.

Functions are organized by data type and discipline

Now you're back in the function reference, looking for something that can count tickets for each date. Where to start? It was obvious when you had to build those dates: you just looked in the date category. But there's no "count ticket sales" category.

There are a bunch of different categories here.

One of these fits our problem.

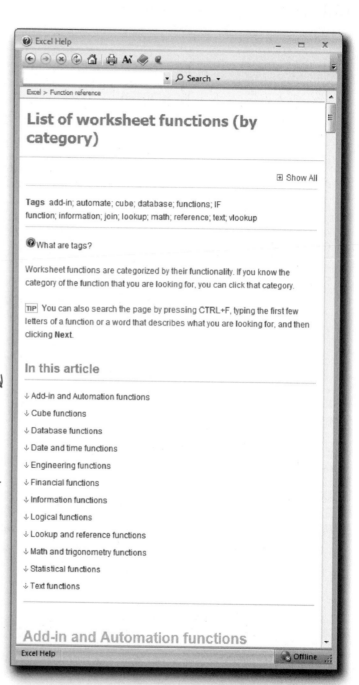

Here's the trick.

When searching for a function, pick a category first by thinking about your problem, and *then* inspect individual formulas in that category. That way, you'll avoid scanning hundreds of irrelevant formulas.

Pool Puzzle

Fill in the blanks with the category names from the pool.

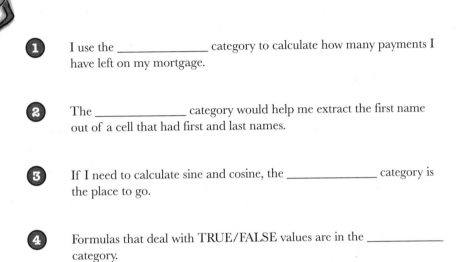

1 I use the _____ category to calculate how many payments I have left on my mortgage.

2 The _____ category would help me extract the first name out of a cell that had first and last names.

3 If I need to calculate sine and cosine, the _____ category is the place to go.

4 Formulas that deal with TRUE/FALSE values are in the _____ category.

5 The _____ category is what I need for counting instances of a date.

Note: Each thing from the pool can be used only once!

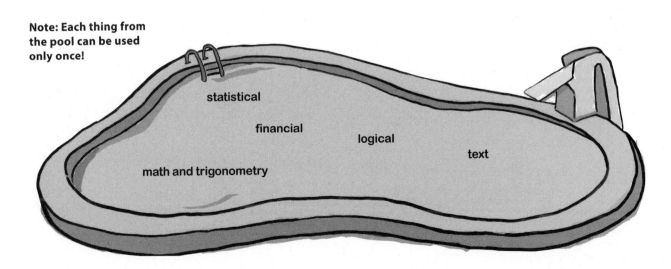

statistical

financial

logical

text

math and trigonometry

Pool Puzzle

Fill in the blanks with the category
names from the pool.

1 I use the _____**financial**_____ category to calculate how many payments I
have left on my mortgage.

2 The _____**text**_____ category would help me extract the first name
out of a cell that had first and last names.

3 If I need to calculate sine and cosine, the _____**math and trigonometry**_____ category is
the place to go.

4 Formulas that deal with TRUE/FALSE values are in the
_____**logical**_____ category.

5 The _____**statistical**_____ category is what I need for counting instances of
a date.

Here's your parking problem.

Better take a look at the statistical functions!

**Note: Each thing from
the pool can be used
only once!**

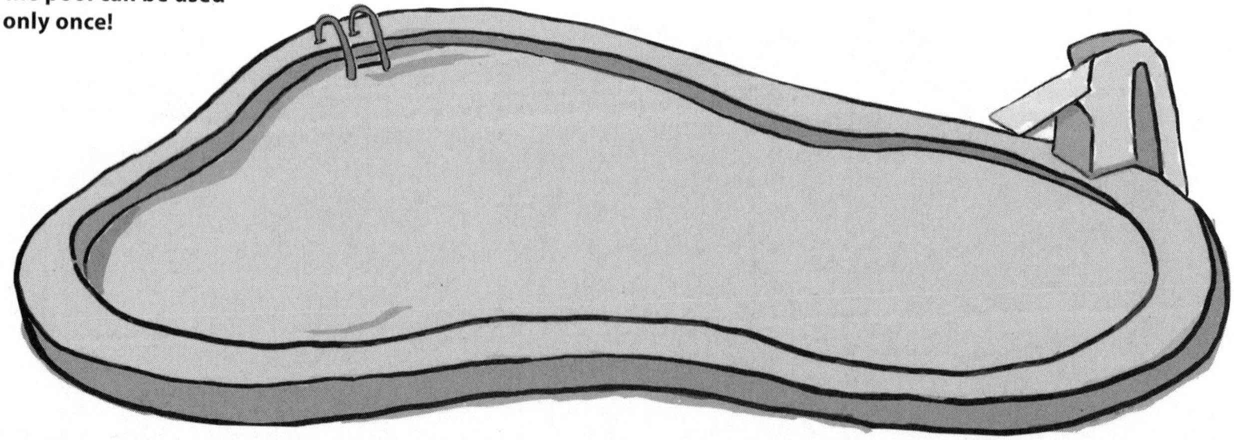

Exercise

1 Under the statistical category, pick the function that will count instances of each date.

Take a look at all these functions.

2 Implement the function to say how much parking you'll need for each date.

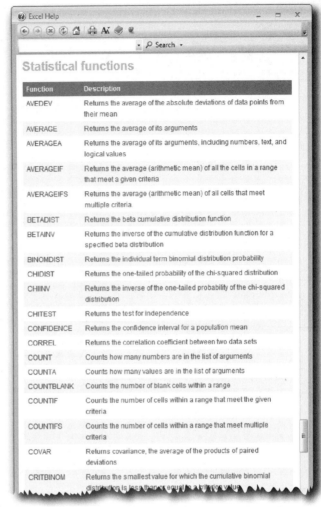

Excel Help

Search

Statistical functions

Function	Description
AVEDEV	Returns the average of the absolute deviations of data points from their mean
AVERAGE	Returns the average of its arguments
AVERAGEA	Returns the average of its arguments, including numbers, text, and logical values
AVERAGEIF	Returns the average (arithmetic mean) of all the cells in a range that meet a given criteria
AVERAGEIFS	Returns the average (arithmetic mean) of all cells that meet multiple criteria
BETADIST	Returns the beta cumulative distribution function
BETAINV	Returns the inverse of the cumulative distribution function for a specified beta distribution
BINOMDIST	Returns the individual term binomial distribution probability
CHIDIST	Returns the one-tailed probability of the chi-squared distribution
CHIINV	Returns the inverse of the one-tailed probability of the chi-squared distribution
CHITEST	Returns the test for independence
CONFIDENCE	Returns the confidence interval for a population mean
CORREL	Returns the correlation coefficient between two data sets
COUNT	Counts how many numbers are in the list of arguments
COUNTA	Counts how many values are in the list of arguments
COUNTBLANK	Counts the number of blank cells within a range
COUNTIF	Counts the number of cells within a range that meet the given criteria
COUNTIFS	Counts the number of cells within a range that meet multiple criteria
COVAR	Returns covariance, the average of the products of paired deviations
CRITBINOM	Returns the smallest value for which the cumulative binomial distribution is less than or equal to a criterion value

You need a function that counts instances of the dates in this column...

...if they match each cell in this column.

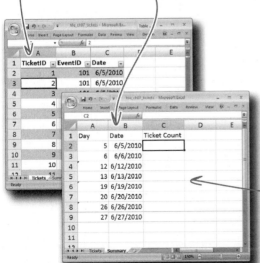

Put your answers here.

Hint: You may want to look carefully at all the COUNT *functions.*

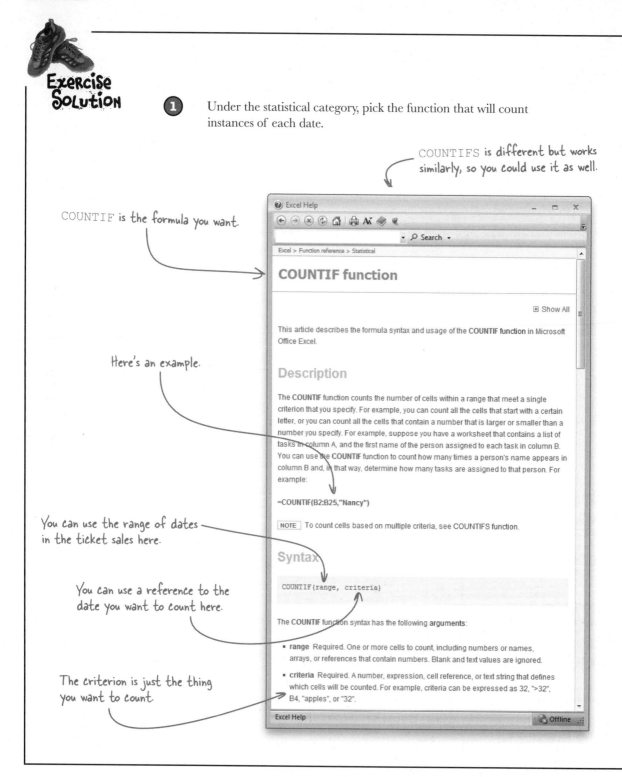

Exercise Solution

1 Under the statistical category, pick the function that will count instances of each date.

COUNTIFS is different but works similarly, so you could use it as well.

COUNTIF is the formula you want.

Excel Help

🔍 Search ▾

Excel > Function reference > Statistical

COUNTIF function

⊞ Show All

This article describes the formula syntax and usage of the **COUNTIF** function in Microsoft Office Excel.

Description

The **COUNTIF** function counts the number of cells within a range that meet a single criterion that you specify. For example, you can count all the cells that start with a certain letter, or you can count all the cells that contain a number that is larger or smaller than a number you specify. For example, suppose you have a worksheet that contains a list of tasks in column A, and the first name of the person assigned to each task in column B. You can use the COUNTIF function to count how many times a person's name appears in column B and, in that way, determine how many tasks are assigned to that person. For example:

Here's an example.

=COUNTIF(B2:B25,"Nancy")

NOTE   To count cells based on multiple criteria, see COUNTIFS function.

Syntax

You can use the range of dates in the ticket sales here.

COUNTIF(range, criteria)

You can use a reference to the date you want to count here.

The **COUNTIF** function syntax has the following **arguments**:

- **range** Required. One or more cells to count, including numbers or names, arrays, or references that contain numbers. Blank and text values are ignored.

- **criteria** Required. A number, expression, cell reference, or text string that defines which cells will be counted. For example, criteria can be expressed as 32, ">32", B4, "apples", or "32".

The criterion is just the thing you want to count.

Excel Help

☁ Offline

2 Implement the function to say how much parking you'll need for each date.

Here's the first argument: the range containing elements you want to count.

Here's the thing you want to count inside that range.

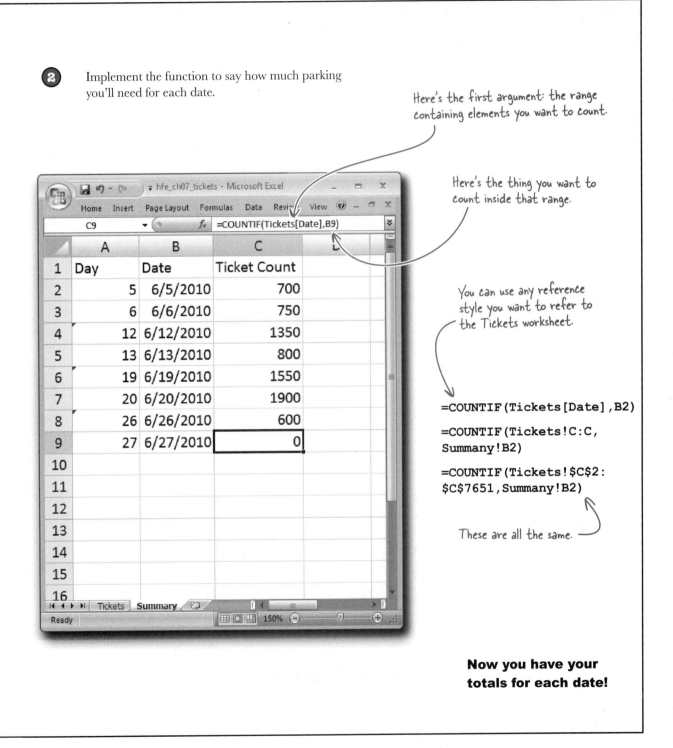

You can use any reference style you want to refer to the Tickets worksheet.

```
=COUNTIF(Tickets[Date],B2)
```

```
=COUNTIF(Tickets!C:C,
Summary!B2)
```

```
=COUNTIF(Tickets!$C$2:
$C$7651,Summary!B2)
```

These are all the same.

Now you have your totals for each date!

Your spreadsheet shows ticket counts summarized for each date

The COUNT family of formulas is a really versatile way to analyze repetitive elements in a list. The formulas enable you to get the size of a list, count the numbers in a list, count the blank cells in a list, and count based on multiple criteria.

You'll almost certainly have use for one or more of these formulas in the future, and when you do, you can just head over to the help docs and use your understanding of them to figure out which formula matches your problem.

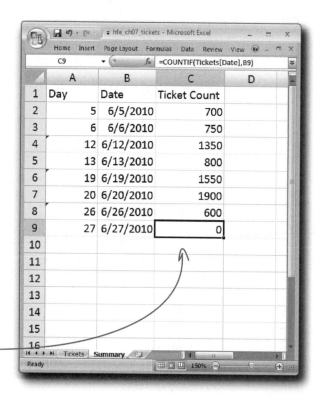

This spreadsheet shows just what you need to know.

From: Dataville Convention Ctr. COO
To: Head First
Subject:

Dear Head First,

Good, but...

Any chance you could show me *only* the list of dates that expect more than 1,000 people?

—COO

---

there are no
Dumb Questions

Q: Now that I know how to look up functions, does this mean that I know all I need to know?

A: You're definitely well on your way to being an Excel master. A strong knowledge of how to use formulas is what really separates people who use Excel casually to keep lists and people who use it to make their data *sing*.

Q: I'm serious: how much about Excel is there left for me to know, if I know how to use the help screens to get functions?

A: In the remainder of the book, there are two more chapters (one on text data and one on Boolean data) that are about functions, and the other chapters are about other powerful features of Excel. But you've learned most of what you need to know to be good with formulas. What is left—for functions, at least—is mainly just figuring out which ones you need for your own work, and then the techniques you need to use to make them work well.

Q: What's the difference between knowing functions and using "techniques" with formulas?

A: This is where the magic happens with Excel—when you use formulas together in clever combinations to achieve your analytic goals. It's one thing to understand your problem, another to understand Excel functions, and another thing entirely to be clever when it comes to matching up the problem with Excel functions.

Q: Sounds like something that just needs practice and experimentation.

A: That's right. People who are good at Excel have generally spent a lot of time working and reworking their data in a bunch of different ways with a bunch of different formulas. It's only through that process that they discover the mind-blowing, clever solutions for the analysis of their own problems.

Q: So, practice, practice, practice.

A: And be aware of features and functions of Excel that you've never used before. You never know whether something will be useful for you unless you try it out.

Q: What about these pivot tables I've heard about? Are they a type of function?

A: Good question. Pivot tables are one of the most powerful features of Excel besides functions, and we haven't touched on them yet, even though they're coming up. But first, we need to clean up the Convention Center's data for the COO....

Exercise

Use an Excel feature you've learned to generate a list of days where expected attendance is greater than 1,000 people.

Exercise Solution

What Excel operation did you need to generate the list of dates where expected attendance is 1,000 or more?

Just use a filter!

Filters are a fast way to display only the data you want to see.

No problem here.....

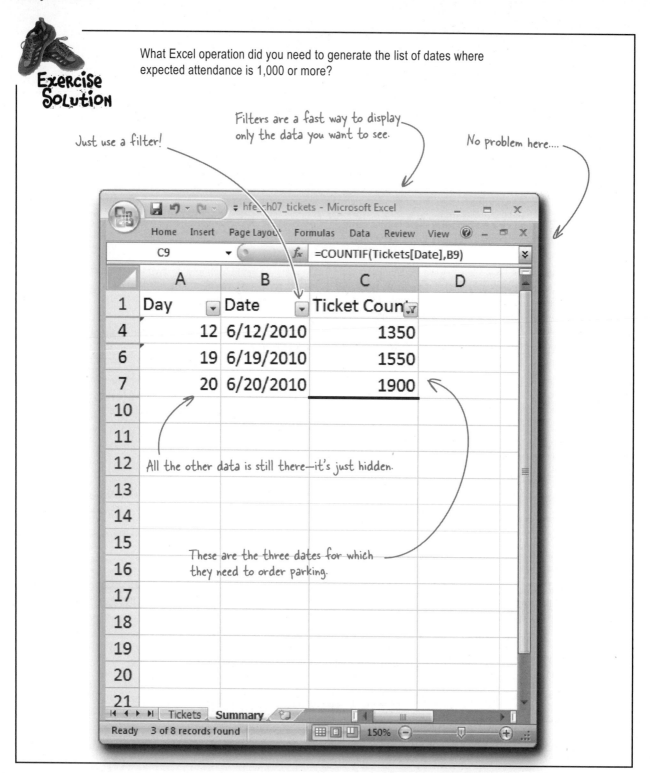

All the other data is still there—it's just hidden.

These are the three dates for which they need to order parking.

Box tickets for you!

Thanks to your diligent efforts, the convention center knows when it's going to need to order more parking. You've saved the convention center money and made spectators happy. Now to enjoy your reward....

Excellent!

8 formula auditing

Visualize your formulas

> If only I had seen where this formula was taking us—downhill fast—I might have chosen a different one....

Excel formulas can get really complicated.

And that is the point, right? If all you wanted to do was simple calculation, you'd be fine with a paper, pen, and calculator. But those complicated formulas can get unwieldy—especially ones written by other people, which can be almost impossible to decipher if you don't know what they were thinking. In this chapter, you'll learn to use a simple but powerful graphical feature of Excel called **formula auditing**, which will dramatically illustrate the flow of data throughout the *models* in your spreadsheet.

Should you buy a house or rent?

It's a perennial question. Both options have good reasons in their favor, and deciding which one is right for you is an important analytical project.

You need to develop a model to compare the cost of both options. You and your **better half** want to move in five years, which in some cases would be enough time to make financial sense for buying a house, but in some cases would not.

You could buy one of these...

...or you could rent a place inside of one of these!

Your choice will have big financial consequences in your life!

It's important to choose wisely.

Exercise

Let's run some basic numbers to see what sort of house you'd be able to afford if you did purchase a home. Use the PV (present value) function to calculate how much money you can borrow.

1 Take a look at the Help files under the PV function. How does the function work?

2 Using what you've learned about the PV function, implement it using the following assumptions about the hypothetical loan you want to take out.

BULLET POINTS

- Annual interest: 5%
- Term of loan: 30 years
- Monthly payment: $1,500

3 What other information do you need to compare buying a house versus renting?

....

....

....

....

Exercise Solution

You just looked into the Excel Help files to learn about the PV function, and then you implemented it to calculate how large of a mortgage you could afford. What did you find?

1 Take a look at the Help files under the PV function. How does the function work?

The rate is the interest for your loan.

NPER refers to the term of your loan—your agreement with the lender of how long you'll need to pay it off.

PMT refers to your expected periodic payment.

In this case, you expect to pay $1,500 every month.

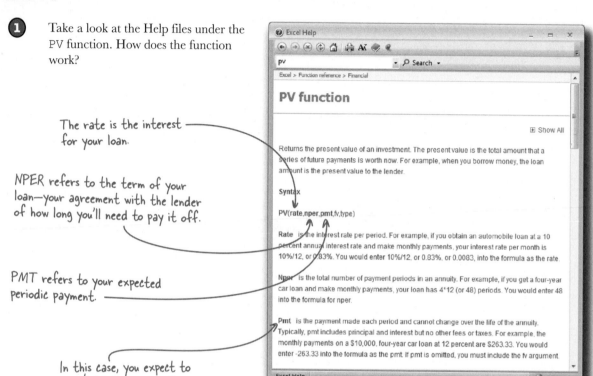

Excel Help

pv — Search

Excel > Function reference > Financial

PV function

⊞ Show All

Returns the present value of an investment. The present value is the total amount that a series of future payments is worth now. For example, when you borrow money, the loan amount is the present value to the lender.

Syntax

PV(rate,nper,pmt,fv,type)

Rate is the interest rate per period. For example, if you obtain an automobile loan at a 10 percent annual interest rate and make monthly payments, your interest rate per month is 10%/12, or 0.83%. You would enter 10%/12, or 0.83%, or 0.0083, into the formula as the rate.

Nper is the total number of payment periods in an annuity. For example, if you get a four-year car loan and make monthly payments, your loan has 4*12 (or 48) periods. You would enter 48 into the formula for nper.

Pmt is the payment made each period and cannot change over the life of the annuity. Typically, pmt includes principal and interest but no other fees or taxes. For example, the monthly payments on a $10,000, four-year car loan at 12 percent are $263.33. You would enter -263.33 into the formula as the pmt. If pmt is omitted, you must include the fv argument.

Excel Help — Offline

2 Using what you've learned about the PV function, implement it using the following assumptions about the hypothetical loan you want to take out.

Here's your PV formula.

Here's the total number of months in your 30-year loan.

=PV(B3/12,B4*12,B5)

This argument is the monthly interest rate.

Here's your monthly payment.

BULLET POINTS

- Annual interest: 5%
- Term of loan: 30 years
- Monthly payment: $1,500

Your spreadsheet with the PV function...

Your interest rate and loan term is in years, but your payment is monthly.

You need to convert the rate and term to months, so you're using the same unit.

This is how much you can borrow, given your assumptions.

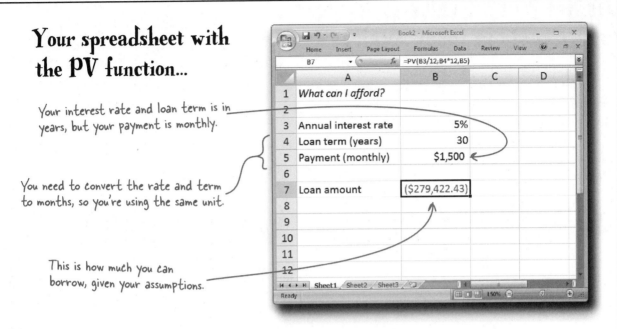

Book2 - Microsoft Excel

B7   =PV(B3/12,B4*12,B5)

	A	B	C	D
1	What can I afford?			
2				
3	Annual interest rate	5%		
4	Loan term (years)	30		
5	Payment (monthly)	$1,500		
6				
7	Loan amount	($279,422.43)		
8				
9				
10				
11				
12				

3 What other information do you need to compare housing versus rent?

This PV calculation is really just a start. Once I've bought a house, that house is either going to rise or fall in value, so I need to know how my investment will look when I sell the house. Plus, I need to compare all those figures with some assumptions about what renting will cost me during the same period of time.

You need a way to compare costs over time.

Here's your real estate broker.

How would you compare the costs of renting and buying over time?

Use Net Present Value to discount future costs to today's values

You can use the NPV function to calculate the Net Present Value of the costs of your two options. NPV discounts future costs to today's dollars, enabling you to do an apples-to-apples comparison of renting and buying.

Whichever option costs less, given your assumptions, is the one you want to pursue.

Here's the syntax of NPV.

=NPV(rate, values)

The rate is the <u>discount rate</u>, which could be a bunch of different values depending on what you are modeling.

The values are the stream of cash flows that you want to discount.

Here's a simple example. Say someone paid you $100 a year (with an annual 3% increase) for the next 5 years. NPV shows that **today** that stream of payments is worth $500.

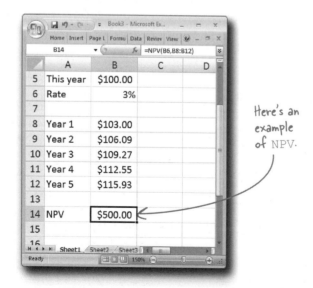

Here's an example of NPV.

Geek Bits: NPV

Aren't familiar with NPV? Here's the idea. Say you have a savings account with $100 this year and 3% interest. $100 **today** is worth $103 **next year**. And *next year*'s $103 is worth $100 *today*.

Now imagine you're the one paying the interest rather than your bank. Paying someone $103 next year is the same as paying them $100 today. Paying them $106.09 in two years is also the same as paying them $100 today.

If you add up all your future renting and buying costs **discounted** using NPV, you have a basis for comparing the two.

Exercise

Let's take NPV for a spin. Here is an example of how your annual cash flows might look for renting an apartment and paying a mortgage.

Your task is to get the NPV of these two streams of costs. Use a **3.5%** **discount rate** to represent inflation.

Type these values into a spreadsheet, then get the NPV of each of these streams of cash.

This is the annual total amount you spend on rent.

This number is the annual payment for a mortgage.

Year	Rent	Mortgage
1	$9,000	$14,389
2	$9,090	$14,389
3	$9,181	$14,389
4	$9,273	$14,389
5	$9,365	$14,389

These values are all annual, so you don't have to convert to monthly payments here.

This figure represents a $200,000 mortgage that lasts 30 years and has a 6% interest rate.

You just used NPV to compare renting and a mortgage under two sample scenarios. Which scenario is the least expensive?

Exercise Solution

=NPV($B$3,C6:C10)

Here is your formula.

Use an absolute reference to make sure your formula stays fixed on cell B3 after you copy it.

You can use the same formula for both of these cells.

Your real estate broker

Book4 - Microsoft Excel

Home   Insert   Page Layout   Formulas   Data   Review   View

C12   fx =NPV($B$3,C6:C10)

	A	B	C	D
1	NPV of rent versus mortgage			
2				
3	Discount	3.5%		
4				
5	Time	Rent	Mortgage	
6	1	$ 9,000	$ 14,389	
7	2	$ 9,090	$ 14,389	
8	3	$ 9,181	$ 14,389	
9	4	$ 9,273	$ 14,389	
10	5	$ 9,365	$ 14,389	
11				
12	NPV	$41,427.96	$64,967.09	
13				
14				
15				

Sheet1 Sheet2 Sheet3

Ready   150%

Your NPV is correct, but you need a more complex model. Here's one I created....

It looks like renting costs less than the mortgage...

...at least, renting costs less using these assumptions.

The broker has a spreadsheet for you

Her crack at the rent vs. buy problem is a lot more elaborate
than the exercise you just completed, even though ultimately
she's using a comparison of NPVs as well. Here's her
spreadsheet.

Load this!

www.headfirstlabs.com/books/hfexcel/
hfe_ch08_models.xlsx

This spreadsheet is a
lot more complex.

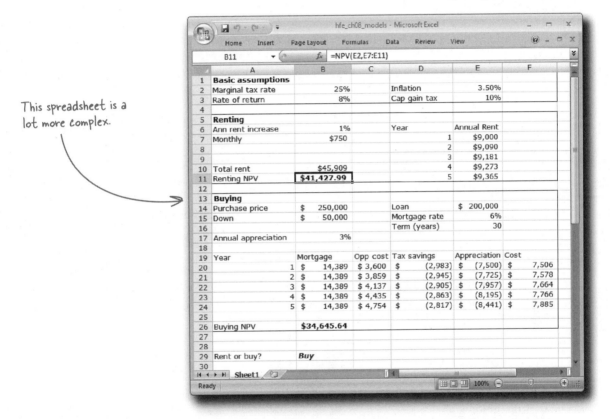

This spreadsheet contains a much larger array
of assumptions about how your calculation will
work. And this is promising, since the world is
complex and it's a good idea to think through all
the variables in such an important decision.

BRAIN POWER

How do you think this spreadsheet works?
Take a close look at the formulas.

Models in Excel can get complicated

You can define **models** in a number of ways, depending on what you're trying to do, but in Excel a "model" is a network of formulas designed to answer a question.

Models can get complicated, and it can be hard to sort them all out. Unless you can understand the workings of this particular model, how do you trust the real estate broker?

This spreadsheet shows models for calculating rent and mortgage NPVs.

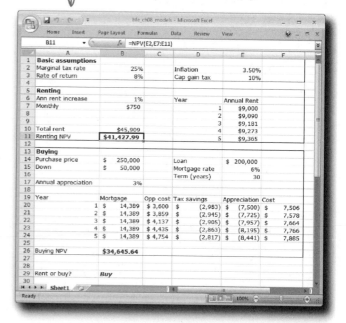

Rent model

The rent model is like the mortgage model in that its spreadsheet representation consists of cells full of data that flow into formulas, which flow into more formulas.

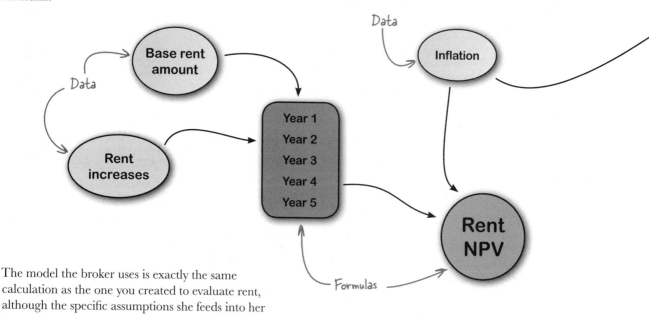

The model the broker uses is exactly the same calculation as the one you created to evaluate rent, although the specific assumptions she feeds into her model are slightly different from the ones you used.

Mortgage model

The mortgage model is a lot more complicated than the rent model. Take a look at all the variables that her model incorporates. They all flow together into the ultimate NPV calculation.

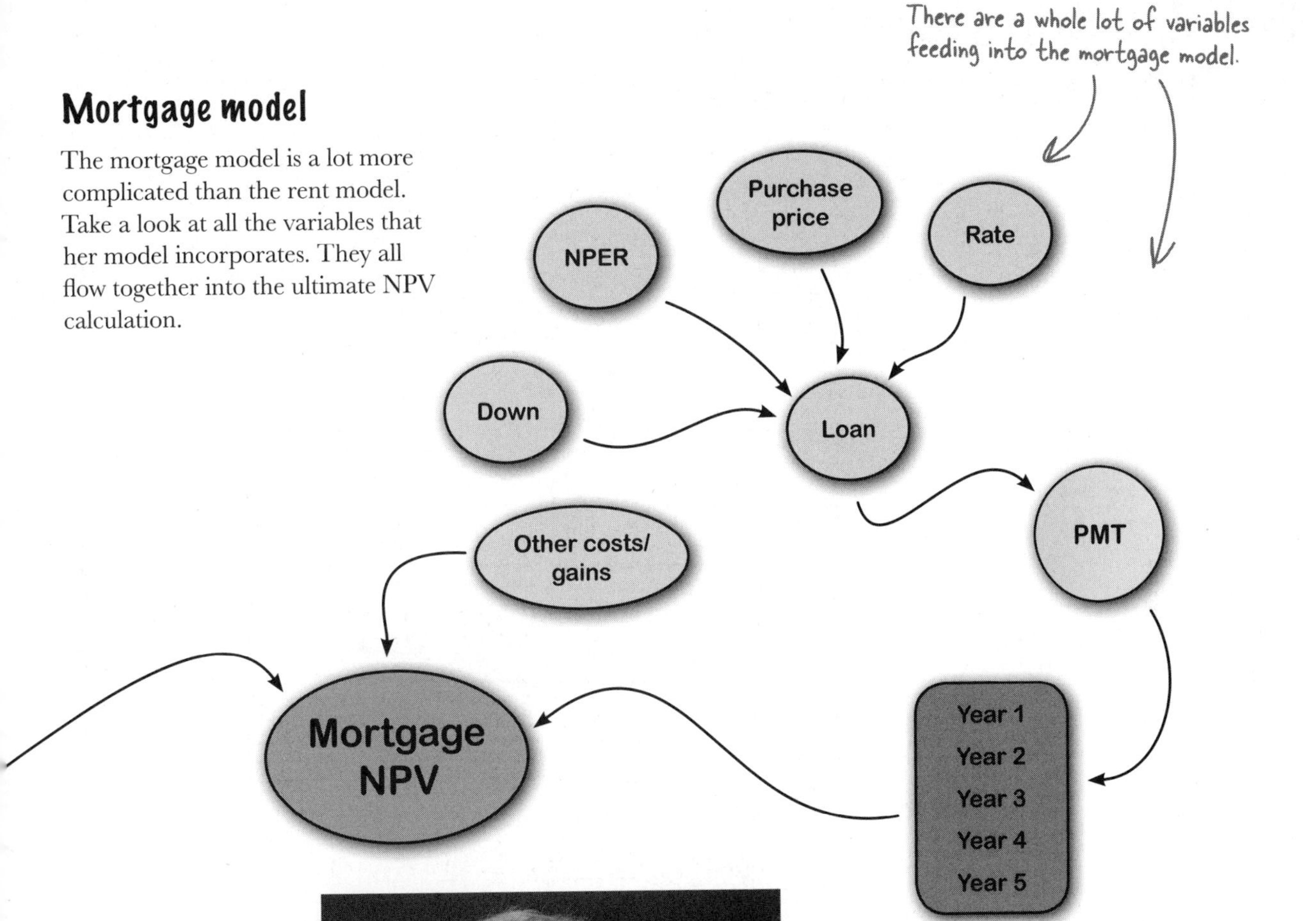

There are a whole lot of variables feeding into the mortgage model.

NPER

Purchase price

Rate

Down

Loan

Other costs/ gains

PMT

Mortgage NPV

Year 1
Year 2
Year 3
Year 4
Year 5

Wouldn't it be dreamy if Excel could show model relationships graphically, so I don't have to imagine this complex data flow? But I know it's just a fantasy...

Formula auditing shows you the location of your formula's arguments

Formula auditing is an Excel feature that allows you to trace the flow of data through complex formulas. Here are the models you saw on the previous page, with arrows drawn by Excel.

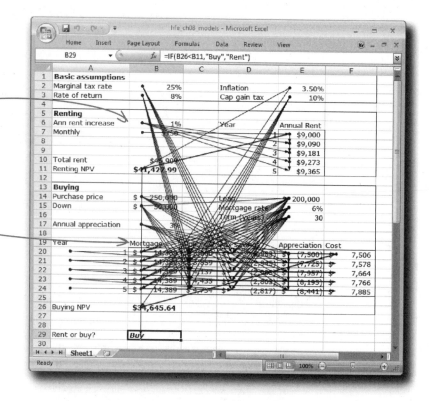

These arrows show how data feeds through formulas into the rent/buy formula.

The formula auditing buttons can be found under the formula tab.

Select a formula and click Trace Precedents to see which cells' data flows into it.

This network of arrows looks complicated, and it is—the model is complicated!

Try recreating these arrows yourself. Put your cursor on cell B29, and then click Trace Precedents until you see this grid. Can you see how data flows through the model?

Click Remove Arrows to get rid of arrows you've created.

Let's take a close look at the rent model to see how its formulas work....

Exercise

Select the rent NPV formula in cell B11. This formula takes data from other formulas in the rent box, and you want to use formula auditing to see how those formulas work together.

Click Trace Precedents on cell B11 *and on the formulas that feed into it.*

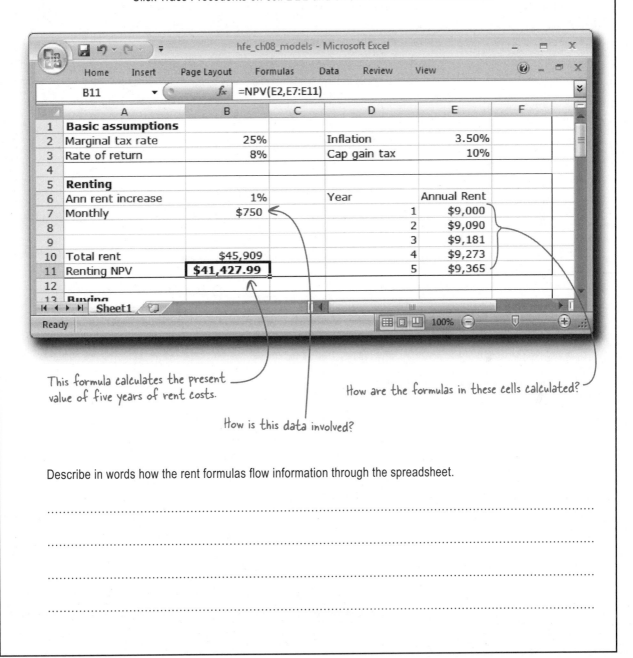

This formula calculates the present value of five years of rent costs.

How is this data involved?

How are the formulas in these cells calculated?

Describe in words how the rent formulas flow information through the spreadsheet.

....

....

....

....

Exercise Solution

Were you able to use formula auditing to figure out how the rent model works?

Here's the Trace Precedents button being pressed.

The rent NPV is selected, so the audit will be of this formula.

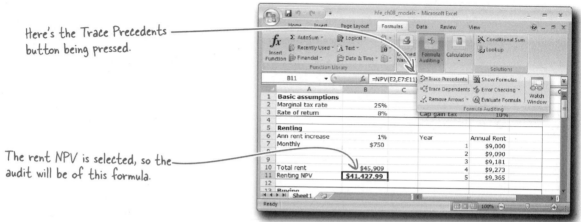

Describe in words how the rent formulas flow information through the spreadsheet.

The NPV formula is pretty straightforward. It points to the cash flows from the Annual Rent column and uses Inflation as the discount rate. As for the Annual Rent formula, Year 1 is the monthly rent (cell B7) times 12, and Year 2 adds an annual 1% increase (from cell B6) to the previous year. Years 3 through 5 do the same thing.

The NPV formula points to the cash flows in the Annual Rent column...

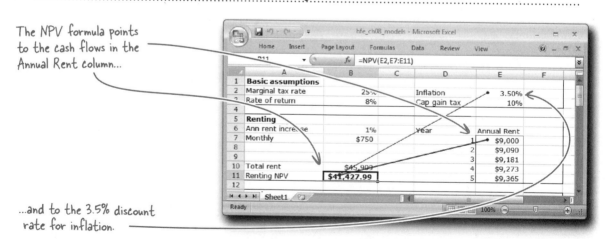

...and to the 3.5% discount rate for inflation.

The rent for Year 1 is the $750/month times 12.

=B7*12

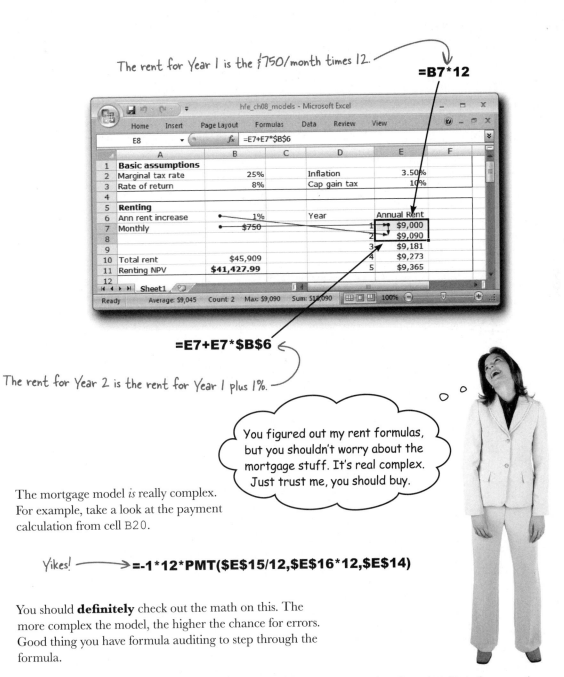

=E7+E7*$B$6

The rent for Year 2 is the rent for Year 1 plus 1%.

> You figured out my rent formulas, but you shouldn't worry about the mortgage stuff. It's real complex. Just trust me, you should buy.

The mortgage model *is* really complex. For example, take a look at the payment calculation from cell B20.

Yikes! ⟶ **=-1*12*PMT($E$15/12,$E$16*12,$E$14)**

You should **definitely** check out the math on this. The more complex the model, the higher the chance for errors. Good thing you have formula auditing to step through the formula.

How do you think the PMT formula works?

Excel's loan functions all use the same basic elements

Excel has a bunch of financial functions, but the core functions are the ones that calculate loan values, payments, rates, and terms. The neat thing about these functions is that they take the same arguments—each other—so if you know a few, you can generally derive the others.

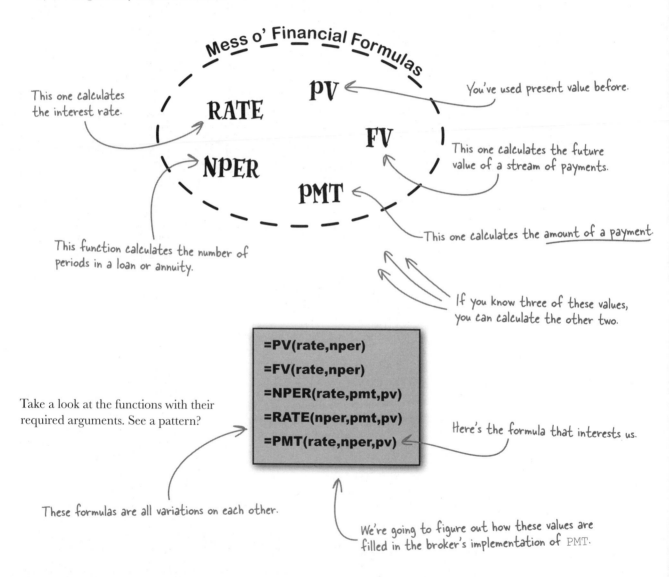

Mess o' Financial Formulas

This one calculates the interest rate.

RATE

PV

You've used present value before.

NPER

FV

This one calculates the future value of a stream of payments.

PMT

This function calculates the number of periods in a loan or annuity.

This one calculates the amount of a payment.

If you know three of these values, you can calculate the other two.

Take a look at the functions with their required arguments. See a pattern?

```
=PV(rate,nper)
=FV(rate,nper)
=NPER(rate,pmt,pv)
=RATE(nper,pmt,pv)
=PMT(rate,nper,pv)
```

Here's the formula that interests us.

These formulas are all variations on each other.

We're going to figure out how these values are filled in the broker's implementation of PMT.

The PMT formula in the broker's spreadsheet calculates your monthly payment

When you click Trace Precedents on the mortgage amount calculation, you can see how the formula looks elsewhere on the spreadsheet for the RATE, NPER, and PV amounts.

Use formula auditing to see how the arguments of this formula are filled.

=-1*12*PMT($E$15/12,$E$16*12,$E$14)

Here's the monthly interest rate.

Here's the term (NPER).

Here's the present value (PV).

Excel spreadsheet: hfe_ch08_models - Microsoft Excel

Cell B20: =-1*12*PMT($E$15/12,$E$16*12,$E$14)

	A	B	C	D	E	F
11	Renting NPV	$41,427.99		5	$9,365	
12						
13	**Buying**					
14	Purchase price	$ 250,000		Loan	$ 200,000	
15	Down	$ 50,000		Mortgage rate	6%	
16				Term (years)	30	
17	Annual appreciation	3%				
18						
19	Year	Mortgage	Opp cost	Tax savings	Appreciation	Cost
20	1	$ 14,389	$ 3,600	$ (2,983)	$ (7,500)	$ 7,506
21	2	$ 14,389	$ 3,859	$ (2,945)	$ (7,725)	$ 7,578
22	3	$ 14,389	$ 4,137	$ (2,905)	$ (7,957)	$ 7,664
23	4	$ 14,389	$ 4,435	$ (2,863)	$ (8,195)	$ 7,766
24	5	$ 14,389	$ 4,754	$ (2,817)	$ (8,441)	$ 7,885
25						
26	Buying NPV	$34,645.64				
27						

When the broker wrote this formula, she multiplied the result by 12 to make the calculation show the total mortgage amount for the year, and then she multiplied the amount by −1 to make it a positive number.

What about the rest of the real estate broker's formulas?

Long Exercise

Take a close look at the formulas the broker uses in her mortgage model. How do they work? Write your answers in the blanks below.

You will need to use both formula auditing and the help screens to decode these formulas.

1 Use what you've learned so far to figure out how the "Tax savings" formula works.

> **Tax savings**
>
> **=CUMIPMT($E$15/12,$E$16*12,$E$14,1,A20*12,0)*$B$2**

This ones's a bear!

....

....

....

....

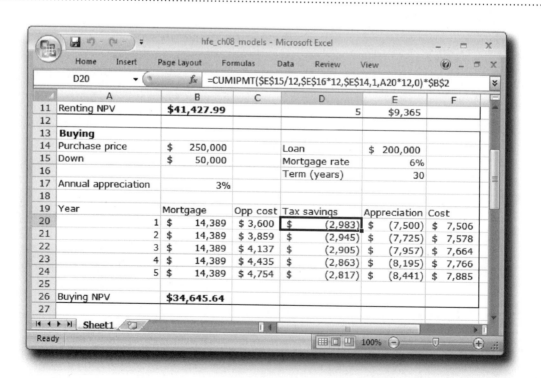

2 Do the same for the "Opp cost" and "Appreciation" formulas.

Write how you think these formulas work in the blanks.

> **Opp cost**
> =$B$15*$B$3*(1-$E$3)

> **Appreciation**
> =-1*$B$17*$B$14

....

....

....

....

	hfe_ch08_models - Microsoft Excel					
Home	Insert	Page Layout	Formulas	Data	Review	View

C20   *fx*   =$B$15*$B$3*(1-$E$3)

	A	B	C	D	E	F
11	Renting NPV	**$41,427.99**		5	$9,365	
12						
13	**Buying**					
14	Purchase price	$ 250,000		Loan	$ 200,000	
15	Down	$ 50,000		Mortgage rate	6%	
16				Term (years)	30	
17	Annual appreciation	3%				
18						
19	Year	Mortgage	Opp cost	Tax savings	Appreciation	Cost
20	1	$ 14,389	$ 3,600	$ (2,983)	$ (7,500)	$ 7,506
21	2	$ 14,389	$ 3,859	$ (2,945)	$ (7,725)	$ 7,578
22	3	$ 14,389	$ 4,137	$ (2,905)	$ (7,957)	$ 7,664
23	4	$ 14,389	$ 4,435	$ (2,863)	$ (8,195)	$ 7,766
24	5	$ 14,389	$ 4,754	$ (2,817)	$ (8,441)	$ 7,885
25						
26	Buying NPV	**$34,645.64**				
27						

Sheet1

Ready   100%

LONG EXERCISE SOLUTION

Were you able to use Excel tools to decode the Tax savings, Opp cost, and Appreciate formulas?

1 Use what you've learned so far to figure out how the "Tax savings" formula works.

> ### Tax savings
> **=CUMIPMT($E$15/12,$E$16*12,$E$14,1,A20*12,0)*$B$2**

The CUMIPMT function calculates the amount of interest paid on a loan (or annuity) between two points in time. In this formula, CUMIPMT looks at assumptions about the size, interest rate, and term of the loan to calculate interest paid each year. Then the formula multiplies the amount of interest paid by your tax rate, which returns how much money you save in taxes.

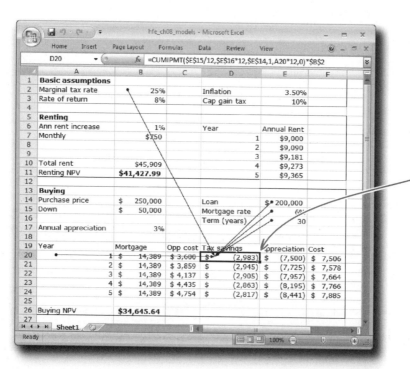

Here's how data flows into the Tax savings formula.

2 Do the same for the "Opp cost" and "Appreciation" formulas.

Opp cost
=$B$15*$B$3*(1-$E$3)

Appreciation
=-1*$B$17*$B$14

The Opp cost formula adds together your down payment and your cumulative mortgage payment and then multiplies the amount by your after-tax rate of return. This is your "opportunity cost." The Appreciation formula looks at the purchase price of your house and adds an annual rate of return.

The Appreciation formula incorporates appreciation from the previous year into its calculation.

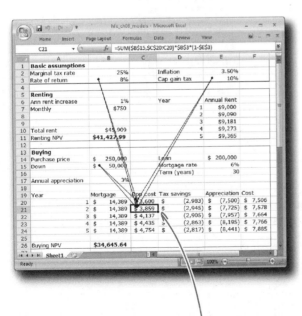

The Opp cost formula draws from three sources.

Here's the Appreciation formula.

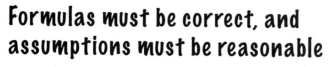

I have to call BS on these models. They're pretty and complex, but who's to say that the assumptions that feed into them are actually true?

Formulas must be correct, and assumptions must be reasonable

Models can get really complicated in Excel, and it always pays to do a sanity check to make sure that the formulas are written correctly and that the numbers that go into them are sensible.

Let's take a look at how the model works if you play around with the broker's assumptions.

Watch it!

Model complexity can obscure a host of ills.

It's easy to create an elaborate spreadsheet that flows data all over the place. It's really hard to devise a complex model that helps you make good real-world decisions. Always make sure you understand the models you use, especially the complex ones.

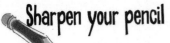

Sharpen your pencil

Here are a couple different scenarios designed to test the broker's model. What happens to your decision when you change the model's assumptions?

1 Say your loan interest is changed to 6.5% and the house appreciates at 1.5% per annum. Does that affect your decision to buy?

....

....

....

....

2 Say it goes to 4% interest and 5% appreciation. What now?

....

....

....

....

3 What would you ask the real estate broker to help tease out her beliefs about the plausibility of her assumptions?

....

....

....

....

Sharpen your pencil
Solution

You tinkered with some of the assumptions in the broker's model. What did you learn about the model?

① Say your loan interest is changed to 6.5% and the house appreciates at 1.5% per annum. Does that affect your decision to buy?

The cost for buying a house goes way up under this circumstance, for two reasons: one, the mortgage interest cost is a lot higher and two, the appreciation of the house isn't high enough to compensate for the increase in mortgage interest. Given the rent assumptions at the top of the spreadsheet, the NPV calculations show renting to be a clear winner.

Here are the two assumptions you changed.

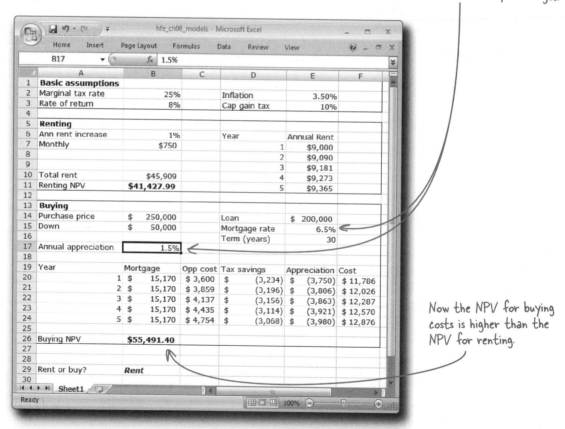

Now the NPV for buying costs is higher than the NPV for renting.

2 Say it goes to 4% interest and 5% appreciation. What now?

Here, interest goes down, and appreciation goes up. In this case, buying a house is a whole

lot more attractive than renting. In fact, you actually make money under this scenario,

which is what the negative NPV means. If you know that this scenario would come to pass,

buying would be a no-brainer. Too bad you don't have a crystal ball....

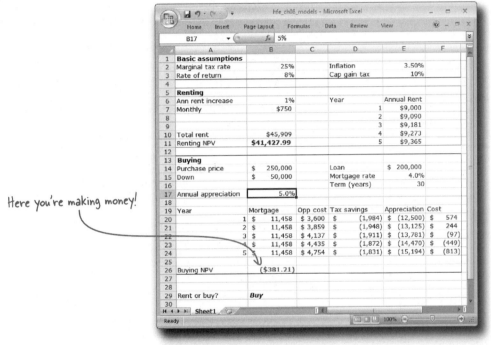

Here you're making money!

3 What would you ask the real estate broker to help tease out her beliefs about the plausibility of her assumptions?

The broker wants to sell the house (wouldn't you, if you were a broker?), so you should be

on guard for overly optimistic assumptions. Small changes in interest and appreciation rates

make all the difference in which strategy is best for you. So the question for the broker is

simply, "Why should I believe your assumptions?!?"

The broker weighs in...

Oh, those are reasonable questions. It's really great that you're thinking through this decision so thoroughly. Your 6.5% interest/1.5% appreciation scenario is possible, but I doubt it'll happen. Here's the deal; I can help you with the model but the decision and risk are ultimately yours. If you feel conservative or speculative in your decision, you need to make sure that you plug in the right assumptions to reflect it.

And BTW, the short answer is this...you should buy a house!

Exercise

An email just came through from your better half talking about the assumptions you two should use for your modeling. And since your purchase of a home is a partnership, you'd better pay attention to those suggestions!

From: Better Half
To: You
Subject:

Hey You,

I've been doing a lot of thinking, and I think that we should use these assumptions. First off, let's go for the $250,000 house.

I think that we should take out a loan for as little as possible, so let's put down $100,000. That way, the present value of our loan will be just $150,000.

The bank officer called and said that we qualify for a 30-year mortgage at 5% interest, and that's the best rate we've seen so far, so I think we should go with it.

And as for the amount we expect the house to appreciate…that's a tough one. The houses we're looking at have been in a pretty up-and-coming neighborhood, and unbiased experts are predicting 7% annual growth over the next five years. But I say we should project 3% just to be on the conservative side.

Love,

Your Better Half

Take these figures and plug them back into your spreadsheet. Using the NPV calculations, should you rent or buy?

Exercise Solution

Your better half provided you with some model parameters for your rent vs. buy decision. What did your spreadsheet tell you to do?

Here's the new down payment.

Change these two cells as well.

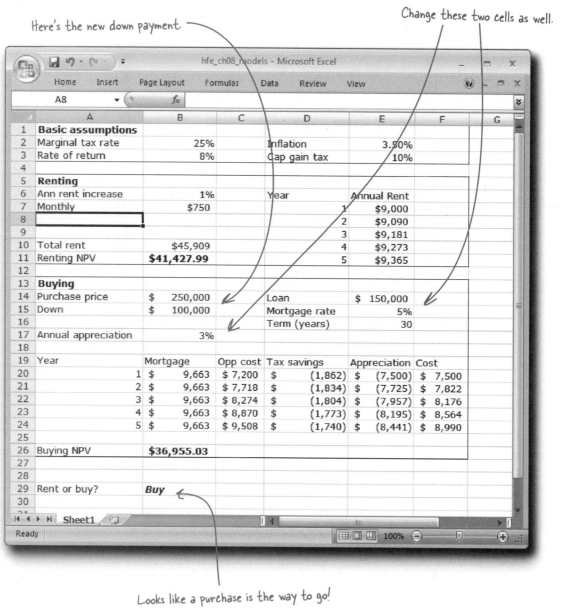

	A	B	C	D	E	F	G
1	**Basic assumptions**						
2	Marginal tax rate	25%		Inflation	3.50%		
3	Rate of return	8%		Cap gain tax	10%		
4							
5	**Renting**						
6	Ann rent increase	1%		Year	Annual Rent		
7	Monthly	$750		1	$9,000		
8				2	$9,090		
9				3	$9,181		
10	Total rent	$45,909		4	$9,273		
11	Renting NPV	**$41,427.99**		5	$9,365		
12							
13	**Buying**						
14	Purchase price	$ 250,000		Loan	$ 150,000		
15	Down	$ 100,000		Mortgage rate	5%		
16				Term (years)	30		
17	Annual appreciation	3%					
18							
19	Year	Mortgage	Opp cost	Tax savings	Appreciation	Cost	
20	1	$ 9,663	$ 7,200	$ (1,862)	$ (7,500)	$ 7,500	
21	2	$ 9,663	$ 7,718	$ (1,834)	$ (7,725)	$ 7,822	
22	3	$ 9,663	$ 8,274	$ (1,804)	$ (7,957)	$ 8,176	
23	4	$ 9,663	$ 8,870	$ (1,773)	$ (8,195)	$ 8,564	
24	5	$ 9,663	$ 9,508	$ (1,740)	$ (8,441)	$ 8,990	
25							
26	Buying NPV	**$36,955.03**					
27							
28							
29	Rent or buy?	**Buy**					
30							

Looks like a purchase is the way to go!

Your house was a good investment!

The purchase of a house is by no means a guaranteed way to make money, but because of your diligence in modeling your decision to buy the house, you and yours have done quite nicely.

Buying the house has definitely proven to be the better strategy.

Nice digs!

9 charts

Graph your data

All this arcane Excel code I have to write...what ever happened to drawing pictures?

Who wants to look at numbers all the time?

Very often a nice graphic is a more engaging way to present data. And sometimes you have so much data that you actually can't see it all without a nice graphic. Excel has extensive charting facilities, and if you just know where to click, you'll unlock the power to make charts and graphs to display your data with drama and lucidity.

Head First Investments needs charts for its investment report

There is a big presentation coming up for Head First Investment's **board of directors**. They have all the data compiled to show their performance over the last year, but they need some charts to make the data easier to read and understand. It's up to you to crank out some attractive charts.

This spreadsheet shows your company's investments.

Load this!

www.headfirstlabs.com/books/hfexcel/
hfe_ch09_allocation.xlsx

We're counting on you.

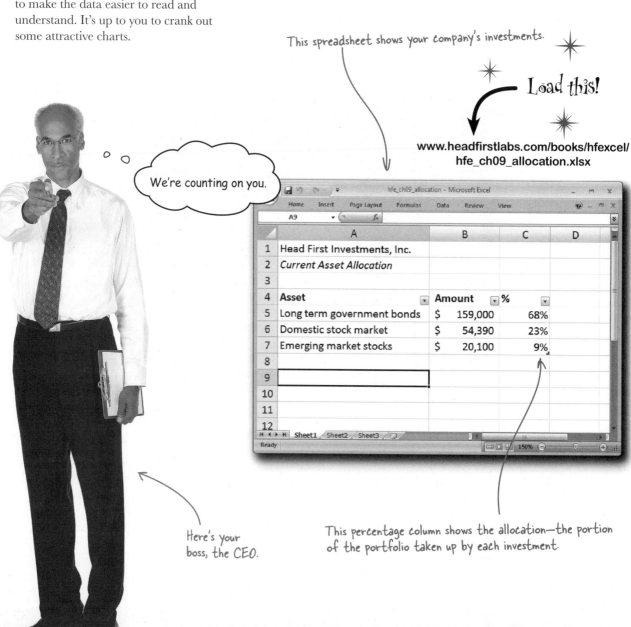

	A	B	C	D
1	Head First Investments, Inc.			
2	*Current Asset Allocation*			
3				
4	**Asset**	**Amount**	**%**	
5	Long term government bonds	$ 159,000	68%	
6	Domestic stock market	$ 54,390	23%	
7	Emerging market stocks	$ 20,100	9%	
8				
9				
10				
11				
12				

Here's your boss, the CEO.

This percentage column shows the allocation—the portion of the portfolio taken up by each investment.

Sharpen your pencil

Look at each chart type. Which is most appropriate to show portfolio allocation?

....

....

....

....

Write your thoughts about the suitability of each chart type in these blanks.

....

....

....

....

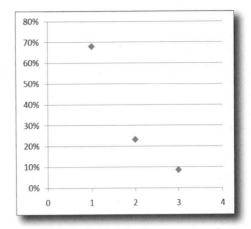

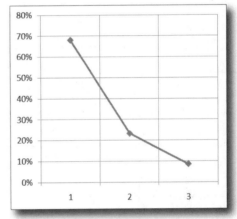

....

....

....

....

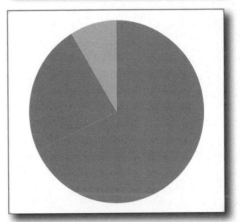

Sharpen your pencil
Solution

Which chart did you conclude would be the most useful way of representing your company's portfolio visually?

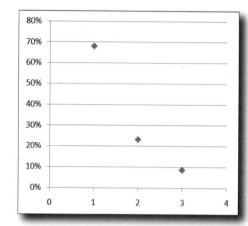

It looks like 1, 2, and 3 on the bottom here represent the different investments, and a dot represents the percentage for each. This isn't a very clear chart.

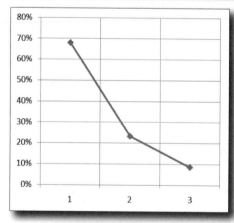

This chart has lines to connect the dots. That doesn't seem very useful either, because the line suggests a trend in the data, like what you'd have if one thing changed over time.

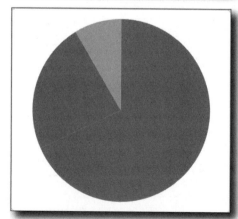

Here's the classic pie chart. This would definitely be a good place to start. The pie itself represents the portfolio, and each slice represents an asset.

Create charts using the Insert tab

Let's try creating one of those pie charts. Making charts in Excel is easy: just start by clicking on the Insert tab of the Ribbon. You'll find everything you need to get started.

Make sure your data isn't selected.

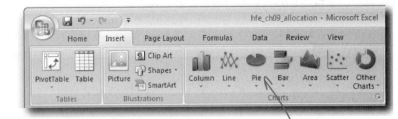

Click on the first option under this drop box.

Do this!

① Make sure your cursor is **outside your data range** in a blank cell. Then insert a pie chart.

② Next, click the Select Data button. Fill in your data range and axis labels.

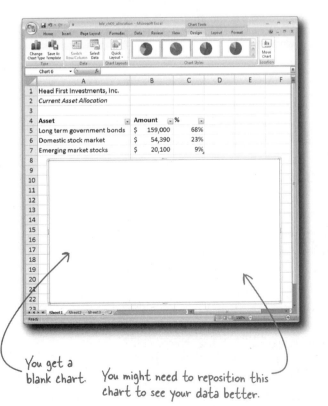

You get a blank chart.

You might need to reposition this chart to see your data better.

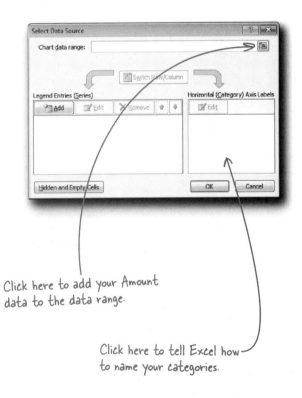

Click here to add your Amount data to the data range.

Click here to tell Excel how to name your categories.

Use the Design and Layout tabs to rework your chart

Inserting a chart in Excel is only the beginning. Once your chart has been created, you'll always head to the Design and Layout tabs under Chart Tools to change elements in your chart like the titles and formatting.

You just hit the **Select Data** button under the Design tab to select your data and labels.

This range includes your data and labels.

This is the legend.

By default, Excel places your labels in the legend.

Exercise

Let's polish up your chart using the Design and Layout tabs.

1 Using the far-right button on the Design tab, move the chart you created to its own sheet. This will clear up the sheet with your data.

Use this button to move the chart to its own sheet.

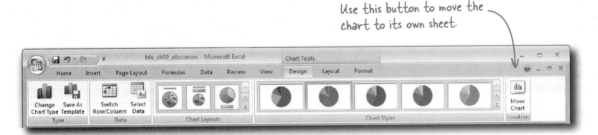

2 Now head over to the Layout tab. Click the Chart Title button to add a title.

Add a title.

Remove the legend.   *Add data labels.*

3 It'd be nice if your labels were actually next to the pie slices rather than in the legend, so let's get rid of the legend. Under the Layout tab, make the legend go away.

4 Add data labels next to the pie slices. Once you've added them, right-click and select Format Data Labels to make sure they refer to the Category Name rather than the Values.

5 Finally, increase the font size of all text elements in the chart to make them more readable. You can change the font size using the Home tab.

ExerCise Solution

You just executed a variety of modifications to your pie chart's layout using the Design and Layout tabs. How do your results look?

① Move the chart you created to its own sheet.

② Add a title.

③ Get rid of the legend.

④ Add data labels next to the pie slices, making sure they refer to the Category Name rather than the Values.

⑤ Increase the font size of all text elements in the chart.

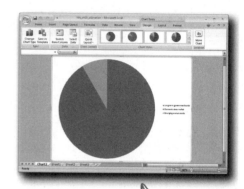

Here's your chart on its own sheet.

Now your labels have moved from the legend to the pie slices.

You needed to open this window to fix your axis labels.

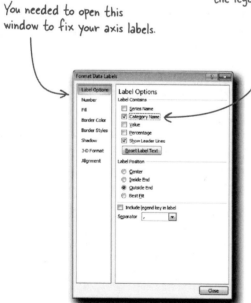

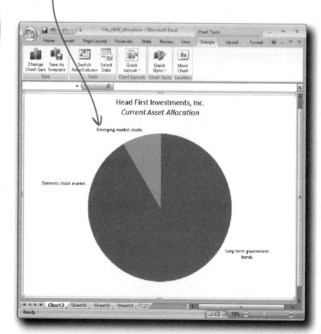

there are no
Dumb Questions

Q: That made sense, but it looks like there are a lot of different options in the chart menus. If I want to change just one thing, how do I know how to find it?

A: That's a great question, and there's a really simple trick. You can right-click on any of the components on your chart, so if you want to change an element of your chart, you can always just right-click on it to search for the menu item that will change that one thing.

Q: So when all else fails, if I want to change something on my chart, I should right-click and explore the menus?

A: That's exactly right.

Q: Are the charts that come with Excel pretty well designed? I mean, if I just go with the defaults, will I generally create pretty attractive, readable charts?

A: Yes and no. The graphic quality of Excel's built-in visualizations is greater than it's ever been. If you look at the Chart Styles under the Design tab, you can see a neat grid of design variations that you can quickly apply to your data. Excel has never been better.

Q: I'm sensing there's a "but" coming.

A: You sense correctly. The "but" is that no software can ever make your design decisions for you, especially when it comes to charts. The fact that your chart came built into Excel is not much help if your visualization is not analytically rigorous or useful.

Q: Is Excel the best spreadsheet charting tool available?

A: It depends on what you're trying to accomplish. If you have data and a problem that fits the built-in charts nicely, then Excel is probably the tool for you. If you need to do high-level, hardcore statistical visualizations, you might want to reach for a program like the open source statistical package R.

Q: What you're telling me is that I have to learn *another* piece of software?

A: Not necessarily! Recent versions of Excel are more powerful and versatile than ever, and Excel's features are more than most people need to manage their data. But it never hurts to be aware of other visualization options, and if you find yourself spending hours and hours trying to force Excel's charting features to create some chart that it wasn't designed to make, then you may want to investigate other graphing programs.

Q: Do people do that—use Excel to make charts that the Excel designers never thought to support?

A: A lot of people use Excel to do things that the original designers of spreadsheets never thought to support. And it's actually one of the coolest things about how people use Excel: users dream up features, then force Excel to implement them (even in weird ways sometimes), and later Microsoft picks them up and implements them in a user-friendly way.

Q: So what's the bottom line?

A: Learn Excel's features. As many as you can. Come up with creative ways to apply those features to your own problems. And if you find yourself spending a huge amount of time forcing Excel to solve your problems, consider the features of more full-fledged computer or statistical programming platforms like R or Python.

Q: Let's get back to charts. How do I know which chart to use with my data?

A: You're about to find out. Your client is almost certainly going to need you to create more charts for the big presentation....

Let's see what the boss thinks....

Your pie chart isn't going over well with the corporate graphic artist

Your pie chart has been passed around, and some guy you've never even dealt with is weighing in with a negative opinion.

Haven't you heard? People judge length better than area. Pie charts show area, so they suck.

This argument makes sense to me, although I'm annoyed that we're dealing with this. Fix it!

The corporate graphic artist

The artist is correct. This is a common critique of pie charts among people who care a lot about data visualizations, so you should probably try a different chart. But no worries: changing the chart type is a snap.

Let's take a look at some other chart types.

WHO DOES WHAT?

Match each Excel chart type to what it does. Which chart do you think would be an improvement over the pie chart?

Lets you plot two variables with the option of fitting a curve to the data points.

A way to plot financial instruments, showing high, low, and closing prices.

Basic comparison, using length and one or more variables.

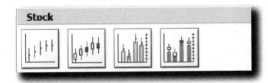

A visualization that lets you add a third dimension of area to a scatterplot.

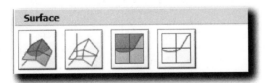

Charts for plotting data with three related variables.

Shows changing trends, generally over time.

compare *chart types*

Match each Excel chart type to what it does. Which chart do you think would be an improvement over the pie chart?

Lets you plot two variables with the option of fitting a curve to the data points.

A way to plot financial instruments, showing high, low, and closing prices.

Basic comparison, using length and one or more variables.

—This is the chart we should use!

A visualization that lets you add a third dimension of area to a scatterplot.

Charts for plotting data with three related variables.

Shows changing trends, generally over time.

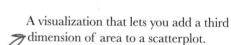

Exercise

Now that you've decided to change your pie chart to a bar chart, go ahead and make that change.

Click this button here.

Excel makes it easy to switch your chart type.

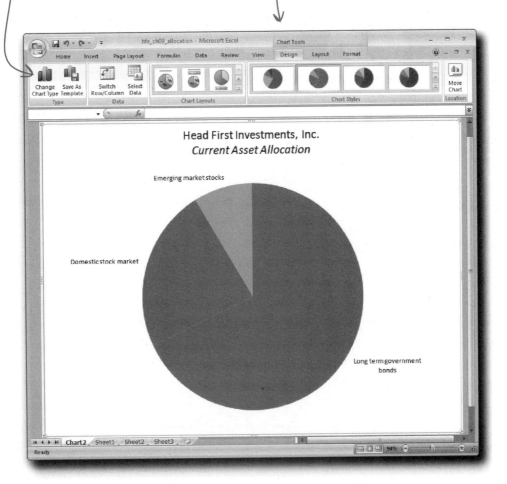

Do the labels update correctly? You might need to adjust the fonts.

Exercise Solution

You just changed your pie chart to a bar chart. How did the conversion go?

Excel remembers your data range.

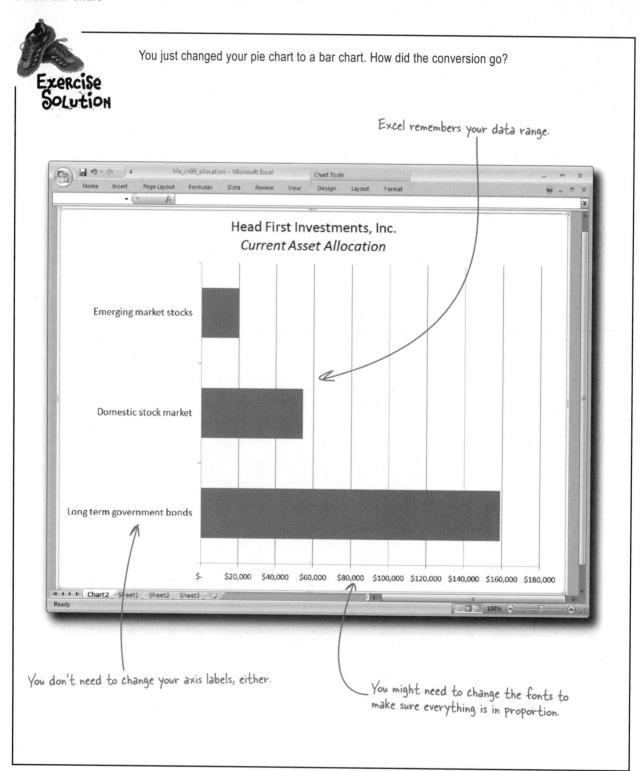

You don't need to change your axis labels, either.

You might need to change the fonts to make sure everything is in proportion.

Nice work! We're very pleased with this visualization. And I think it's time for you to take on a bigger project. Compare these two stocks in our portfolio using a time series line chart.

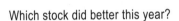

Create a line chart to compare stock 1 and stock 2. Put your cursor inside your data range, and Excel will try to figure out which columns represent your data.

Exercise

Load this!

www.headfirstlabs.com/books/hfexcel/ hfe_ch09_stocks.xlsx

Which stock did better this year?

....

....

....

....

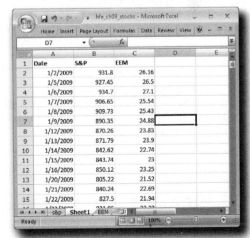

Exercise Solution

You just created a time chart to compare two stocks. Did Excel create a strong visualization?

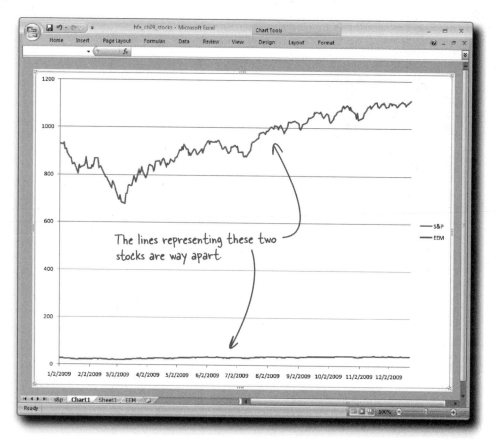

The lines representing these two stocks are way apart.

Which stock did better this year?

It appears that Excel created the visualization correctly, but there's a problem. It's hard to tell which stock performed better, because they have such different values. The starting and ending price of the S&P index stock is way higher than that of the EEM stock. The stocks started from different places, so we might need to do something to the data to get a good comparison.

Maybe you can transform the data so they start from the same basis. You could write formulas that show the percentage change from a baseline.

Sometimes you need to transform the data in order to graph it effectively.
Creating effective graphics isn't just about using the graphical manipulation features of Excel effectively. It's also about making sure that your data is prepped correctly for a good visualization.

Exercise

Write a formula to show a percentage change from Day 1 for each subsequent day.

Set up these zero basis columns.

For the first period, enter zero. For the second period, enter a formula that calculates the percentage change of the S&P from the first period.

Format the columns as percentages to the hundredth decimal place.

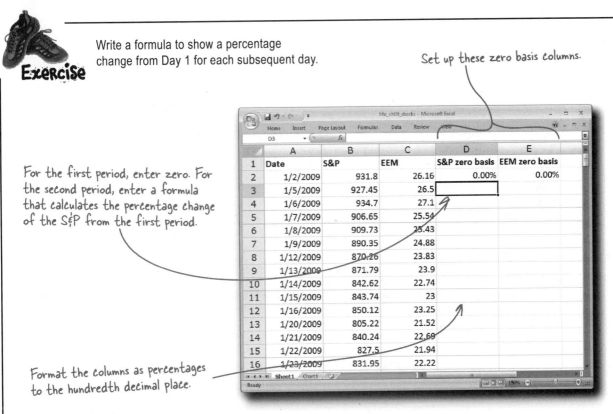

	A	B	C	D	E
1	Date	S&P	EEM	S&P zero basis	EEM zero basis
2	1/2/2009	931.8	26.16	0.00%	0.00%
3	1/5/2009	927.45	26.5		
4	1/6/2009	934.7	27.1		
5	1/7/2009	906.65	25.54		
6	1/8/2009	909.73	25.43		
7	1/9/2009	890.35	24.88		
8	1/12/2009	870.26	23.83		
9	1/13/2009	871.79	23.9		
10	1/14/2009	842.62	22.74		
11	1/15/2009	843.74	23		
12	1/16/2009	850.12	23.25		
13	1/20/2009	805.22	21.52		
14	1/21/2009	840.24	22.69		
15	1/22/2009	827.5	21.94		
16	1/23/2009	831.95	22.22		

Exercise Solution

You just transformed your data to show a percentage change from a zero basis rather than the original value. What did you find?

Here's the formula you want to use.

=(B3–B2)/B2

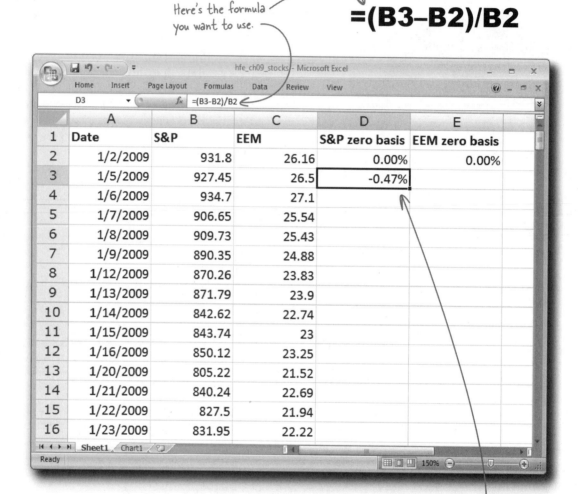

This formula shows that the value of the S&P on 1/5 was 0.47% less than it was on 1/2.

Let's copy the formulas and graph the data....

Exercise

Now that you've written a formula to show the percentage change for one unit of time, copy and paste the formula for all dates. Then graph your new data.

① Copy and paste the formula for both stocks. Make sure you add absolute references where necessary.

$$=(B3–B2)/B2$$

You'll need to add absolute references to make this formula copy correctly.

② Create a new time series line chart.

Head back over to the Insert tab to select the chart you want to create.

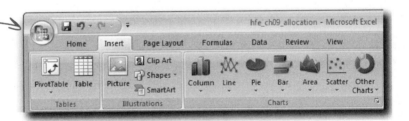

You'll want to pick one of these.

Hint: You might have to go back into the menu that tells Excel which data to select. You want Excel to select only your new data, not all four columns.

Exercise Solution

You just copied and pasted your new data transformation functions, and then you graphed them. How does your chart look now?

Here are your absolute references.

$$=(C3-C\$2)/C\$2$$

This reference makes sure that you're always comparing any given day's asset value with the original value from January 2.

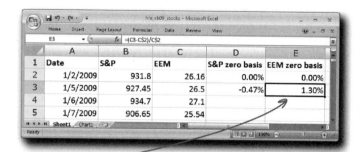

The formula copies and pastes smoothly for all values.

You need to remove these two data entries.

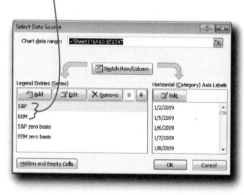

Here's your new chart.

Now it's easier to tell how the stocks performed relative to each other.

You're starting to get tight on time...

Better get your chart formatted for the big presentation....

From: CEO
To: Head First
Subject:

Dear Head First,

I hear the new chart is coming along well. Can you make sure it's really nicely formatted?

The board is a cantankerous bunch, and we need to make sure our data visualizations display the utmost professionalism.

Oh, and BTW, we need your chart really soon. Like yesterday.

I know you can handle this.

—CEO

Exercise

Format your chart according to these parameters.

1 Make this the title: *S&P versus EEM*.

2 Put the legend, which is currently on the right, at the bottom of the chart.

3 The date labels on the y-axis are kind of verbose and also get in the way of the lines. See whether you can fix that issue as well.

Exercise Solution

You just reformatted your new line chart. How did it turn out?

1   Make this the title: *S&P versus EEM*.

2   Put the legend, which is currently on the right, at the bottom of the chart.

3   The date labels on the y-axis are kind of verbose and also get in the way of the lines. See whether you can fix that issue as well.

Your visualization might look different.

Set the axis labels to "Low" to put them at the bottom.

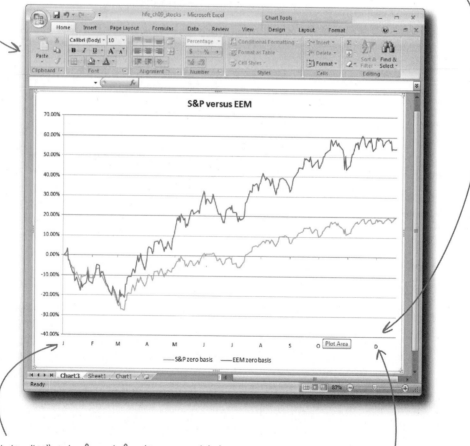

Select the "M" data format for the y-axis labels to show the first letter of the month's name.

The major units of the y-axis are fixed at 1 month.

Your report was a big success...

The two charts you created were a big
hit among the board of directors. You
made the data accessible and elegant
through your graphical visualizations.

These were sharp-looking
charts. Thank you very much!

10 what if analysis

Alternate realities

I said, no, I won't invest in your silly "aeroplanes." People love boats, they want to travel in boats, so I put everything in this boat....

I'm sure you did your research and investigated all the possibilities....

Things could go many different ways.

There are all sorts of **quantitative factors** that can affect how your business will work, how your finances will fare, how your schedule will manage, and so forth. Excel excels at helping you model and manage all your *projections*, evaluating how changes in those factors will affect the variables you care about most. In this chapter, you'll learn about three key features—**scenarios**, **Goal Seek**, and **Solver**—that are designed to make assessing all your "what ifs" a breeze.

Should your friend Betty advertise?

Betty sells the best baguettes in Dataville. But in spite of her renown, she is interested in expanding her business through advertising.

She'd like to add more customers to her already stable customer base. But ads can be expensive. Would advertising be worthwhile? She's enlisted you for help, and if your recommendations pay off, your baguettes will be on the house.

Here's Betty.

Can you help me figure out whether I should advertise? I want to attract new customers.

Here's Betty's famous bread.

Exercise

Here's Betty's weekly cash flow statement. You're going to use this spreadsheet as the basis for your projections about advertising costs and revenue. Rework this spreadsheet to accommodate blanks for **ad costs** and revenue from **baguettes sold to new customers**. Where would you put the new information?

Just make up dummy numbers to fill in the new blanks. You can use real numbers later.

Load this!

www.headfirstlabs.com/books/hfexcel/ hfe_ch10_weekly_income.xlsx

Right-click on the row numbers to insert a new row.

You need to update this formula to accommodate the number of new customer baguettes sold.

Your "Sold to new customers" blank should go somewhere in here.

This formula multiplies the price by the number of baguettes sold.

Costs from advertising should go somewhere in here.

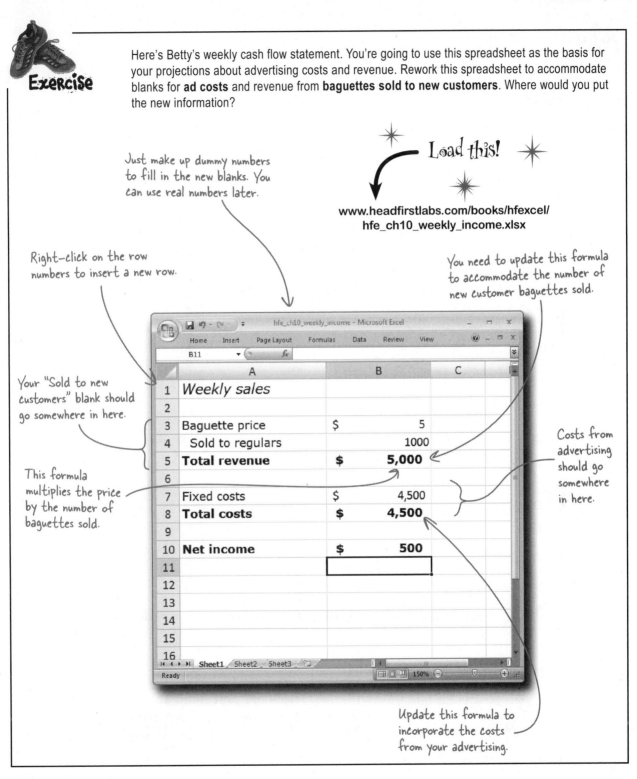

Update this formula to incorporate the costs from your advertising.

Exercise Solution

You just modified Betty's spreadsheet to incorporate figures for new customers and ad costs. How'd it go?

Here are dummy numbers.

They're just placeholders for now.

=B3*SUM(B4:B5)

This formula now adds B4:B5 together before multiplying the result by B3.

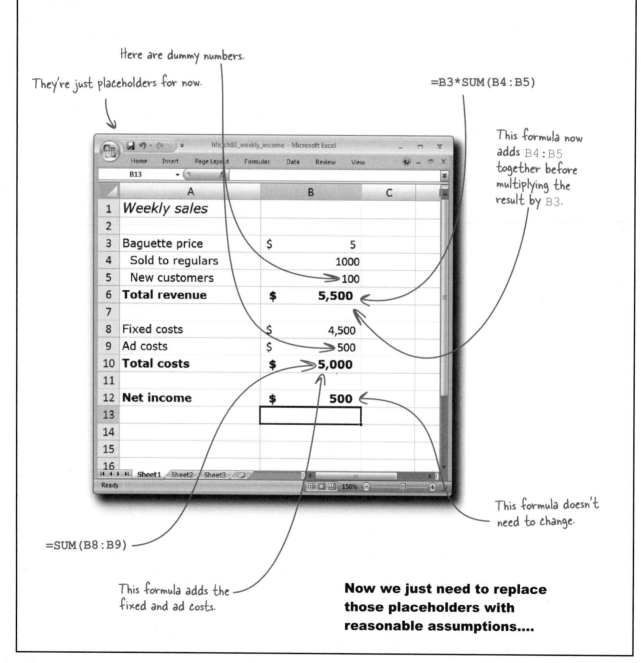

=SUM(B8:B9)

This formula adds the fixed and ad costs.

This formula doesn't need to change.

Now we just need to replace those placeholders with reasonable assumptions....

Betty has projections of best and worst cases for different ad configurations

Betty has already done some thinking about the best- and worst-case scenarios for both TV and magazine advertising. Here are what she takes to be the parameters of her decision.

Betty has projected best- and worst-case scenarios for TV and magazines.

> OK, it costs me $100 to advertise in a magazine. In the best case, I'll pick up 200 new customers. In the worst case, I'm thinking 20 new customers.

> TV is a different beast. It costs $700 to advertise on TV, and the best case for TV is 350 new customers, while the worst case is no new customers.

Let's take one of those configurations and see how it affects net income. What does the spreadsheet say about the best case for magazine advertising?

Exercise

Use your spreadsheet model to implement the best case for magazine advertising.

Plug her assumptions into the blanks you created.

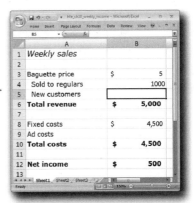

	A	B
1	*Weekly sales*	
2		
3	Baguette price	$ 5
4	Sold to regulars	1000
5	New customers	
6	**Total revenue**	$ 5,000
7		
8	Fixed costs	$ 4,500
9	Ad costs	
10	**Total costs**	$ 4,500
11		
12	**Net income**	$ 500
13		

Does this scenario show a rise in net income?

....

....

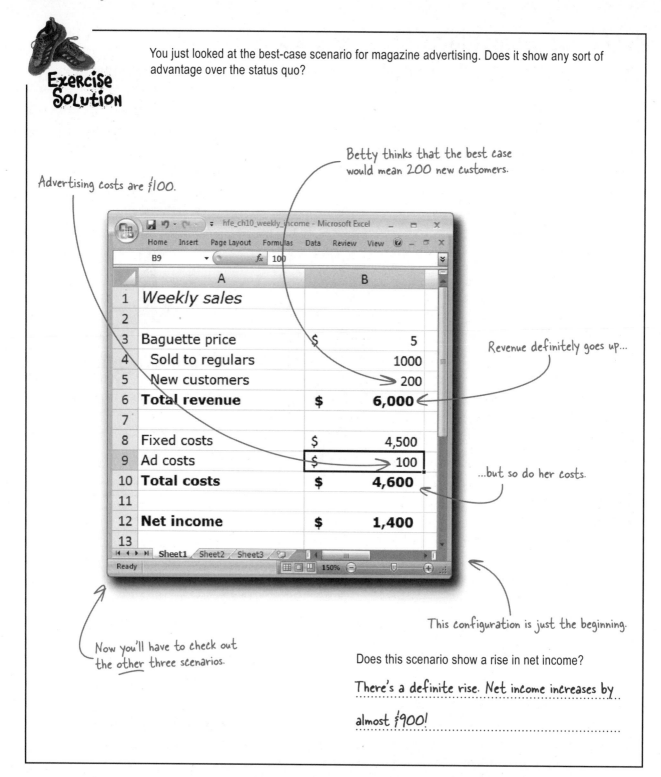

You just looked at the best-case scenario for magazine advertising. Does it show any sort of advantage over the status quo?

EXERCISE SOLUTION

Betty thinks that the best case would mean 200 new customers.

Advertising costs are $100.

Revenue definitely goes up...

...but so do her costs.

This configuration is just the beginning.

Now you'll have to check out the other three scenarios.

Does this scenario show a rise in net income?

There's a definite rise. Net income increases by almost $900!

Spreadsheet: hfe_ch10_weekly_income - Microsoft Excel

B9 | 100

	A	B
1	*Weekly sales*	
2		
3	Baguette price	$ 5
4	Sold to regulars	1000
5	New customers	200
6	**Total revenue**	$ **6,000**
7		
8	Fixed costs	$ 4,500
9	Ad costs	$ 100
10	**Total costs**	$ **4,600**
11		
12	**Net income**	$ **1,400**
13		

You need to evaluate all her scenarios

The best-case scenario for magazine advertising looks good, but is it the best? And what about the worst-case scenarios? In order to make this assessment, you're going to need to look at **all** of her projected possibilities.

Possible situations after ads

Best Magazine

Worst TV

Best TV

Situation before ads

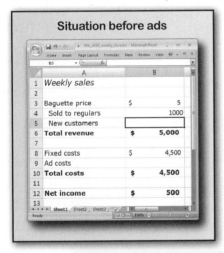

Worst Magazine

Wouldn't it be dreamy if we could elegantly and easily manage these scenarios inside Excel? But I know it's just a fantasy....

Scenarios helps you keep track of different inputs to the same model

When you refined Betty's cash flow model to accommodate an ad expense and the revenue that results from that advertising, you enhanced the **model** she was using to understand her business.

Having the model is one thing, and getting the inputs correct is another. You tried one set of inputs, but what about the other three? Scenarios is a feature in Excel that helps you keep track of all your different sets of model inputs.

There are a bunch of inputs that can fill in these values.

Baguette price

Options

New customers

New customers

New customers

New customers

Fixed costs

Options

Ad costs

Ad costs

Sold to regulars

Total revenue

Total costs

Her projections show certain input elements to change, depending on different outcomes.

Net income

Those various inputs all have an effect on this final output.

Scenarios saves different configurations of the elements that change

To take the Scenarios feature for a spin, first you need to have your network of formulas (your model) set up. Next, head over to the What If Analysis button under the Data tab.

Start setting up scenarios here.

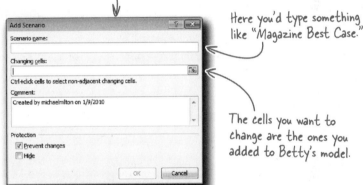

Click on **Scenario Manager...**, which takes you to this dialog box. Here you can name each of your scenarios and specify which cells change and what the values are for those cells in each scenario.

Here's the dialog box you see when you press the Add... button.

Here you'd type something like "Magazine Best Case."

The cells you want to change are the ones you added to Betty's model.

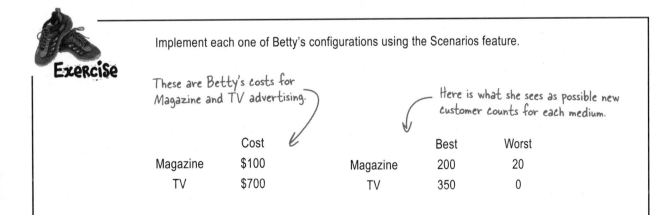

Implement each one of Betty's configurations using the Scenarios feature.

Exercise

These are Betty's costs for Magazine and TV advertising.

Here is what she sees as possible new customer counts for each medium.

	Cost		Best	Worst
Magazine	$100	Magazine	200	20
TV	$700	TV	350	0

You just used Scenarios to implement each of Betty's four projected outcomes for her advertising investment. What did you find?

Exercise Solution

These scenarios show net income projections for different ad cost and customer count increases resulting from the ad.

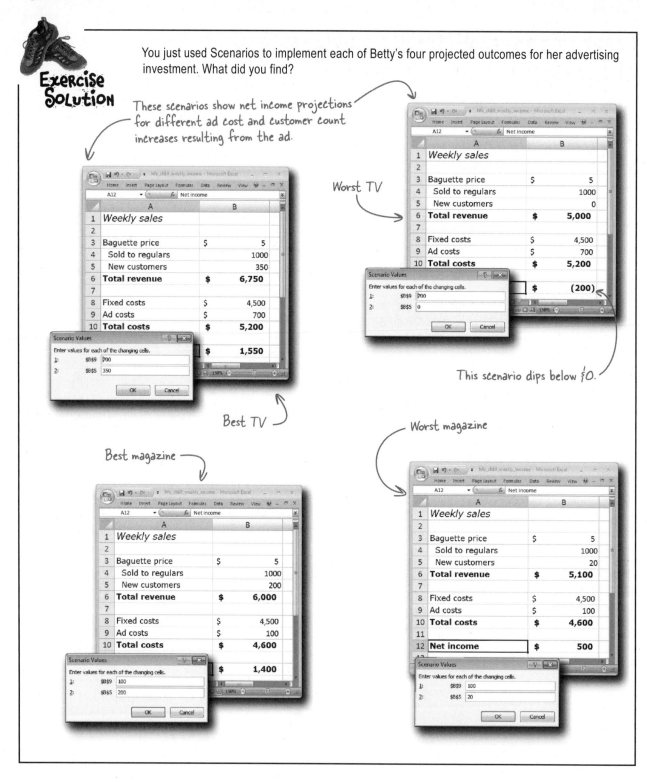

Worst TV

This scenario dips below $0.

Best TV

Best magazine

Worst magazine

Betty wants to know her breakeven

I gave you projections, but now tell me what my breakeven points are for each ad configuration. In other words, how many baguettes do I need to sell in order to recoup my investment on both TV and magazine ads?

You need to create some new scenarios.

But what are they? With the other four, she gave you the inputs. But now you need to do a calculation to find out how many new customers are needed to recoup her costs for TV and magazine ads.

	A	B	C
1	*Weekly sales*		
2			
3	**Baguette price**	$ 5	
4	Sold to regulars	1000	
5	New customers	20	
6	**Total revenue**	$ **5,100**	
7			
8	Fixed costs	$ 4,500	
9	Ad costs	$ 100	
10	**Total costs**	$ **4,600**	
11			
12	**Net income**	$ **500**	
13			
14	**Return on ad**		
15			
16			

You need to add this cell.

If this value is equal to zero, you're at the breakeven point for that type of advertising.

Do this!

Create a new cell in your spreadsheet called "**Return on ad**," and fill this cell with a formula that subtracts your ad cost from your new customer revenue.

Goal Seek optimizes a value by trying a bunch of different candidate values

With your formula to calculate the amount of new money Betty brings in on top of the costs of her advertising, you're in a position to try to figure out the key variable you don't know: the number of new customers she needs to break even.

You need to try a bunch of options in this cell...

Add this formula to your spreadsheet.

=B3*B5-B9

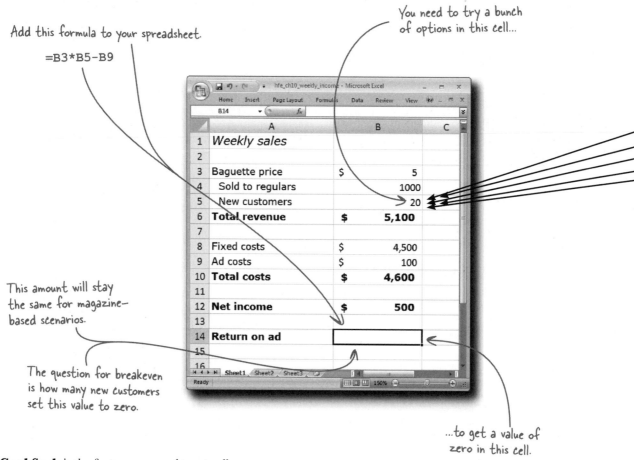

This amount will stay the same for magazine-based scenarios.

The question for breakeven is how many new customers set this value to zero.

...to get a value of zero in this cell.

Goal Seek is the feature you need to set cell B5 (your new customer count) to the value that makes cell B14 (your return) equal to zero.

Goal Seek operates by ***trying a whole bunch of different values in one cell*** in order to get a formula in another cell to be equal to the value you want. In this case, you need Goal Seek to try a bunch of different values in your New Customers cell to figure out which one makes your return equal to zero.

Here's the Goal Seek dialog box.

Make this blank refer to your return formula.

The breakeven point is where B14 is zero.

This is the New Customer cell.

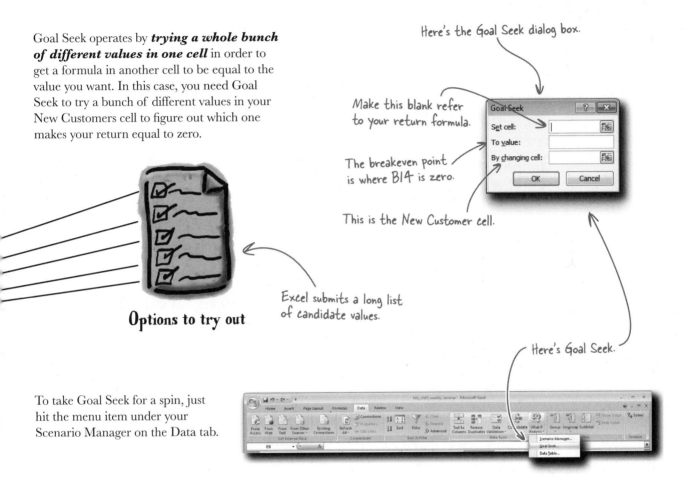

Options to try out

Excel submits a long list of candidate values.

Here's Goal Seek.

To take Goal Seek for a spin, just hit the menu item under your Scenario Manager on the Data tab.

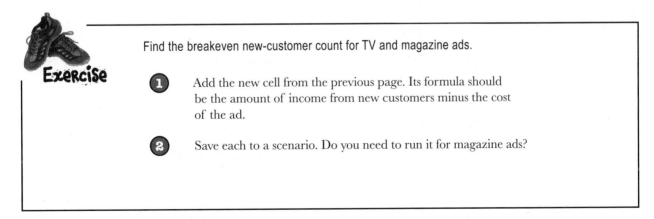

Find the breakeven new-customer count for TV and magazine ads.

Exercise

1   Add the new cell from the previous page. Its formula should be the amount of income from new customers minus the cost of the ad.

2   Save each to a scenario. Do you need to run it for magazine ads?

Exercise Solution

You just ran Goal Seek to figure out the breakeven points for both TV and magazine advertising. What did you find?

Here's how the Goal Seek dialog box should be filled out.

This will calculate the right number of new customers.

This is the magazine breakeven scenario.

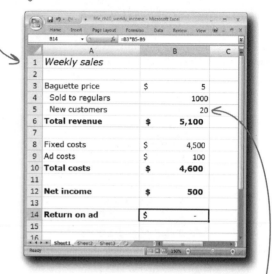

You need 20 customers... the worst case!

Here's how your Scenario Manager should look with your two new scenarios.

This is the TV breakeven scenario.

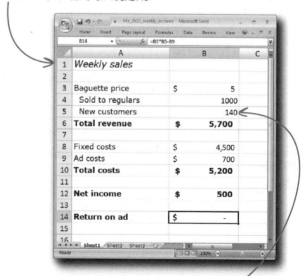

You need 140 new customers to break even.

there are no
Dumb Questions

Q: I'm wondering about the distinction here between "new customers" and "baguettes." What if you have one new customer who buys 50 baguettes? And what if your current customers buy *more* baguettes as a result of the advertising?

A: Good observation. The model we have right now assumes that each customer buys one baguette. That might not be true.

Q: So why not change the model to incorporate these details?

A: You could absolutely do that, and the question for you as an analyst is whether making your model that much more complex is worth the trouble.

Q: It doesn't seem like it'd be that much trouble.

A: It might not be that much trouble to incorporate the details you just mentioned, but there are many other details to reality that also are not incorporated into the model. If you think you should make your model more complex, you need to distinguish between the issues that affect your goals and those that do not.

Q: Sounds like the model itself is really important to get right.

A: Yes, absolutely. We're assuming that Betty's model and our modifications to it have been accurate enough. When you create your own models, you'll need to be really careful to make sure that you incorporate all the relevant variables, that those variables are all linked by the right formulas, and that the values you have for those variables are reasonable.

Q: Goal Seek seems like a nice feature, but it seems like there are other ways of making the same calculation.

A: Oh yeah?

Q: I think I could probably just create more formulas—maybe an ancillary model—to make the calculation we just did.

A: That's definitely true. Goal Seek is not the most powerful tool for optimization in Excel. You could certainly write formulas to calculate what you just found about the breakeven points for magazine and TV advertising.

Q: I could even write a couple of algebra equations and figure it out.

A: You sure could. The reason you'd use Goal Seek, though, is because it's fast and easy. Even once you learn more powerful tools, you'll still use Goal Seek just because it's so handy. The dialog box only has three places for you to enter information.

Q: Does Goal Seek always get the right answer?

A: If there is a single correct answer, Goal Seek can find it. But there's not always an answer to the question you're asking, and it just depends on the formulas in your model.

Q: What if I don't want to set a value to a specific number, I just want to get it as high as it'll go? Like with the Return, for example. I just want the highest return I can get.

A: Goal Seek is really all about setting a single formula to a single value by modifying a single cell.

Q: That gets me to another question. What if I have more than one variable that I want to mess around with?

A: If that's your problem, it sounds like you need a more powerful tool.

Q: OK, you said that Goal Seek isn't the most powerful tool for optimization in Excel. What is?

A: You're about to find out!

Betty needs you to add complexity to the model

> The model is actually too simple: I can change the price of my baguettes, which has an effect on sales. Let's allow baguette prices to move between $3 and $6.

We're still trying to maximize our net income by looking at the best- and worst-case scenarios for new customers. But modelling these scenarios has become harder, because…

> Also, let's drop the magazine option. Your work convinced me to go with the TV ads over the magazine ads.

She needs you to do two things Goal Seek cannot do

Goals Seek sets the output on one formula to one value by changing one cell. But you need to be able to do more, since her problem needs you to…

Goal Seek can't handle either of these.

1 **Change the values of more than one variable.** Now you have both new customers *and* baguette prices to account for as you project net income.

2 **One of the variables is subject to constraints.** Baguette prices can't be any old number: they have to be somewhere between $3 and $6.

You need a more powerful Goal Seek….

Solver can handle much more complex optimization problems

The gold standard for optimization inside Excel is the powerful add-on utility Solver. It comes as an optional installation in every copy of Excel for Windows.

In an **optimization problem**, you have a target cell you want to maximize, minimize, or set to a value by changing other cells that may be subject to constraints.

Don't see Solver in your menus?

Solver is there; it's not just installed yet. Head over to Appendix ii to see how to get Solver up and running.

Max and Min are options you don't have inside Goal Seek.

Here's the Solver window.

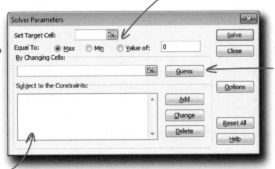

You want to change both the number of possible new customers and the price of the baguettes.

Your constraints affect the bounds of your variables. Betty has constraints for her baguette price, for example.

To get Solver started, head over to the far-right corner of the Data tab on the Ribbon.

Click here for Solver.

Exercise

We'd like to maximize our net income for television advertising. Let's start setting up our optimization with Solver.

1. Open Solver and set your target cell. This is the cell that contains the value you want to maximize.

2. Set the cells you want to change. Solver will try a number of different values for these cells in order to maximize your target cell.

Exercise Solution

You just set up the first part of your Solver optimization. Did you enter the right parameters?

1 Open Solver and set your target cell. This is the cell that contains the value you want to maximize.

2 Set the cells you want to change. Solver will try a number of different values for these cells in order to maximize your target cell.

Your target cell is B12.

B12 is where you have your Net income formula.

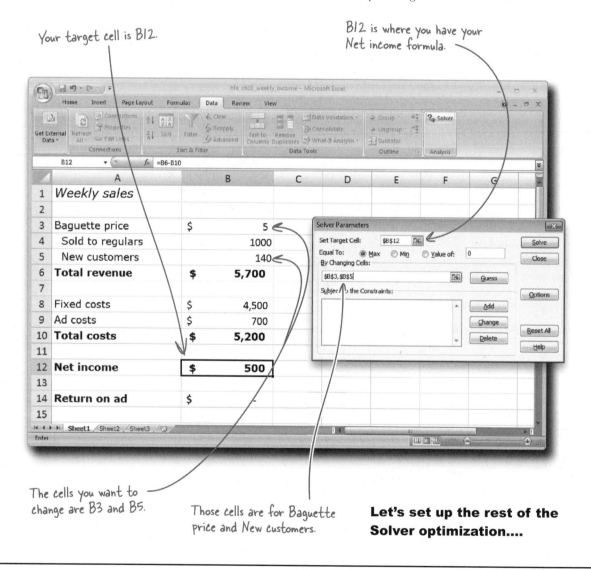

The cells you want to change are B3 and B5.

Those cells are for Baguette price and New customers.

Let's set up the rest of the Solver optimization....

Exercise

Finish your Solver optimization. How much net income can Betty hope to get if she uses television advertising?

1 Finally, set up your constraints. Betty told you that her baguette price can shift between $3 and $6, so that's one constraint. For the purposes of this scenario, set up this one as well: your maximum number of new customers equals 350.

If you don't set an upper bound for your New customers, Solver will take it up to infinity.

2 Click **Solve** to run Solver. What does Solver say to you? Write your answer below.

....

....

....

....

Write your answer here.

Exercise Solution

You just entered your constraints and ran Solver. What happened?

1 Finally, set up your constraints. Betty told you that her baguette price can shift between $3 and $6, so that's one constraint. For the purposes of this scenario, set up this one as well: your maximum number of new customers equals 350.

These constraints are for the baguettes.

This one is for new customers.

Here's the result.

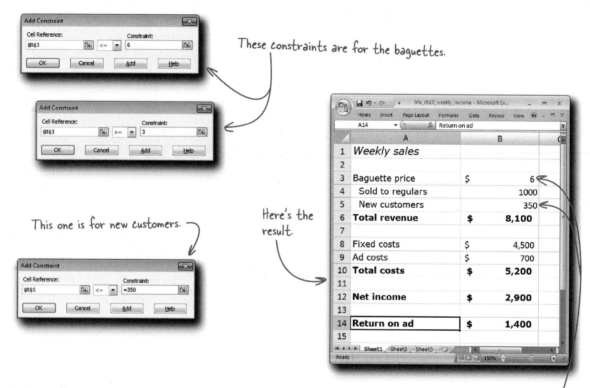

Both of these values are as high as they can go.

2 Click **Solve** to run Solver. What does Solver say to you? Write your answer below.

Solver takes both of the cells we said could change and sets them to their maximum values. Baguettes are at their highest possible price, and the most possible new customers are expected. The resulting net income figure is high: $2,900.

Stop! That model doesn't make any sense. It assumes that changing the price won't affect anything else in the model.

She's right. In the real world, you can't just raise your prices without anyone noticing. Your models somehow needs to recognize that other variables may be changed by a change in the price of baguettes.

BRAIN POWER

How might a change in the price of baguettes affect other variables in the model?

....

....

Do a sanity check on your Solver model

Solver will give you optimal answers, provided that
your model is correct. But it doesn't know whether your
model is based in reality.

You always need to check your formulas to make sure
your model corresponds to reality correctly.

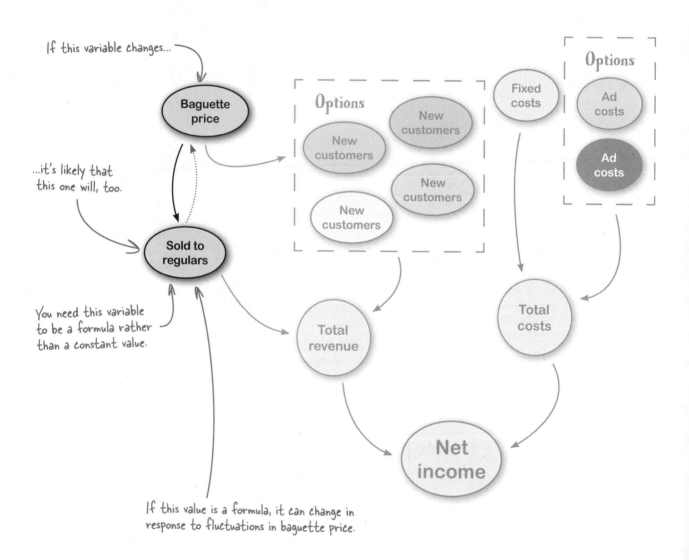

If this variable changes...

...it's likely that
this one will, too.

You need this variable
to be a formula rather
than a constant value.

If this value is a formula, it can change in
response to fluctuations in baguette price.

I commissioned an economist's report to find out the relationship between baguette price and demand.

This equation describes the relation between your variables.

$$y = -300x^2 + 2200x - 2500$$

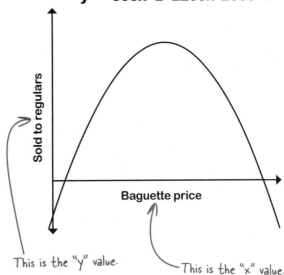

Sold to regulars

Baguette price

This is the "y" value.

This is the "x" value.

Looks like Betty shelled out the big bucks and had an economist create an equation to describe the relationship between the cost of baguettes and the amount sold to regulars. This sort of thing just screams to be made into an Excel formula.

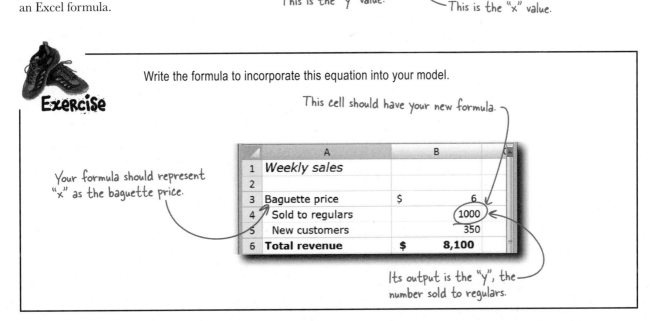

Exercise

Write the formula to incorporate this equation into your model.

This cell should have your new formula.

Your formula should represent "x" as the baguette price.

	A	B
1	*Weekly sales*	
2		
3	Baguette price	$ 6
4	Sold to regulars	1000
5	New customers	350
6	**Total revenue**	**$ 8,100**

Its output is the "y", the number sold to regulars.

Exercise Solution

You just entered a new formula to calculate the number of regulars who'll buy Betty's baguettes in light of the price of those baguettes. What formula did you use?

Here's your formula.

The "x" in the formula is replaced by a reference to cell B3.

$$=-300*B3\wedge2+2200*B3-2500$$

There must be a big drop-off by the time she hits $6, because the equation returns a negative customer count here.

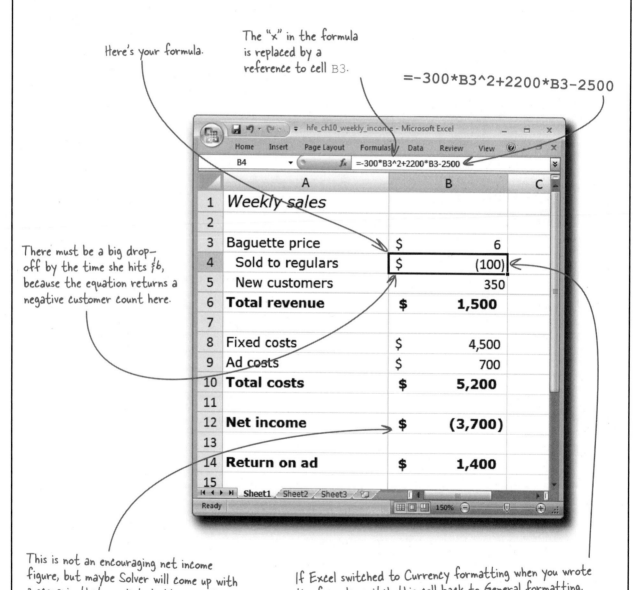

This is not an encouraging net income figure, but maybe Solver will come up with a scenario that predicts better results.

If Excel switched to Currency formatting when you wrote the formula, switch this cell back to General formatting.

Now you just have to re-run Solver and you'll have your projections! You'll probably get a different answer this time.

Do this!

Go ahead and run Solver again.

Since you've set it up already, you won't have to make any sort of modifications to your target cells, constraints, or any other element of the optimization problem. The change you made is in the model itself, so Solver will just try to maximize your profits like it did previously, but this time with a slightly different model.

Solver calculated your projections

When you reran Solver, it used the same
assumptions you gave it previously, but this time
the formula outputs were all different because
you added a formula to provide a better
prediction of the number of regulars who
would buy baguettes at whatever price Solver
thinks is best. Here's what happened:

This is a Solver solution you want to keep.

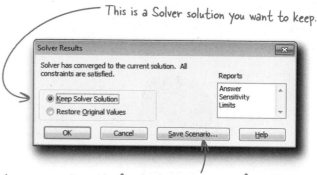

You can name this set of outputs as a scenario if you like.

Solver thinks Betty should
lower her baguette price.

This is a significant projected increase
in the number of regular customers.

Net income under this
scenario is looking solid.

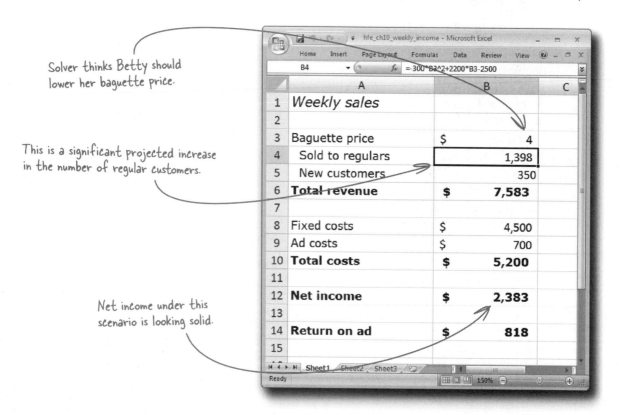

Solver thinks Betty should bring her price down
to $4, which will optimize her regular customer
purchases, but not any further down, which
could hurt her revenue. This configuration
represents a final best-case scenario for TV
advertisement.

Betty's best-case scenario came to pass...

...and she's a very, very happy client. The public reaction to her TV advertisements appears overwhelmingly positive.

That was fantastic. I really felt like looking through all those scenarios—especially the ones Solver created—gave me a better sense of my options. And wouldn't you know it? Reality fit the model. Free baguettes for you!

All sorts of new clients are lining up for Betty's baguettes!

11 text functions

Letters as data

Hi there! I'm here to mince words....

Excel loves your numbers, but it can also handle your text.

It contains a suite of functions designed to enable you to manipulate **text data**. There are many applications to these functions, but one that all data people must deal with is what to do with *messy* data. A lot of times, you'll receive data that isn't at all in the format you need it to be in—it might come out of a strange database, for example. Text functions shine at letting you pull elements out of messy data so that you can make analytic use of it, as you're about to find out....

Your database of analytic customers just crashed!

Lightning smashed into your office and wiped out all your hard drives, including your **customer database**. No problem. Just go get the backup disks, right?

Wrong. The guy in charge of backups forgot to do them (he sends his apologies). Fortunately, you have **something** you might be able to use. Word is, a garbled scrap of email sent a few days ago might have salvageable information about your contacts....

Uh, I tore this thing up and still could not make it work. What a piece of junk. How am I going to deal with our clients if I don't know who they are?

This computer crashed.

It had all your customer data on it.

Your panicked employee

Here's the data

That email has your client list, all right, but the list isn't looking so hot. All the data is mashed together. One of your employees loaded it and saved it to an Excel file for you....

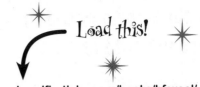

Load this!

www.headfirstlabs.com/books/hfexcel/
hfe_ch11_messy_data.xlsx

All the information appears to be in one column of the spreadsheet.

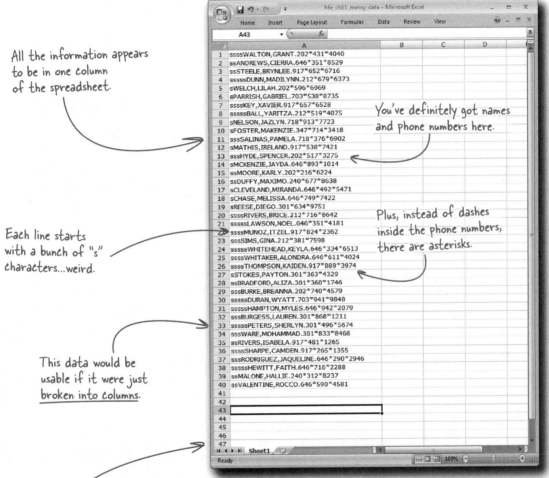

You've definitely got names and phone numbers here.

Plus, instead of dashes inside the phone numbers, there are asterisks.

Each line starts with a bunch of "s" characters...weird.

This data would be usable if it were just broken into columns.

Your messy data is all mashed together in the same column. How do you separate the good data from the garbage?

BRAIN POWER

Look at the toolbar. What feature of Excel do you think would break this data into multiple columns?

Text to Columns uses a delimiter to split up your data

Text to Columns is a great feature that lets you split your data into columns using a **delimiter**, which is simply a text character that signifies the breaks between the different data points. If your delimiter is, say, a period, Text to Columns will put the data to the left of the period in one column, the data to the right in another, and then it'll delete the period.

Geek Bits

CSV is a really popular file format for data. The letters stand for **C**omma **S**eparated **V**alue. For these files, commas act as the delimiter. The format is so common that when you load a CSV file, Excel automatically splits the data into columns using the comma delimiter.

Here everything is mashed into one column.

Text to Columns splits your data into columns.

If you have more than one type of delimiter, you might have to run Text to Columns more than once. In this case, you have a period acting as a delimiter, as well as a comma, and you could even treat those weird "s" characters as delimiters, which would make Excel throw them out.

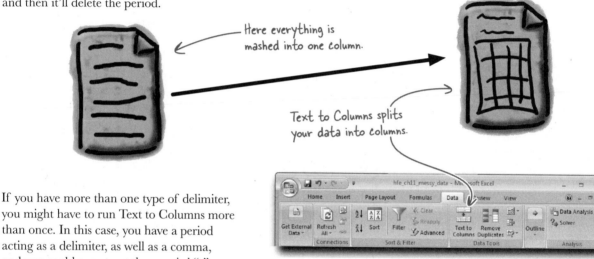

Here you tell Excel what character(s) serve as delimiters.

If your data points are arranged in columns with the data separated by spaces, click "Fixed width."

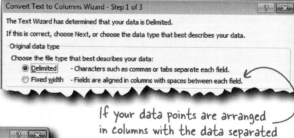

Click Finish to skip step 3 of the Wizard, which is about number formatting.

Exercise

Try using Text to Columns to fix this messy data. Make sure your cursor is inside your data first.

You'll probably have to **run it a second time** to get the period delimiter.

You'll have to run Text to Columns more than once to get rid of all your delimiters.

You don't need to treat the asterisk as a delimiter, because the data on the right is a phone number.

Be sure to tell Excel to treat consecutive "s" delimiters as one, because you have a lot of them.

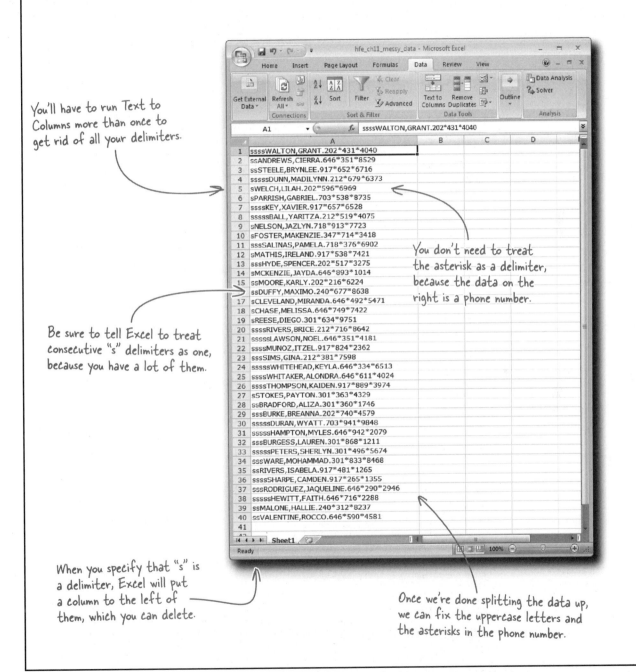

When you specify that "s" is a delimiter, Excel will put a column to the left of them, which you can delete.

Once we're done splitting the data up, we can fix the uppercase letters and the asterisks in the phone number.

You just used Text to Columns to break your data into multiple pieces. How'd it go?

Exercise
Solution

Here are your last names.

Here are your first names.

This is the phone number.

This is a lot better
looking than the messy
data you received!

Text to Columns
did a good job.

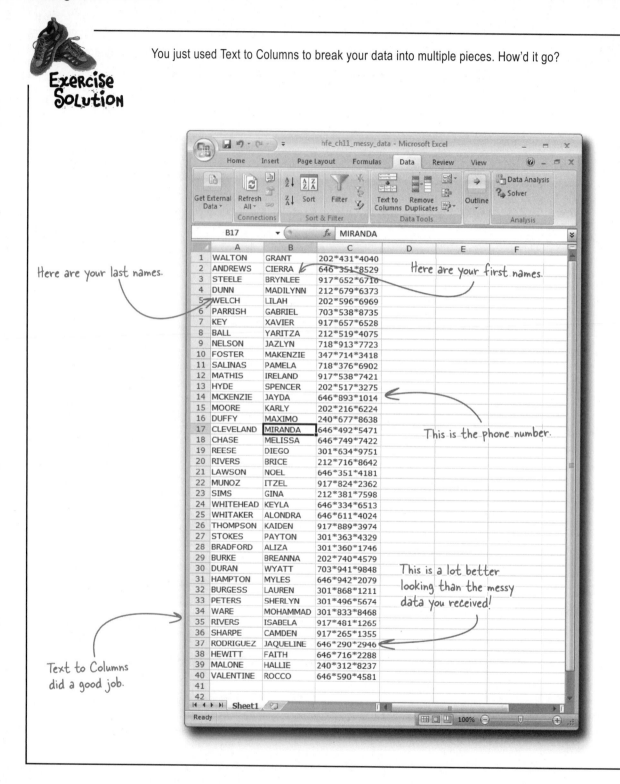

> Uh, we need the "s" characters. They are actually data! They stand for "stars," and they're a ranking of the quality of our customers. We need them, so is there any chance you can bring them back?

Text to Columns doesn't work in all cases

For starters, you need a delimiter, or at least you need the data elements to be evenly spaced. Here you have neither: the "s" characters aren't evenly spaced, they aren't delimiters, and there's nothing that separates them from the next data element: the last name.

	A	B
1	ssssWALTON,GRANT.202*431*4040	
2	ssANDREWS,CIERRA.646*351*8529	
3	ssSTEELE,BRYNLEE.917*652*6716	
4	sssssDUNN,MADILYNN.212*679*6373	

There's no delimiter between these two data fields.

Better click **Undo** a couple times to start from scratch. You're going to need some more firepower for this problem. Weren't there formulas for dealing with text data?

Do this!

Press Undo a few times to get the data back to its original messy state, and then look up text formulas in Help files.

Excel has a suite of functions for dealing with text

Earlier you used the function VALUE () to convert text data to numbers, but VALUE () is just the beginning of Excel's text functions. Excel has a whole suite of functions to deal with all sorts of situations in which you need to change or query text data.

Click here to get to the reference on text functions.

Here are all of Excel's text formulas.

There are a whole bunch!

You're going to use a few of these to clean up this database, and in the future when you have text problems that Text to Columns can't solve, you should check out the Help files for other function-based solutions.

Match each Excel text function to what it does. Which functions would you use to extract the "s" characters and the phone numbers from your messy data?

LEFT   Removes duplicate spaces and spaces on each end of text in a cell.

RIGHT   Grabs the leftmost text in a cell. You tell it how many characters you want.

FIND   Returns a value equal to two or more text cells mashed together.

TRIM   Returns a number that represents the position of a search string in a cell.

CONCATENATE   Returns text from the righthand side of the cell.

WHO DOES WHAT? SOLUTION

You were to match each Excel text function to what it does. Which functions would you use to extract the "s" characters and the phone numbers from your messy data?

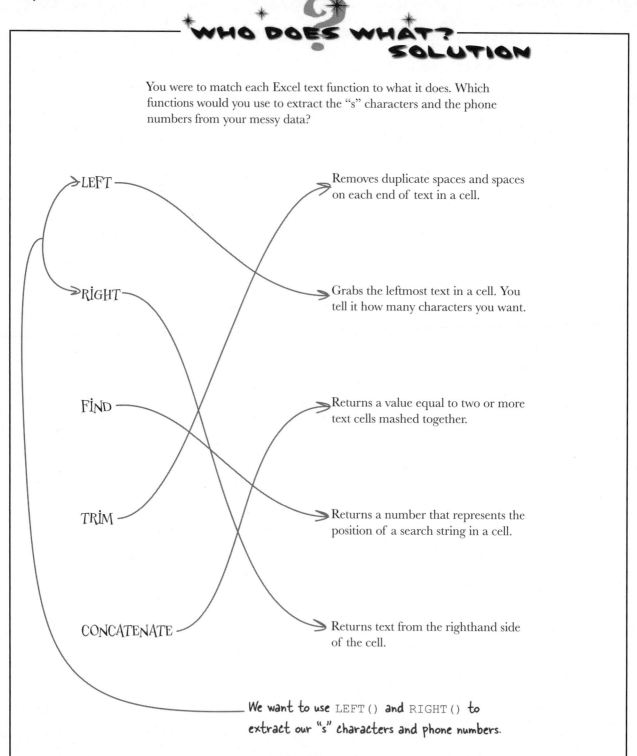

LEFT

RIGHT

FIND

TRIM

CONCATENATE

Removes duplicate spaces and spaces on each end of text in a cell.

Grabs the leftmost text in a cell. You tell it how many characters you want.

Returns a value equal to two or more text cells mashed together.

Returns a number that represents the position of a search string in a cell.

Returns text from the righthand side of the cell.

We want to use LEFT() and RIGHT() to extract our "s" characters and phone numbers.

LEFT and RIGHT are basic text extraction functions

You need to extract characters on the left side of your cells (the "s" characters) and on the right side of your cells (the phone numbers). To do this, you can use the LEFT() and RIGHT() functions. Here's the syntax.

This has the text or cell reference where you want to extract characters.

=RIGHT(target cell, # of characters)

This is a value or formula saying how many characters to grab.

You'll put a formula with this function in a new cell, and the formula will point to your original raw data and say how many characters to grab.

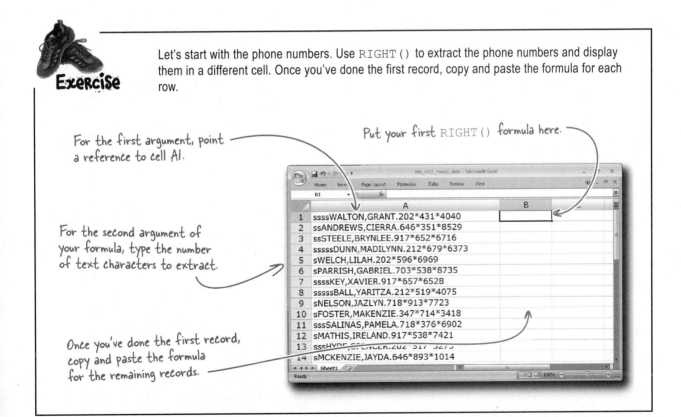

Exercise

Let's start with the phone numbers. Use RIGHT() to extract the phone numbers and display them in a different cell. Once you've done the first record, copy and paste the formula for each row.

For the first argument, point a reference to cell A1.

Put your first RIGHT() formula here.

For the second argument of your formula, type the number of text characters to extract.

Once you've done the first record, copy and paste the formula for the remaining records.

	A	B
1	ssssWALTON,GRANT.202*431*4040	
2	ssANDREWS,CIERRA.646*351*8529	
3	ssSTEELE,BRYNLEE.917*652*6716	
4	sssssDUNN,MADILYNN.212*679*6373	
5	sWELCH,LILAH.202*596*6969	
6	sPARRISH,GABRIEL.703*538*8735	
7	ssssKEY,XAVIER.917*657*6528	
8	sssssBALL,YARITZA.212*519*4075	
9	sNELSON,JAZLYN.718*913*7723	
10	sFOSTER,MAKENZIE.347*714*3418	
11	sssSALINAS,PAMELA.718*376*6902	
12	sMATHIS,IRELAND.917*538*7421	
13	sssHYDE,SPENCER.202*317*3273	
14	sMCKENZIE,JAYDA.646*893*1014	

try out right()

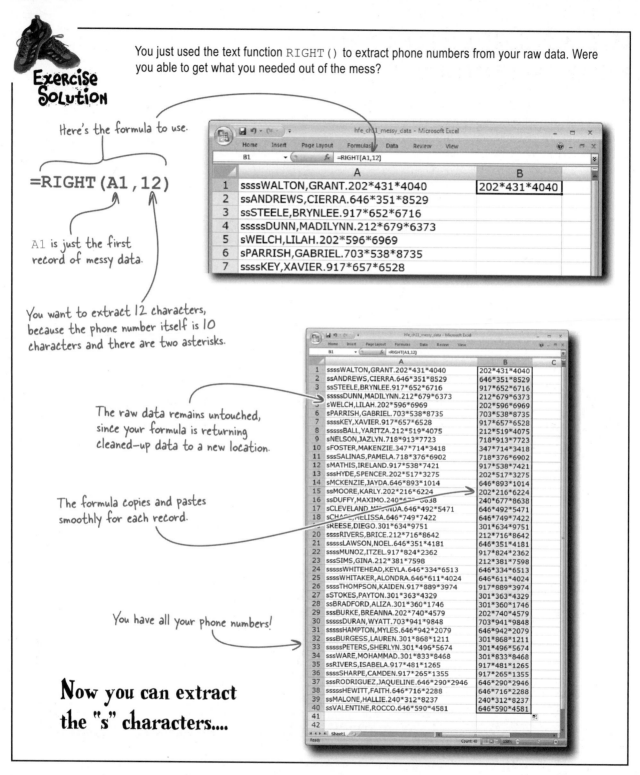

You just used the text function `RIGHT()` to extract phone numbers from your raw data. Were you able to get what you needed out of the mess?

Here's the formula to use.

=RIGHT(A1,12)

A1 is just the first record of messy data.

You want to extract 12 characters, because the phone number itself is 10 characters and there are two asterisks.

The raw data remains untouched, since your formula is returning cleaned-up data to a new location.

The formula copies and pastes smoothly for each record.

You have all your phone numbers!

Now you can extract the "s" characters....

You need to vary the values that go into the second argument

In the `RIGHT()` formula you used to extract phone numbers, you told Excel to extract 12 characters, which works for all the phone numbers. But the count of "s" characters varies among the cells—from one character to five.

...two here...

Here are four "s" characters...

1	ssssWALTON,GRANT.202*431*4040
2	ssANDREWS,CIERRA.646*351*8529
3	ssSTEELE,BRYNLEE.917*652*6716
4	sssssDUNN,MADILYNN.212*679*6373
	WELCH,LILAH.202*596*6969

So when you create a `LEFT()` formula to extract the "s" characters, the value of your second argument somehow needs to vary among the cells.

...and five here.

Exercise

① Create column headings, because you're about to have a number of columns. Right-click on the 1 button to the left of the first row, and tell Excel to insert a row. Then type some column headings.

② Sort your data by column A. This will mostly group together records that have a similar number of "s" characters.

③ In column C, type the number of "s" characters in each row. Since similar records will be grouped together, you should be able to copy and paste.

④ Finally, in column D, create the `LEFT()` formula that will return the "s" characters. Have your second argument refer to the number you just created in column C.

Put your `LEFT()` formula here.

Be sure to add column headers in your new row.

Sort your data and type the number of "s" characters in this column.

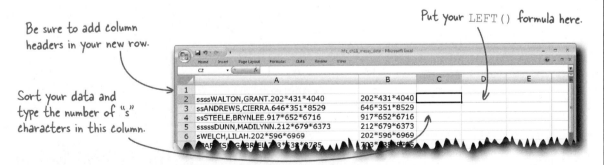

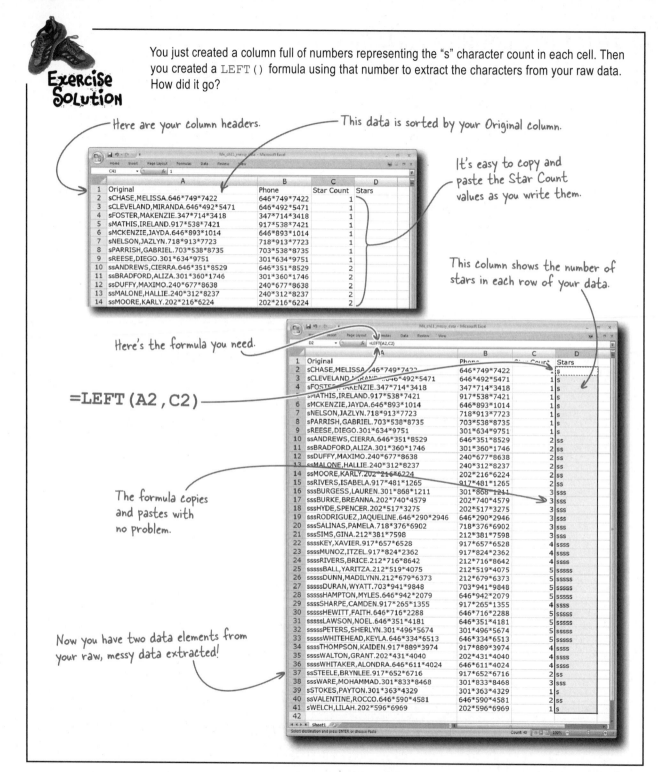

Exercise Solution

You just created a column full of numbers representing the "s" character count in each cell. Then you created a LEFT() formula using that number to extract the characters from your raw data. How did it go?

Here are your column headers.

This data is sorted by your Original column.

It's easy to copy and paste the Star Count values as you write them.

This column shows the number of stars in each row of your data.

Here's the formula you need.

=LEFT(A2,C2)

The formula copies and pastes with no problem.

Now you have two data elements from your raw, messy data extracted!

Business is starting to suffer for lack of customer data

That data you're working on is really important, and without it your employees are starting to have problems.

> Hate to bug you about this, but I need our customer data! Right now, I can't get in touch with anyone, which is seriously hurting business!

Better punch through those first and last names really quickly!

You know, because you already extracted values on both ends of your raw data, it'd be nice if you could use that information to get the name out. It'd be nice if you could use the data you've extracted to trim the ends off of your raw data.

s**CHASE,MELISSA.646*749*7422**

...you could use a LEFT() *formula here...*

If you had a formula that told you the length of things...

s**CHASE,MELISSA**

...and a RIGHT() *formula here.*

Let's use the stars and phone fields to whittle down the original. That way, breaking apart the last name and first name will be easier.

This will be easy to break apart.

CHASE,MELISSA

Exercise

The LEN() function returns the number of characters in its argument, and it can help you extract the names from your raw data.

If you give LEN() a text value...

You can type text or use a reference.

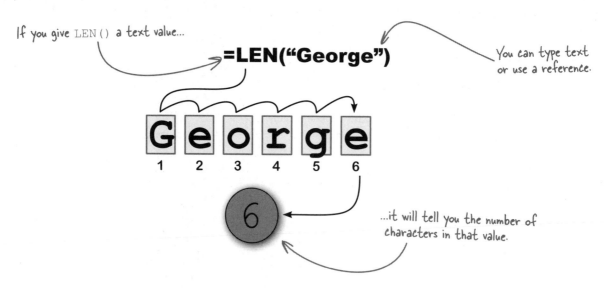

=LEN("George")

...it will tell you the number of characters in that value.

1 Create two columns for transitional messy data. In the first column, you'll peel the phone number out of the original data. In the second column, you'll peel the stars out of the original data.

Create these two columns.

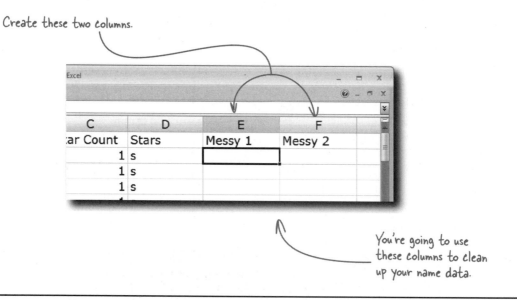

You're going to use these columns to clean up your name data.

2 Write a function that takes the leftmost characters out of the original data.

How many characters? An amount equal to the **length of the original data** minus the **length of the phone number**. The second argument of your `LEFT()` formula should contain another formula that makes this calculation.

`LEN(A2)` is the length of the original data.

`LEN(B2)` is the length of the phone number.

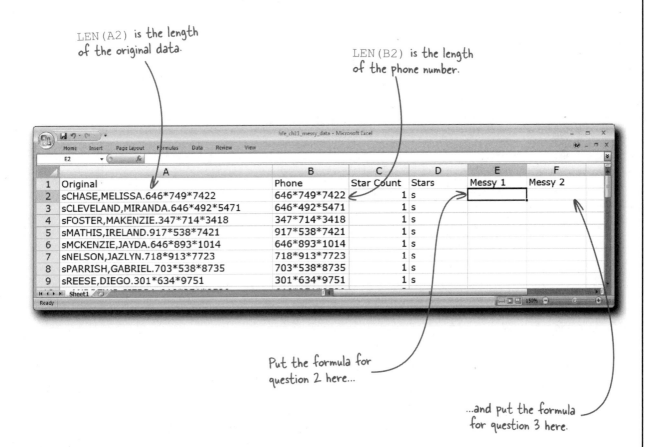

	A	B	C	D	E	F
1	Original	Phone	Star Count	Stars	Messy 1	Messy 2
2	sCHASE,MELISSA.646*749*7422	646*749*7422	1	s		
3	sCLEVELAND,MIRANDA.646*492*5471	646*492*5471	1	s		
4	sFOSTER,MAKENZIE.347*714*3418	347*714*3418	1	s		
5	sMATHIS,IRELAND.917*538*7421	917*538*7421	1	s		
6	sMCKENZIE,JAYDA.646*893*1014	646*893*1014	1	s		
7	sNELSON,JAZLYN.718*913*7723	718*913*7723	1	s		
8	sPARRISH,GABRIEL.703*538*8735	703*538*8735	1	s		
9	sREESE,DIEGO.301*634*9751	301*634*9751	1	s		

Put the formula for question 2 here...

...and put the formula for question 3 here.

3 Now write a function that takes the rightmost characters out of your new value. How many? An amount equal to the length of your new value minus the length of your star value.

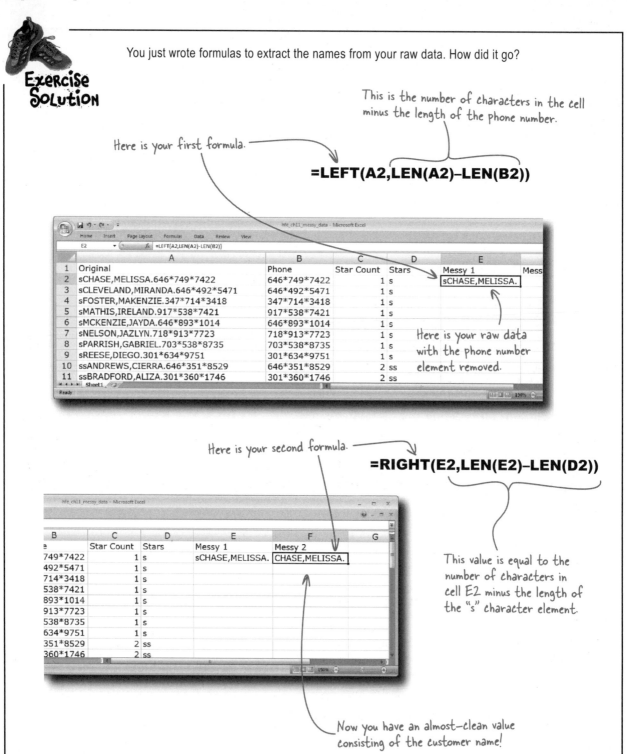

You just wrote formulas to extract the names from your raw data. How did it go?

Exercise Solution

This is the number of characters in the cell minus the length of the phone number.

Here is your first formula.

=LEFT(A2,LEN(A2)–LEN(B2))

Here is your raw data with the phone number element removed.

Here is your second formula.

=RIGHT(E2,LEN(E2)–LEN(D2))

This value is equal to the number of characters in cell E2 minus the length of the "s" character element.

Now you have an almost-clean value consisting of the customer name!

This spreadsheet is starting to get large!

The spreadsheet is getting complex, but we're making lots of progress. Go ahead and copy/paste the two formulas you just created for the remaining rows in your spreadsheet.

These are intermediary values you've created to clean your data.

Here's your clean data so far.

Next step: extract the last names.

You need a way to extract the last name from the data you created in column D. It seems clear that you can use a LEFT() formula, but you need to create another formula-based argument to specify the number of characters to grab.

You need a formula that will state the **numerical position of the comma**. When you use it as your argument, your LEFT() formula will know just how many characters to grab to return the last name.

What formula will state the numerical position of the comma?

FIND returns a number specifying the position of text

FIND() is a function that returns a number that states where a search string can be found within a piece of text. Say you were looking for the position of the text "x" in the expression "Head First Excel".

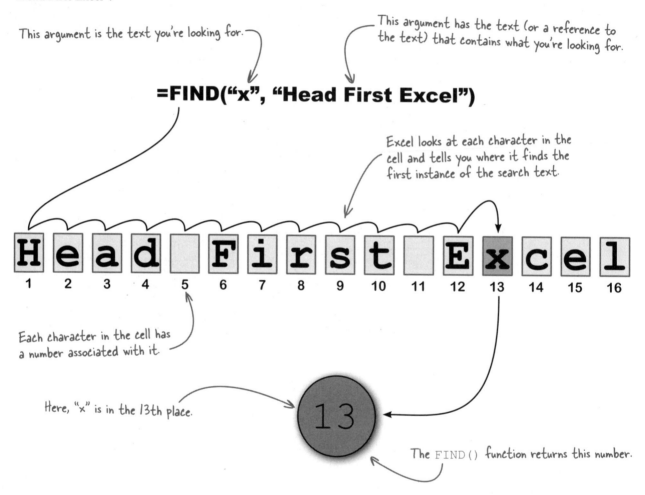

This argument is the text you're looking for.

This argument has the text (or a reference to the text) that contains what you're looking for.

=FIND("x", "Head First Excel")

Excel looks at each character in the cell and tells you where it finds the first instance of the search text.

Head First Excel

1 2 3 4 5 6 7 8 9 10 11 12 13 14 15 16

Each character in the cell has a number associated with it.

Here, "x" is in the 13th place.

13

The FIND() function returns this number.

Why would you need a function like this? Well, for starters, you could use it in conjunction with a LEFT() or RIGHT() formula to extract a number of characters that varies from formula to formula.

Let's use FIND() to extract our Last Name field....

Use FIND() inside your LEFT() formula to specify the position of the comma, telling LEFT() how many characters to grab to return your **Last Name** value.

1 Combine LEFT() and FIND() into a formula that extracts last names from column F.

2 Copy and paste for each line of messy data.

FIND() should look for the comma in cell F2.

Put your formula in a new *Last Name* column.

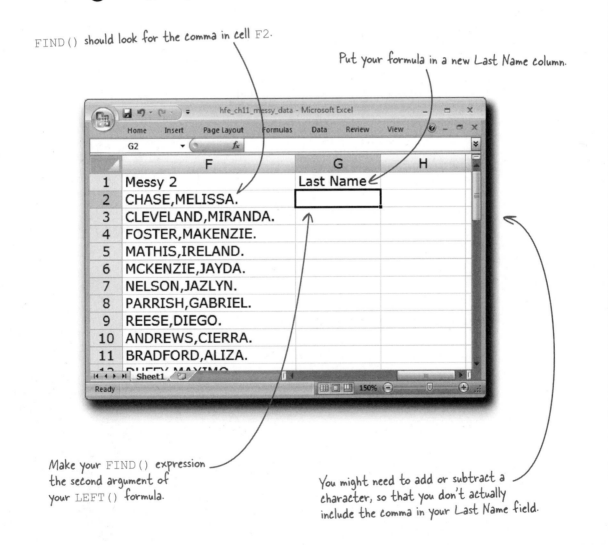

Make your FIND() expression the second argument of your LEFT() formula.

You might need to add or subtract a character, so that you don't actually include the comma in your Last Name field.

Exercise Solution

You just combined two formulas to get your Last Name field. What happened?

This formula searches for the comma, and it returns the last name...

=LEFT(F2,FIND(",",F2))

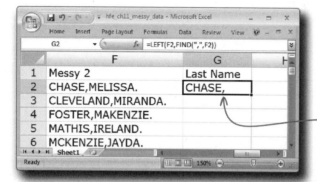

...but it also includes the comma in the result, so you need a formula that will exclude the comma.

All you have to do is subtract 1 from the value of your FIND() formula, and your comma is excluded.

=LEFT(F2,FIND(",",F2)–1)

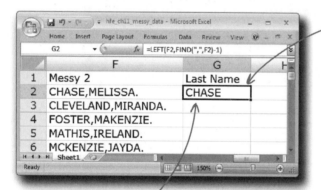

That LEFT/FIND formula is cool and everything, but wouldn't it be easier in this case just to use Text to Columns? We have a simple delimiter here, why not use it?

Now your Last Name has been extracted!

there are no
Dumb Questions

Q: Wouldn't Text to Columns be an easier way to deal with this problem?

A: Text to Columns is definitely quick and easy. You could use it in this case.

Q: So why didn't we?

A: Whether and when you use Text to Columns versus formulas is really a personal preference, and there is nothing wrong with using it here. But there is one big, fat reason to use formulas primarily.

Q: Because it's the harder way, so it's easier to show off?

A: Not at all! You'd always want to use formulas in situations where you think you might want to go back and trace exactly how your clean data was derived from your messy data.

Q: Why would you care? As long as the clean data works correctly, aren't you in good shape?

A: If you have messy data that has a single, simple pattern to it, you probably wouldn't have to go back and see how you derived your clean data. If every data point is separated by a delimiter, and you run a Text to Columns, you probably won't have problems with your cleaned data not squaring with your original data.

Q: But if the original data is complicated, it's a different story.

A: Exactly. The customer data you salvaged from the email has several patterns to the messiness: the first two fields (stars and names) aren't separated by a delimiter, the last name and the first name are separated by a comma, the first name and the phone number are separated by a period, and don't forget the asterisks inside the phone number.

Q: The data is really messy.

A: And because it's so messy, you've had to do a bunch of things to fix it. In creating the big, formula-filled spreadsheet you used to clean the data, you've also set up an audit that you can review if your clean data doesn't match your messy data perfectly later on.

Q: But there are still a lot of cases where I need to use Text to Columns, right?

A: Totally. Cleaning messy data—which all of us have to do at one point or another—is about finding the boundary conditions between your individual data points. And those boundaries are usually delimiters of some sort. If it's not a comma or a period, it might be spaces. So most of the field of cleaning messy data involves identifying those boundary conditions and making the software split the data using them.

Q: Which is what Text to Columns does.

A: Right. And if you run it over and over, Text to Columns can usually make some pretty complicated breaks. Just remember that you sacrifice the ability to go back and tweak the formulas you used to get different results. Once you run Text to Columns on data, it deletes the original data and leaves you with new columns.

Q: I think that on the first name, which is the last data field we have, we're safe to go with Text to Columns. By now, all the formulaic work we've done to break up the original mess has made what's left pretty simple.

A: Then go right ahead and use Text to Columns!

Can you run Text to Columns on column Messy 2? What happens when you try?

Text to Columns sees your formulas, not their results

There's a little snag when it comes to running this operation on the data you created in the Messy 2 column:

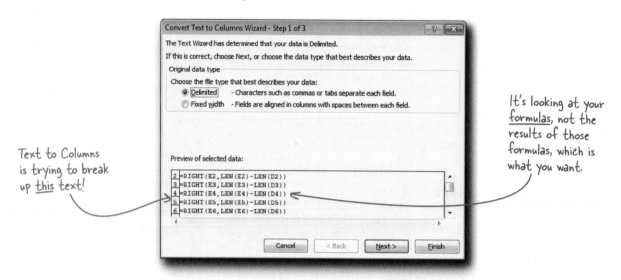

Text to Columns is trying to break up this text!

It's looking at your formulas, not the results of those formulas, which is what you want.

Text to Columns does what it says it does: take **text** and break it into columns. But here Excel wants to treat your *formulas* as text. This won't work: you need to take the formulas and render them as **values**.

Paste Special lets you paste with options

Paste Special is a fantastically helpful operation in Excel that lets you copy something and then—rather than paste an exact copy of the original—paste a modification of the original.

You can use Paste Special to paste the values that the formulas you've copied return, rather than the formulas themselves. And that is just what you need to do with your Messy 2 column data.

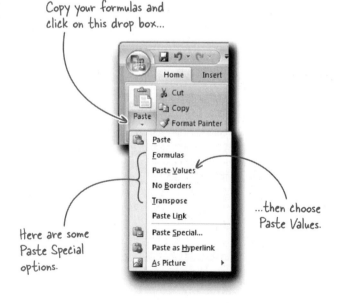

Copy your formulas and click on this drop box...

Here are some Paste Special options.

...then choose Paste Values.

Exercise

In order to run Text to Columns on your Messy 2 column, you need to Paste Special > Values its contents to a new column first. Do this and then run Text to Columns to break your first and last names apart while getting rid of the comma and period.

Copy this data.

Put your cursor here and choose Paste Special > Values.

Then run Text to Columns on your new data.

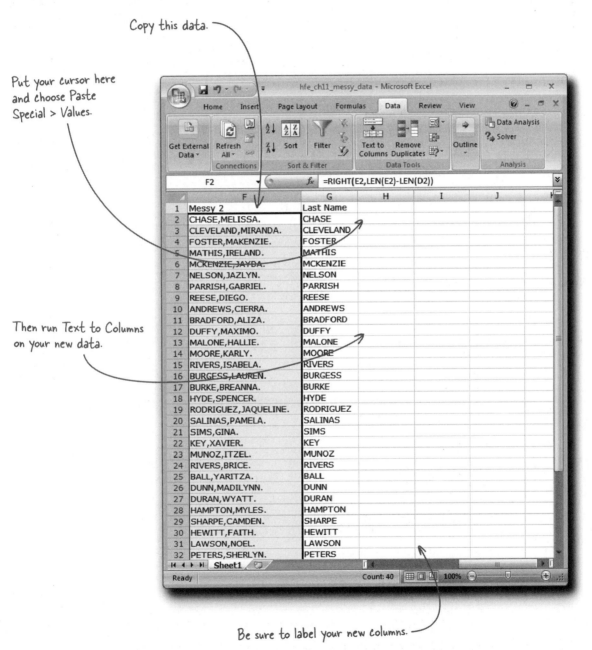

Be sure to label your new columns.

You just ran Paste Special > Values to make your data ready for the
Text to Columns operation. What happened?

Exercise Solution

Paste your data here.

Text to Columns has no problem
reading your data this time around.

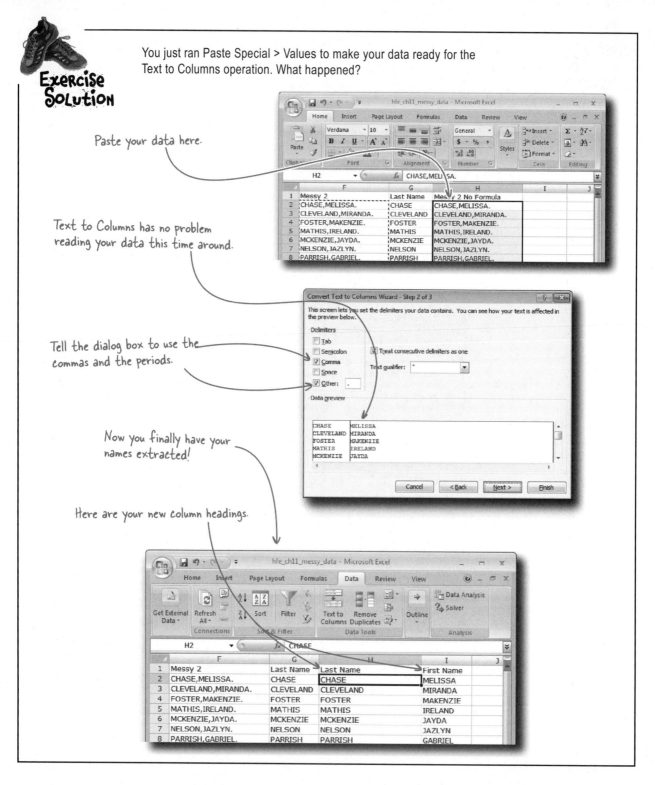

Tell the dialog box to use the
commas and the periods.

Now you finally have your
names extracted!

Here are your new column headings.

Looks like time's running out...

From: Employee
To: Head First
Subject: That database…

Dear Head First,

You know, could I get that data? I know fixing it up is a pain, but I'm starting to get angry phone calls from customers who are wondering whether we've forgotten them. It's getting really rough.

There's still time to patch things up with everyone, but not much. Can I get that data?

—Your Employee

Wow...she's starting to get worked up!

Better take care of this.

Exercise

You've successfully extracted all your data from the original mess, but in order for your employee to use your work, you'll need a perfectly clean version.

1   **Fix the case of your names.** Use the PROPER() function to make your names look like This rather than THIS. Look up the function in Help if you need to learn how to use it.

2   **Change the asterisks in the phone number to dashes.** Use the SUBSTITUTE() function, looking it up in Help if you need to.

3   **Copy everything to a new sheet with Paste Special > Values.**

4   **Delete the columns you no longer need from your new sheet.**

These steps will perfect your work.

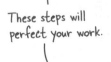

Exercise Solution

You just went through the final steps to fix your data so that your employee can use it. How did it go?

① **Fix the case of your names.** Use the PROPER() function to make your names look like This rather than THIS. Look up the function in help if you need to learn how to use it.

This formula is pretty simple—it just takes one argument.

=PROPER(H2)

You can copy and paste this formula for all the name values.

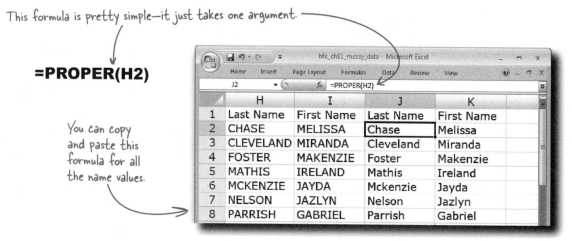

② **Change the asterisks in the phone number to dashes.** Use the SUBSTITUTE() function, looking it up in Help if you need to.

The second and third arguments are what you want to replace and what you want to replace it with.

=SUBSTITUTE(B2,"*","-")

Here's SUBSTITUTE() in action.

3   **Copy everything to a new sheet with Paste Special > Values.**

These tasks are pretty straightforward.

4   **Delete the columns you no longer need from your new sheet.**

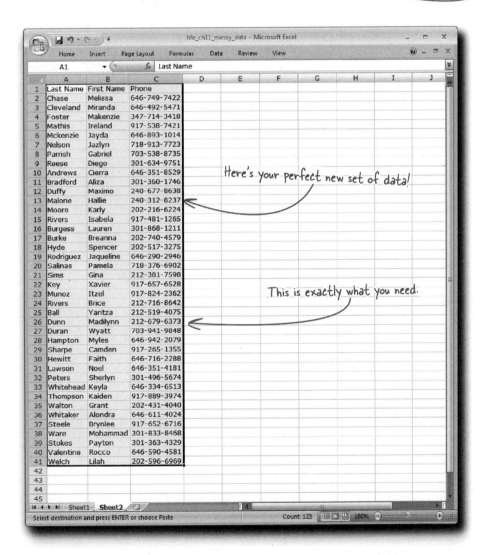

Here's your perfect new set of data!

This is exactly what you need.

Your data crisis is solved!

This chapter started off with a real mess: you received a pile of jumbled-up data, which was all you had left of your customer database. But with the help of Excel's powerful text formulas, you fixed that messy data right up.

> We're back in business!

The spreadsheet started as a mess...

...and now it shows your progress as you cleaned it up!

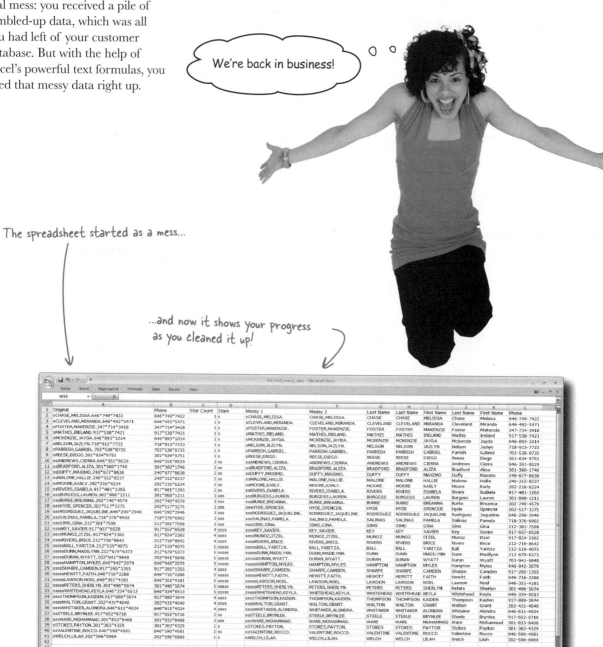

12 pivot tables

Hardcore grouping

Such glorious stuff. But everything rides on the boxes I put it in. Did I choose the right positions?

Pivot tables are among Excel's most powerful features.

But what are they? And why should we care? For Excel newbies, pivot tables can also be among Excel's most *intimidating* features. But their purpose is quite simple: **to group data quickly** so that you can analyze it. And as you're about to see, grouping and summarizing data using pivot tables is *much faster* than creating the same groupings using formulas alone. By the time you finish this chapter, you'll be slicing and dicing your data in Excel faster than you'd ever thought possible.

Head First Automotive Weekly needs an analysis for their annual car review issue

Head First Automotive Weekly has signed you on to help them create some **table visualizations** out of their annual car test data.

The magazine's readers are serious data junkies; they just love looking at stats on all the cars available. On the one hand, it's great that you have such passionate readers, but on the other hand, it's kind of a drag that you have to slice and dice the car data in so many ways in order to satisfy them.

Load this!

www.headfirstlabs.com/books/hfexcel/
hfe_ch12_pivot_tables.xlsx

This is going to be a big project, so you'd better brew up a pot of Starbuzz coffee. I need you to summarize, slice, and dice the car data in every way you can. Especially the cars' mileage. Why don't you start there?

The HFAW editor

Here's the ratings data.

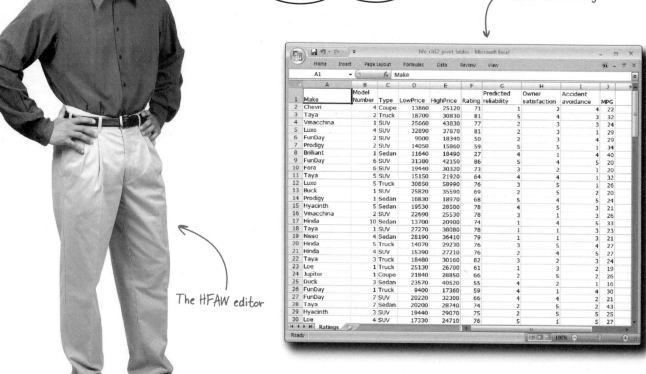

Sharpen your pencil

The editor has just given you a pretty broad request. Using the fields in your data, come up with four ways you might group and summarize the MPG (miles per gallon) information. One is provided for you.

1 The average MPGs grouped by Make and Type.

Here's an example.

2 ....

3 ....

4 ....

5 ....

Put your answers in the blanks.

Describe some of the steps you'd have to undertake to implement these summaries using formulas. How long do you think it would take to do all this?

....

....

....

....

Sharpen your pencil
Solution

You just brainstormed a bunch of ways to summarize the data on the basis of MPG. What did you find?

1 The average MPGs grouped by Make and Type.

2 The minimum MPG for each Make.

3 The maximum MPG for each type of car.

4 The average MPG grouped by reliability and Make.

5 The average MPG of SUVs under $40,000.

Describe some of the steps you'd have to undertake to implement these summaries using formulas. How long do you think it would take to do all this?

This would take quite a while. For each one of these, I'd have to write formulas to group the data in one or more ways, and I'd have to write formulas like AVERAGE or MAX that would actually calculate the summaries.

You've been asked to do a lot of repetitive operations

There is **complexity** in these data summaries that you've envisioned. You can slice the data in a million different ways, and it could take forever.

But there's **simplicity** as well. These summaries basically have you doing the same sort of operation over and over again: applying formulas to various groups and sub-groups of data.

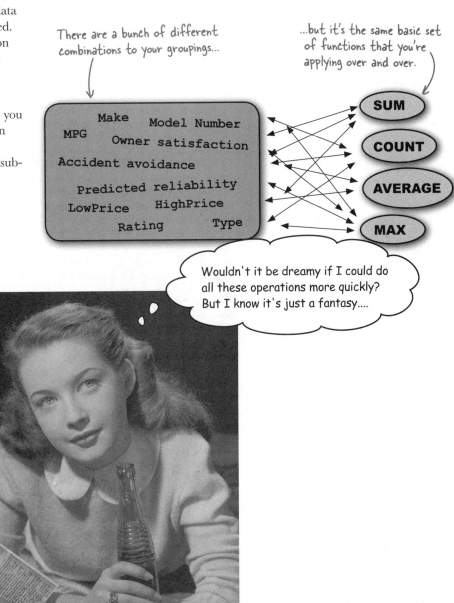

There are a bunch of different combinations to your groupings...

...but it's the same basic set of functions that you're applying over and over.

Make   Model Number

MPG   Owner satisfaction

Accident avoidance

Predicted reliability

LowPrice   HighPrice

Rating   Type

SUM

COUNT

AVERAGE

MAX

Wouldn't it be dreamy if I could do all these operations more quickly? But I know it's just a fantasy....

Pivot tables are an incredibly powerful tool for summarizing data

How do you group data in a bunch of different ways and summarize the groupings with formulas? The best approach is to use Excel's pivot tables. Pivot tables are an extraordinarily powerful feature of Excel that let you quickly and visually run these operations. Here's the basic idea behind how to make them.

Suppose this is your data.

Raw data

Each one of these ellipses is a spreadsheet cell with a data point inside.

What you want to do is take your data and put the different fields together into a new summary table.

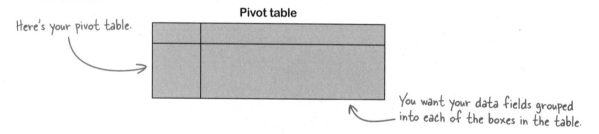

Pivot table

Here's your pivot table.

You want your data fields grouped into each of the boxes in the table.

Drag one of your fields to the row blank. This will show unique values from that field as row elements. That is the sort of grouping that takes place in pivot tables.

In the pivot table dialog box, drag a field into the row blank.

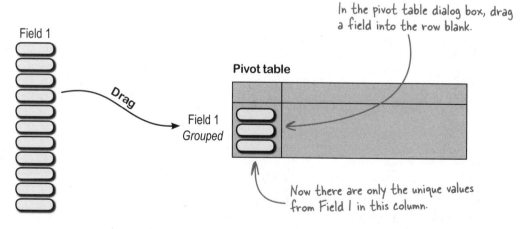

Field 1

Drag

Field 1
Grouped

Pivot table

Now there are only the unique values from Field 1 in this column.

Next, you do the same thing for the element you want to represent in your column. Drag the field name into the column blanks on the pivot table.

─Drag Field 2 into your column blank.

Do the same thing for columns.

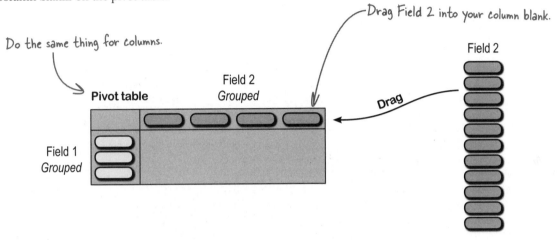

Field 2

Pivot table

Field 2
Grouped

Drag

Field 1
Grouped

Finally, pick the quantitative field that you'd like to see summarized and pick the function you want to use. Generally (but not always), your rows and columns will be categories, and your data blank will be the numerical thing you want to group and summarize by the row and column categories.

This summary is a pivot table.─

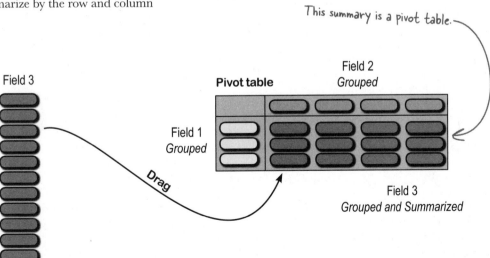

Field 3

Pivot table

Field 2
Grouped

Field 1
Grouped

Drag

Field 3
Grouped and Summarized

Pivot table construction is all about previsualizing where your fields should go

Pivot tables are their own little universe inside Excel, and people get intimidated at first by all the options. The thing you need to remember is this: stay focused on your analytical objectives, and try to create tables that help you understand your data better.

What are your analytical objectives?

Lots of raw data

Field 1	Field 2	Field 3	Field 4	Field 5	Field 6	Field 7	Field 8	Field 9

Pivot table

What table would help you understand your data and fulfill your objectives?

Try out creating your first pivot table from the summary you envisioned in the first exercise of this chapter.

Let's make a pivot table out of this idea.

Sharpen your pencil

The editor has just given you a pretty broad request. Using the fields in your data, come up with four ways you might group and summarize the MPG (miles per gallon) information. One is provided for you.

1 The average MPGs grouped by Make and Type.

Your table should look like this:

	Type
Make	Average MPG

Use these fields.

Go through these steps to create your pivot table.

1 Select a cell in your data, and click Insert > Pivot Table.

2 Drag fields from the Field List to the column, row, and data blanks.

3 Click the "Sum of MPG" drop box, and change the Value Field Settings so that you're taking the **Average**. Also, tweak the Number Format so that you don't end up with a bunch of decimal zeros.

Here's your data.

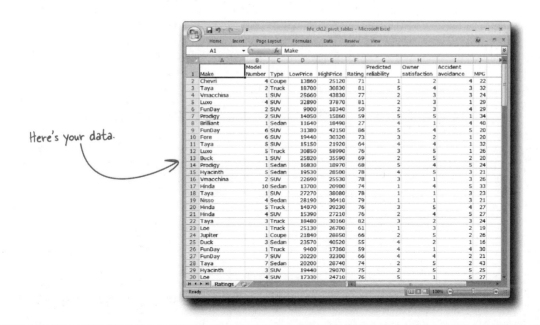

Exercise Solution

You just created your first pivot table, summarizing average MPG by Make and Type. How did it go?

① Select a cell in your data, and click Insert > Pivot Table.

Here's the window you use to make sure you have the correct data selected.

② Drag fields from the Field List to the column, row, and data blanks.

Drag the field names to the boxes where you want them to be.

③ Click the "Sum of MPG" drop box, and change the Value Field Settings so that you're taking the **Average**. Also, tweak the Number Format so that you don't end up with a bunch of decimal zeros.

We need a different formula here, because the sum of MPG values doesn't make any sense.

Tell Excel to take the Average of your MPG field.

Click this button to change the number format.

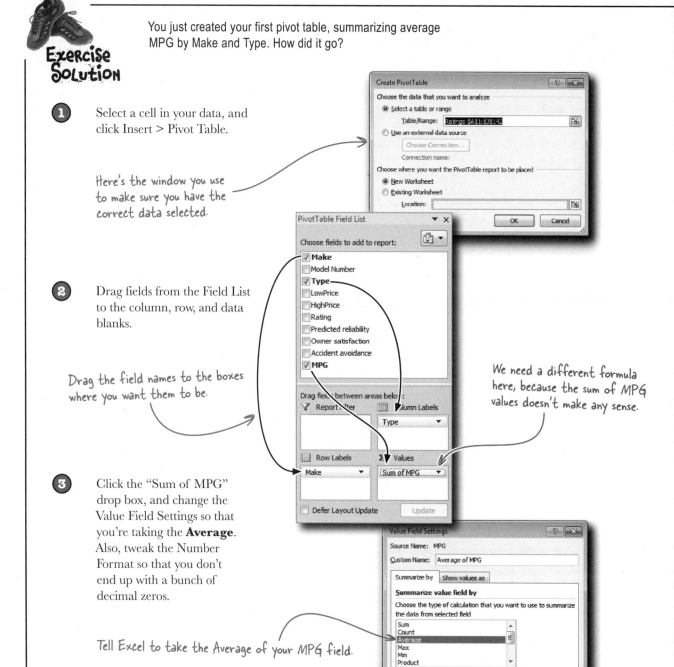

You want to reduce the decimal places.

No need for currency formatting or anything like that.

Here's your final pivot table.

This table summarizes average MPG by Type and Make.

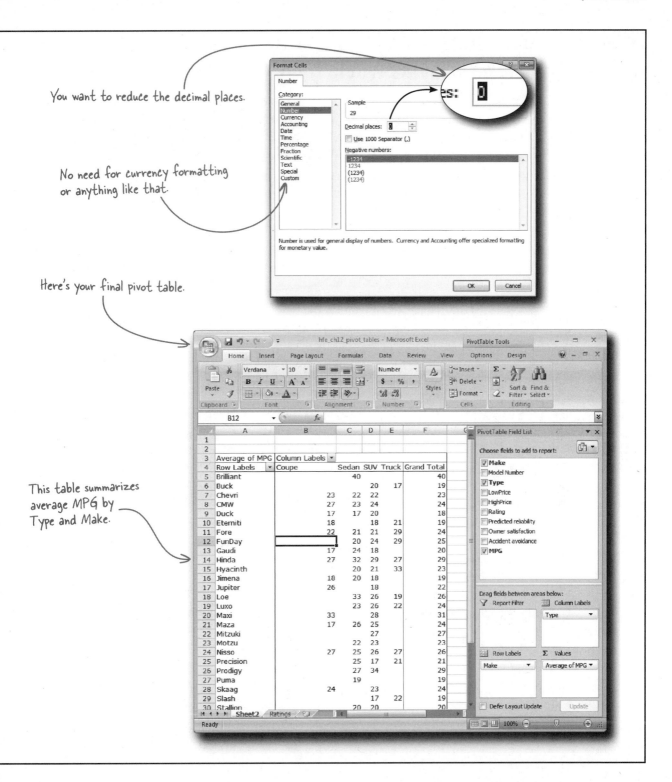

The pivot table summarized your data way faster than formulas would have

The steps to create a pivot table are pretty simple. Just select your data and drag your fields where you want them to be.

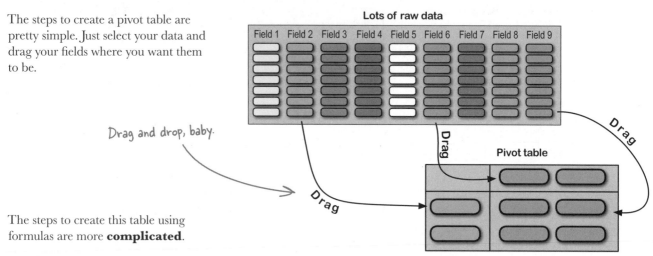

Drag and drop, baby.

The steps to create this table using formulas are more **complicated**.

Using formulas to create something like a pivot table

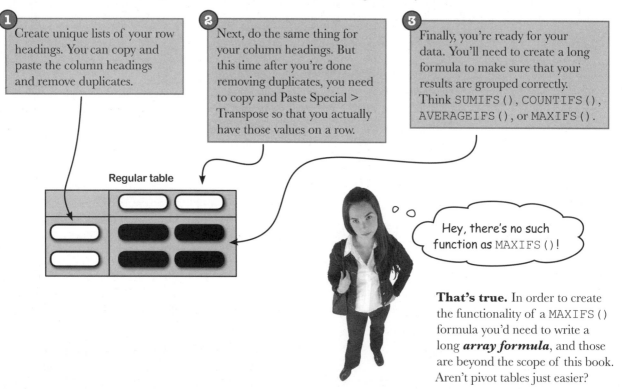

1 Create unique lists of your row headings. You can copy and paste the column headings and remove duplicates.

2 Next, do the same thing for your column headings. But this time after you're done removing duplicates, you need to copy and Paste Special > Transpose so that you actually have those values on a row.

3 Finally, you're ready for your data. You'll need to create a long formula to make sure that your results are grouped correctly. Think SUMIFS(), COUNTIFS(), AVERAGEIFS(), or MAXIFS().

Hey, there's no such function as MAXIFS()!

That's true. In order to create the functionality of a MAXIFS() formula you'd need to write a long *array formula*, and those are beyond the scope of this book. Aren't pivot tables just easier?

there are no
Dumb Questions

Q: **Where does the word "pivot" come into play? Have we been pivoting the data somehow?**

A: You "pivot" the data when you look at it from different angles. One of the things that pivot tables enable you to do is switch around your data summaries really quickly, so if you wanted to "pivot" your rows and columns literally you'd be able to do it easily.

Q: **But what if I just wanted to make groups and summarize them, but not actually *pivot* the data?**

A: Don't get too hung up on the word "pivot." If you think of pivot tables as efficient ways to group and summarize, you've grasped what they're all about.

Q: **How would I use pivot tables in a workflow for data analysis?**

A: They are great for doing exploratory data analysis, where you are looking at data from a bunch of different angles in order to prepare your ideas for the use of more advanced data analysis techniques.

Q: **So if there was something in the data I wanted to optimize with Solver, for example, I might knock around inside the data with pivot tables in order to develop my ideas about what I wanted to optimize?**

A: That's exactly it. And the reason that pivot tables are good for dealing with data in this way is because they are so fast. As long as it would take to create the formulas you'd need to create one summary table, you can create a whole mess of pivot tables.

Q: **Speaking of formulas, what if I want the speed and flexibility of pivot tables but just want a little scrap of summary data rather than a full-blown table? Got anything for me?**

A: There are a bunch of ways to do this. First, even though you want a piece or two of data, you can still create a pivot table for it. Just be judicious in your use of grouping and filtering, and you can get the answers you need quickly.

Q: **I was thinking more along the lines of a pivot *formula*.**

A: Check out the `GETPIVOTDATA()` function. You'll need to create a pivot table, but once you have it you can call it from another worksheet using that function.

Q: **What else?**

A: You can also replicate a lot of the functionality of pivot tables using structured references. The more advanced structured reference syntax enables you to group data in ways you can't using conventional references. Yet another reason to deepen your skills as a formula master.

Q: **Nice. Another question: so I liked the fact that I can use different functions to calculate the "Data" portion of the pivot table. But what if I want to do something really fancy—say, use a function that compares my data field to some other data field?**

A: Not a problem. Under your field's settings, click "Show values as..." for some options to compare the data to other fields.

Q: **Impressive. Here's another question: say I wanted to use pivot tables that aren't actually in my document. Like, say they're inside a corporate database.**

A: Again, this is no problem. Excel uses a technology called OLAP (Online Analytical Processing) that enables it to plug into (potentially huge) databases. This usage of pivot tables is beyond the scope of this book, but using pivot tables to access and evaluate external data is one of the powerful uses of Excel.

Q: **Hmm.**

A: You know, you're throwing a lot of questions at pivot tables and seem to be having a hard time stumping the feature.

Q: **Yeah, pivot tables sound pretty powerful.**

A: It's a good idea to use them every time you can, and to stay on the lookout for opportunities to use them. Chances are, if it's possible at all to do a task with pivot tables, doing that task with pivot tables is faster than the alternatives.

Q: **Got it. OK, so here's a question. How does this filtering thing work? With all the power of pivot tables, what does filtering get me?**

A: Let's take a look....

Your editor is impressed!

Nice table! We're definitely making progress. Now could you show me the table only for vehicles with reliability equal to 5?

You need to filter.

Pivot tables have yet another dimension: filtering. Filters allow you to take the elements you've assigned to your Values box and calculate only the ones that meet your criteria. In this case, you want to look at average MPG only for cars with a reliability of 5. Let's take filters for a spin....

Exercise

Go back to your pivot table and tell it to show the summary only for highest reliability cars. What box do you use?

Use the filter option in your pivot table.

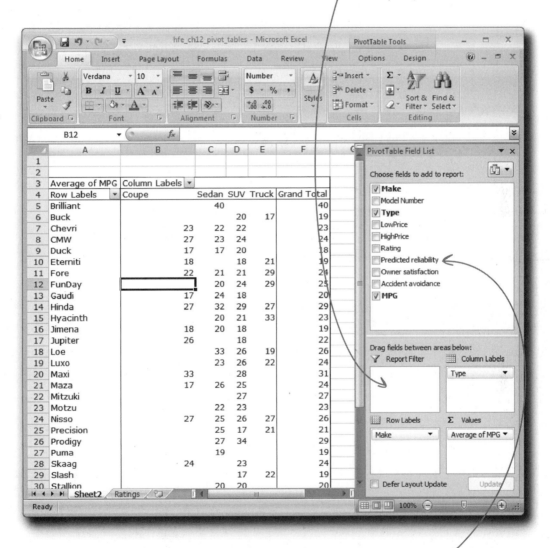

Drag your Predicted reliability field to filters and access the drop box in cell B2 to specify that you want the value to equal 5.

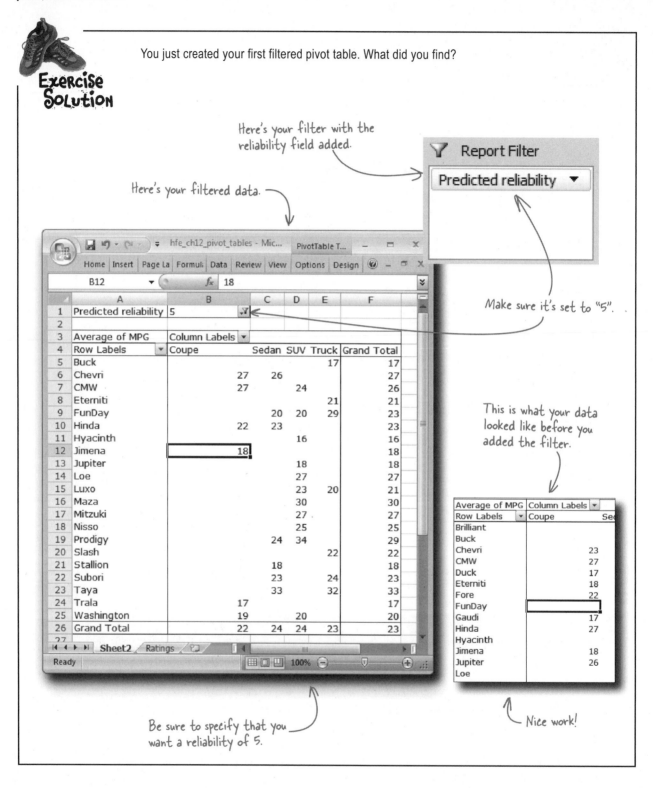

You just created your first filtered pivot table. What did you find?

Here's your filter with the reliability field added.

Here's your filtered data.

Make sure it's set to "5".

This is what your data looked like before you added the filter.

Be sure to specify that you want a reliability of 5.

Nice work!

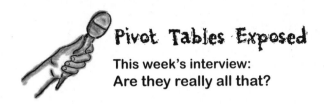

Pivot Tables Exposed

**This week's interview:
Are they really all that?**

Pivot Table: I must say that I'm delighted to be here. It's always such a joy to spread the word about me and what I do. People need to recognize that there is nothing inside of Excel that matches my ***raw analytic power***.

Head First: Well, we're happy you're here and you're welcome any time. But I have to ask, is it true that there is *nothing* in Excel that matches your *analytic power*? Actually, let me rephrase the question. Isn't the analytic power something the analyst brings to the game, not something you do?

Pivot Table: OK, touché. The user needs to be a good analyst in order to use me to come up with good analytic results. But I'm a big deal.

Head First: Just to play devil's advocate here, are you? It seems that all you can do is group data on two dimensions and run a calculation.

Pivot Table: Two dimensions? You should think bigger than that. Try dragging more than one field to my column, row, data, and filter blanks. You can insert as many levels of dimensionality into your pivot table analysis as you like.

Head First: Yep, that's pretty powerful.

Pivot Table: Told you so.

Head First: But wouldn't that clutter up the spreadsheet big time to have four or five or ten dimensions of summary?

Pivot Table: I would point you to your previous observation. It takes a good analyst to do good pivot table-based analysis. Yes, dragging a whole mess of fields into a pivot table makes the resulting table full of fields, but if a user has the analytic chops for it, then creating such a table may be exactly what is in order.

Head First: But there must be something to be said for keeping things simple.

Pivot Table: There is indeed. Even the most brilliant analyst is going to have to present results to someone who isn't a brilliant analyst, so keeping things simple for an audience's sake is a good idea.

Head First: Well, suppose that brilliant analyst wanted to make a chart rather than a table. They'd need make to a chart off the pivot table—they can't make a pivot *chart*.

Pivot Table: *Au contraire, mon frère.* I can make pivot charts. The feature is called Pivot Charts, and it's right under the Pivot Table button under the Insert tab. Charts are no problem.

Head First: What if we want to do some more subtle formatting of our pivot table? Can we just format the pivot table directly as if it were a regular spreadsheet?

Pivot Table: You can, but a lot of people will copy and Paste Special > Values the result of a pivot table to another sheet and then format the pasted results. The downside of that approach is that you lose your formulas. But the upside of the approach is that your formatting doesn't mess up if you want to change your pivot table to look at another set of summaries.

Head First: Last question. This is possibly a weird one. You've been dropping some interesting terminology: *touché* and *au contraire*, for example. Are you French?

Pivot Table: Let's just say my versatility in processing different types of data has enabled me to cultivate a certain cosmopolitanism. But no, I'm not French. I'm a feature in a computer program, silly.

You're ready to finish the magazine's data tables

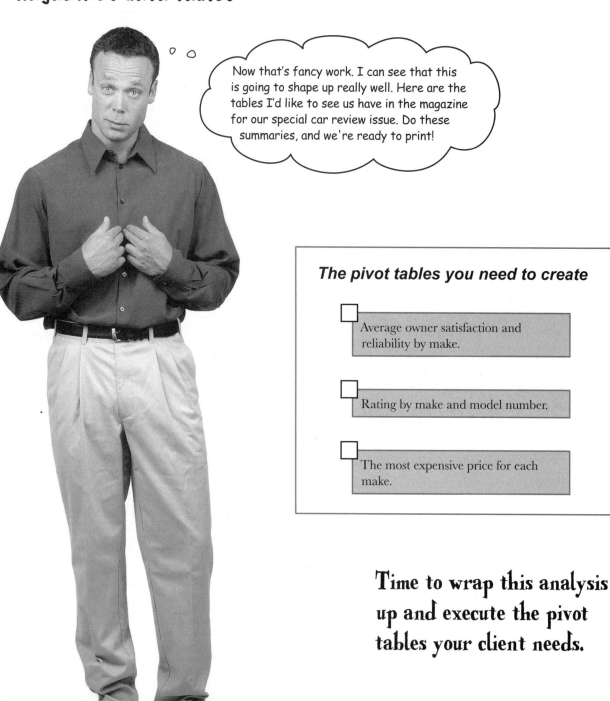

Now that's fancy work. I can see that this is going to shape up really well. Here are the tables I'd like to see us have in the magazine for our special car review issue. Do these summaries, and we're ready to print!

The pivot tables you need to create

☐ Average owner satisfaction and reliability by make.

☐ Rating by make and model number.

☐ The most expensive price for each make.

Time to wrap this analysis up and execute the pivot tables your client needs.

Long Exercise

Create the data summaries that your client needs using Excel's pivot tables.

① Implement the tables that the editor describes on the facing page. You might have to get a little creative....

Here's your blank pivot table.

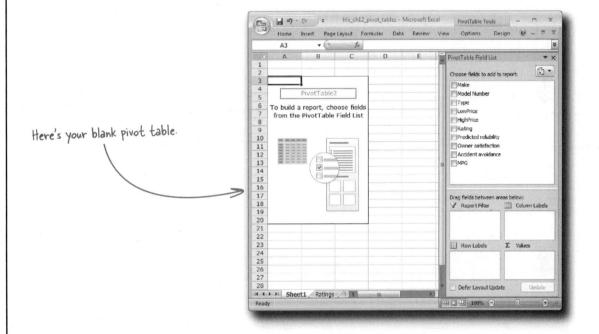

② In order to create a presentation, copy and Paste Special > Values each to a new sheet. Format the results as you see fit.

LONG EXERCISE SOLUTION

With your new knowledge of pivot tables, you created the tables the *Head First Automotive Weekly* needed for its review issue. How'd it go?

① Implement the tables that the editor describes on the facing page. You might have to get a little creative....

② In order to create a presentation, copy and Paste Special > Values each to a new sheet. Format the results as you see fit.

Set your number formatting to round off the extra zeros.

Here's your first pivot table.

☑ Average owner satisfaction and reliability by make.

You can actually put both satisfaction and reliability in the Values box.

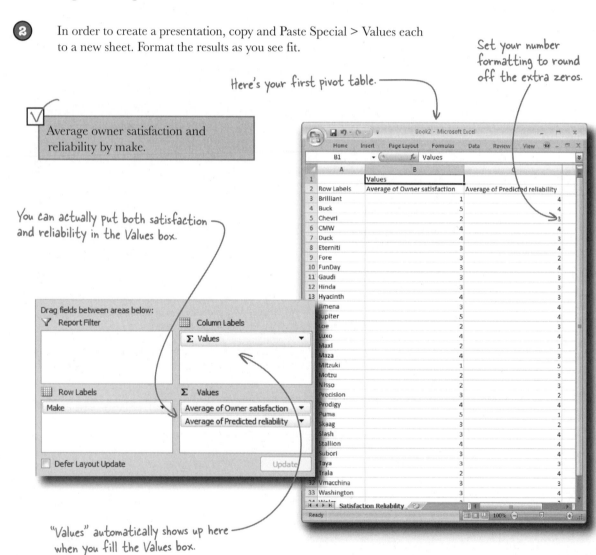

"Values" automatically shows up here when you fill the Values box.

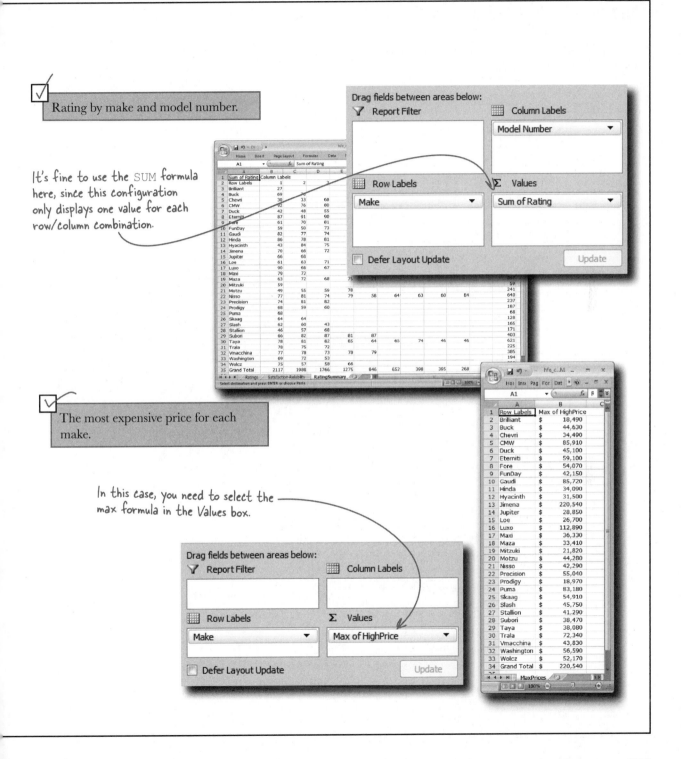

Rating by make and model number.

It's fine to use the SUM formula here, since this configuration only displays one value for each row/column combination.

The most expensive price for each make.

In this case, you need to select the max formula in the Values box.

Your pivot tables are a big hit!

Head First Automotive Weekly released a
particularly illuminating annual car review
this year, all thanks to your well-crafted
pivot tables. Reader response has been
overwhelmingly positive.

Man, that issue of HFAW was the best. It
helped me figure out which car I wanted to buy.
This baby doesn't have the best reliability, but
man, the stats were right about satisfaction!

One of your (very happy) readers

13 booleans

TRUE and FALSE

The values in this spreadsheet are too good to be **TRUE**....

There's a deceptively simple data type available in Excel.

They're called **Boolean values**, and they're just plain ol' TRUE and FALSE. You might think that they are too basic and elementary to be useful in serious data analysis, but nothing could be further from the truth. In this chapter, you'll plug Boolean values into **logical formulas** to do a variety of tasks, from cleaning up data to making whole new data points.

Are fishermen behaving on Lake Dataville?

Lake Dataville has so many enthusiastic fishermen that the Dataville government has had to impose limits on fishermen to make sure they don't take all the fish!

Most fishermen love the rules, because they guarantee the supply of fish. But there's always a handful of bad apples, and the government needs your help sifting through the catch records to find them.

Here's one of the Dataville fishing boats

I need your help finding the violators!

Here are the regulations that state how many fish different types of boats can catch.

You need to help fill in these blanks.

Load this!

www.headfirstlabs.com/books/hfexcel/
hfe_ch13_boolean.xlsx

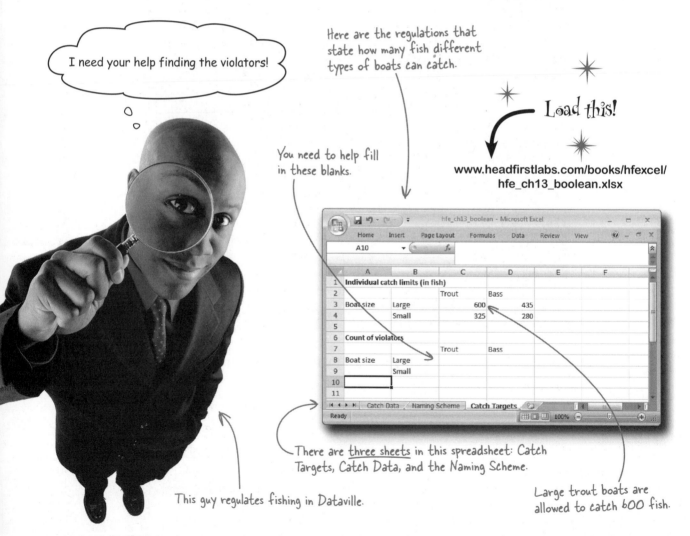

There are _three sheets_ in this spreadsheet: Catch Targets, Catch Data, and the Naming Scheme.

This guy regulates fishing in Dataville.

Large trout boats are allowed to catch 600 fish.

You have data on catch amounts for each boat

There's a complex system for each boat ID. Each ID tells you whether the boat is small or large and what kind of fish it catches. That determines the catch regulations for each boat.

The problem in dealing with this data is that you don't have cells to tell you the type and size of each boat. That information is all mashed up inside the ID cells.

The IDs are written in code.

Here is the number of fish caught by each boat.

This sheet describes the codes.

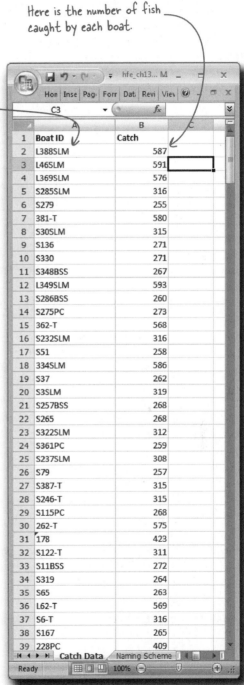

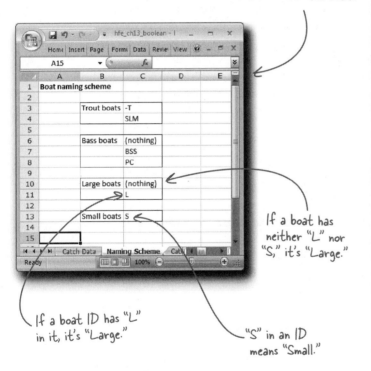

If a boat has neither "L" nor "S," it's "Large."

If a boat ID has "L" in it, it's "Large."

"S" in an ID means "Small."

If that information isn't broken out of the ID cell, you'll never be able to cross-reference each boat with the catch limits.

You need a formula that can tag each boat as small and large, and as bass and trout. It'd be nice to have a field for each boat that says "Large" or "Small," and one that says "Bass" or "Trout."

Boolean expressions return a result of TRUE or FALSE

A Boolean expression is a formula or argument to a formula that returns a value of TRUE or FALSE. It's often used to compare two values.

One is equal to one.

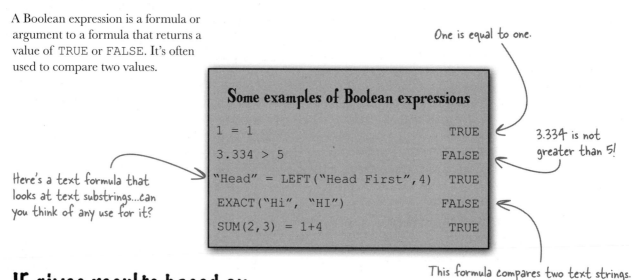

Some examples of Boolean expressions

1 = 1	TRUE
3.334 > 5	FALSE
"Head" = LEFT("Head First",4)	TRUE
EXACT("Hi", "HI")	FALSE
SUM(2,3) = 1+4	TRUE

Here's a text formula that looks at text substrings...can you think of any use for it?

3.334 is not greater than 5!

This formula compares two text strings.

IF gives results based on a Boolean condition

If you stick a Boolean expression inside an IF formula, you can have your formula return any value you want instead of returning TRUE or FALSE.

Your Boolean goes into the first argument.

The results you want go into the second and third arguments.

=IF(*boolean expression, value if true, value if false*)

You can put text, numbers, or even another formula in these arguments.

This formula won't apply to all the boats, but it's getting close to what you need.

This expression evaluates to TRUE.

=IF(LEFT(A2,1)="L", "Large", "Small")   **"Large"**

It looks at the first character of A2...

...then it returns "Large" if that character is "L" and "Small" if it's not.

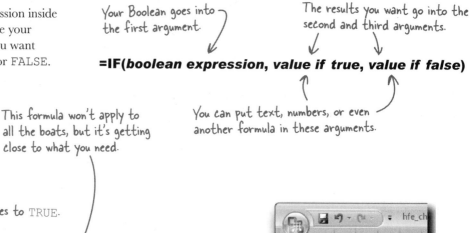

Booleans Exposed

**This week's interview:
Is what we've heard about
Booleans TRUE or FALSE?**

Head First: I have to say, as simple as the TRUE and FALSE data values are, you're definitely looking promising as a tool to help with data analysis in Excel.

Boolean: You bet! And you've only seen the beginning of what I can do. I'm going to rock your brains out.

Head First: OK, relax and let's talk through your features slowly.

Boolean: Fire away.

Head First: Are there other formulas besides IF that accept Boolean expressions?

Boolean: Are you kidding? I'm all over the place. The most obvious place to find me is in the category of logical functions, and IF is one of those. But there is also AND, OR, NOT, and a bunch of others.

Head First: I assume that those three functions are similar to IF in how they work?

Boolean: Yep. I bet you can guess what they do. But even if you can't, don't worry, because you'll need them soon enough. I've been looking at that fishing boat problem of yours, and you're going to need to throw a lot more Booleans at it to get what you want.

Head First: We'll get to that in a moment. So you show up in logical functions...what else?

Boolean: I'm in logical functions, but I'm in all sorts of functions throughout Excel. A lot of the time, the third or fourth argument of a function that's totally unrelated to the logical functions will take a Boolean expression.

Head First: Why is that?

Boolean: The heavy-duty functions in Excel often have a lot of subtle permutations to how they can run. So it's a good idea to put in a Boolean or two so that you tell Excel the specifics of what you want.

Don't worry, if you spend enough time in the Help files, you'll notice me all over the place.

Head First: So what about the equals sign and the greater-than sign?

Boolean: Sure. You can also use less than (<), greater than or equal to (>=), and less than or equal to (<=).

Head First: What if I wanted to see whether something wasn't equal to something, like whether 1 is not equal to 3?

Boolean: You'd type this formula: =1<>3. That Boolean expression asks whether 1 is *unequal* to 3, and since it is, the expression returns TRUE.

Head First: Cool. So you can use Booleans in a bunch of ways to compare values. And you can use IF to return values different from TRUE and FALSE.

Boolean: Oh, you're just getting started with IF. It's one of the most powerful functions in Excel.

Head First: Yeah, I wanted to ask. What if I wanted to compare three values rather than two using an IF formula?

Boolean: Now you're talking. This is the sort of question that makes you an Excel power user. This sort of thing makes your friends stare in awe at the breadth of your mastery over spreadsheets....

Head First: Could you just answer the question?

Boolean: To compare three things, you nest IF formulas inside each other. Like this:

```
=IF(exp1,value2,IF(exp2,value3,value4))
```

If you want to compare x, y, and z, you compare x and y in exp1 and then y and z in exp2.

Head First: Heavy!

Boolean: Why don't you try it?

Your IF formulas need to accommodate the complete naming scheme

The boats are coded by fish type using a complex logic. The presence of one of five special codes is what determines whether a boat is Trout or Bass.

Your IF formula can't think through options like this.

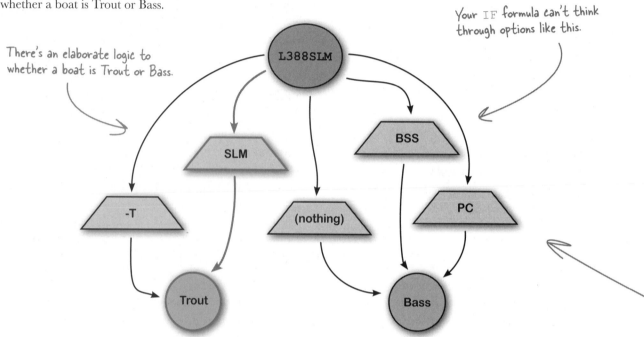

There's an elaborate logic to whether a boat is Trout or Bass.

The problem is that IF doesn't evaluate five options in order to return one or two answers. It just looks at one Boolean expression at a time. So you need to take the complex logic of boat ID assignments and convert it into a series of **linear** decisions. That way, you'll be able to write the IF formula that gives you the right answer.

IF wants its choices to be one right after the other.

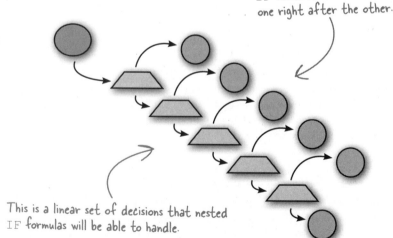

This is a linear set of decisions that nested IF formulas will be able to handle.

Pool Puzzle

Your **job** is to take text strings from the pool and place them into the blank lines in the logic structure. You may **not** use the same text string more than once. Your **goal** is to make a logical structure that you'll be able to represent in nested IF formulas.

Fill in this logical structure.

IF it has _____ the type of fish is _____,

  otherwise, if it has _____ the type of fish is _____,

    otherwise, if it has _____ the type of fish is _____,

      otherwise, if it has _____ the type of fish is _____,

        otherwise, the type of fish is _____.

Use the diagram on the facing page.

Nope, "(nothing)" is not in here...you don't need it!

Note: Each thing from the pool can be used only once!

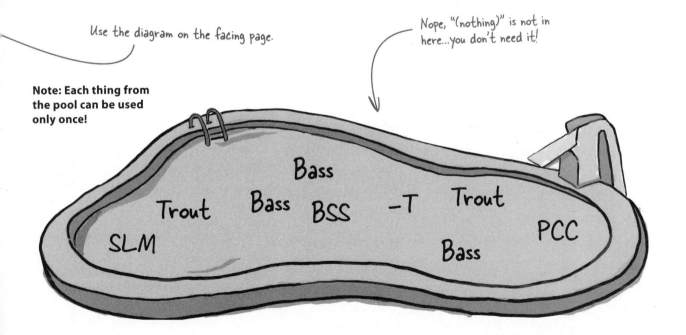

Bass
Trout Bass BSS -T Trout
SLM Bass PCC

Pool Puzzle Answers

You just created a logical diagram to describe the **linear** way in which you want your nested IF formulas to decide the value to assign to each boat. How did it go?

1	Boat naming scheme		
2			
3		Trout boats	-T
4			SLM
5			
6		Bass boats	(nothing)
7			BSS
8			PC
9			
10		Large boats	(nothing)
11			L
12			
13		Small boats	S
14			
15			

Here's how the logic works.

Excel will be able to make sense of this.

IF it has ___-T___ **the type of fish is** _Trout_,

otherwise, if it has ___SLM___ **the type of fish is** _Trout_,

otherwise, if it has ___BSS___ **the type of fish is** _Bass_,

otherwise, if it has ___PCC___ **the type of fish is** _Bass_,

otherwise, the type of fish is _Bass_.

Now let's write the formula....

Note: Each thing from the pool can be used only once!

Nested IF Magnets

Use the logic diagram you created to complete your nested `IF` formula.

Then **implement that formula in your spreadsheet.**

Here's the `IF` formula.

Match the Boolean expressions with the logic you created.

Where should the extra parentheses go?

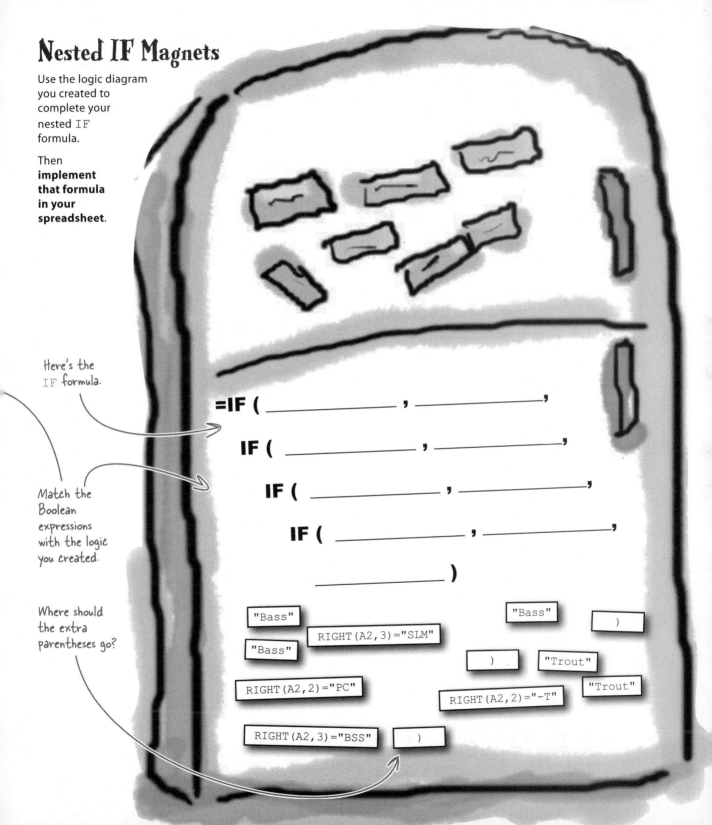

=IF (_____ **,** _____ **,**

IF (_____ **,** _____ **,**

IF (_____ **,** _____ **,**

IF (_____ **,** _____ **,**

_____ **)**

`"Bass"`	`"Bass"`	`)`

`RIGHT(A2,3)="SLM"`

`"Bass"`

`)` . `"Trout"`

`RIGHT(A2,2)="PC"`

`RIGHT(A2,2)="-T"` `"Trout"`

`RIGHT(A2,3)="BSS"` `)`

Nested IF Magnets

Were you able to create the formula that tags each boat as either Trout or Bass?

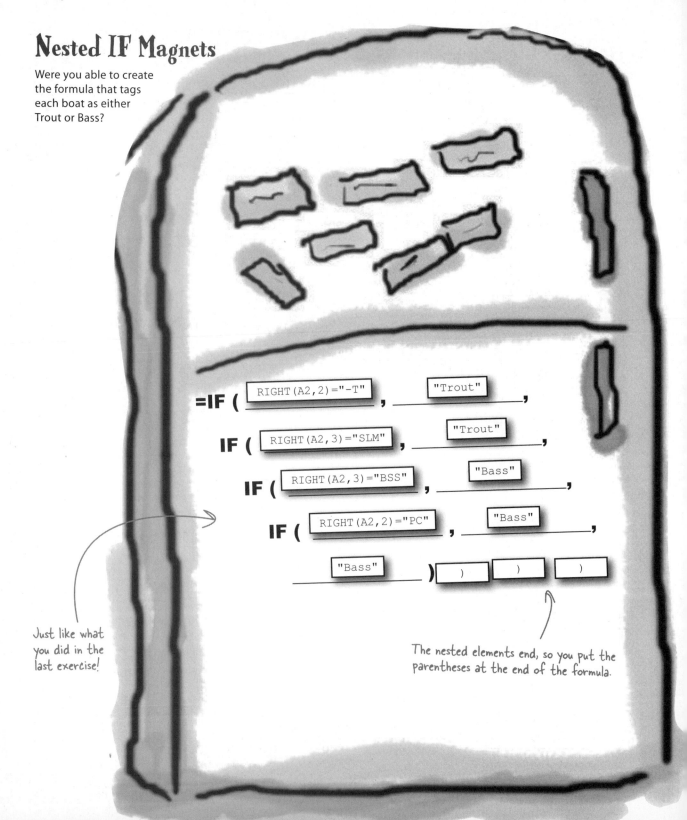

=IF (`RIGHT(A2,2)="-T"` , _____ `"Trout"` _____ ,

    IF (`RIGHT(A2,3)="SLM"` , _____ `"Trout"` _____ ,

        IF (`RIGHT(A2,3)="BSS"` , _____ `"Bass"` _____ ,

            IF (`RIGHT(A2,2)="PC"` , _____ `"Bass"` _____ ,

            _____ `"Bass"` _____))))

Just like what you did in the last exercise!

The nested elements end, so you put the parentheses at the end of the formula.

Exercise

Now that you've created the formula to tag each boat as being Trout or Bass, it's time to write another formula that tags each boat as being either Large or Small.

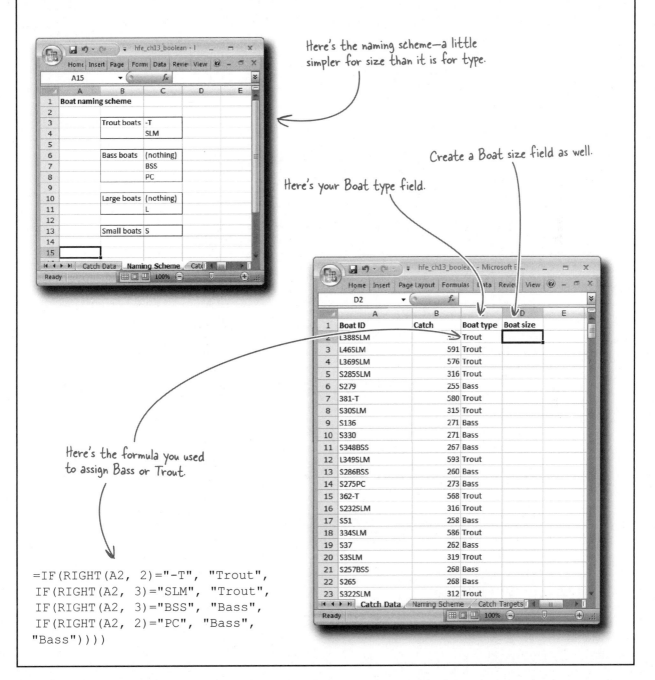

Here's the naming scheme—a little simpler for size than it is for type.

Create a Boat size field as well.

Here's your Boat type field.

Here's the formula you used to assign Bass or Trout.

```
=IF(RIGHT(A2, 2)="-T", "Trout",
IF(RIGHT(A2, 3)="SLM", "Trout",
IF(RIGHT(A2, 3)="BSS", "Bass",
IF(RIGHT(A2, 2)="PC", "Bass",
"Bass"))))
```

ExercisE SolutioN

You just created a formula to assign a size amount to each boat. What does it look like?

If you had nested IF formulas in this exercise like you did in the last one, your formula might look like this.

```
=IF(LEFT(A2, 1)="S", "Small",
IF(LEFT(A2, 1)="L", "Large",
"Large"))
```

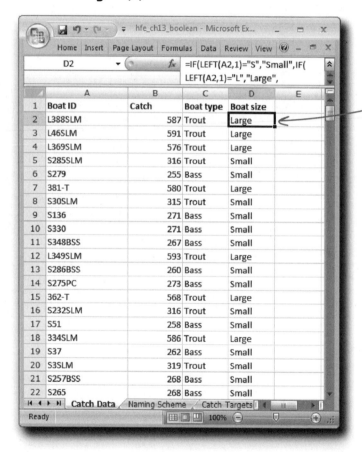

Here it is in action.

Since all small boats are marked "S", you know that all boats not marked "S" are large.

But you also could have written a simpler formula that looks like this.

```
=IF(LEFT(A2, 1)="S", "Small", "Large")
```

Summarize how many boats
fall into each category

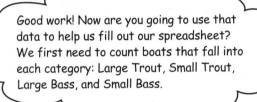

Good work! Now are you going to use that data to help us fill out our spreadsheet? We first need to count boats that fall into each category: Large Trout, Small Trout, Large Bass, and Small Bass.

He's asking you to fill up these cells on your spreadsheet.

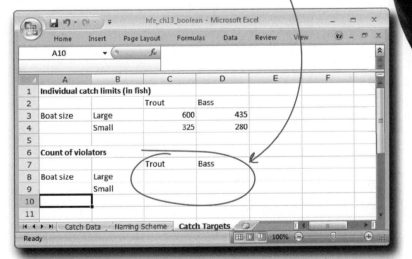

You won't be able to use IF for this problem. IF just returns one or two values depending on your calculation. You'll need a formula that **counts** based on a Boolean expression. Or rather, a formula that will count based on *two* expressions, because each boat is part of two **categories**, size and type....

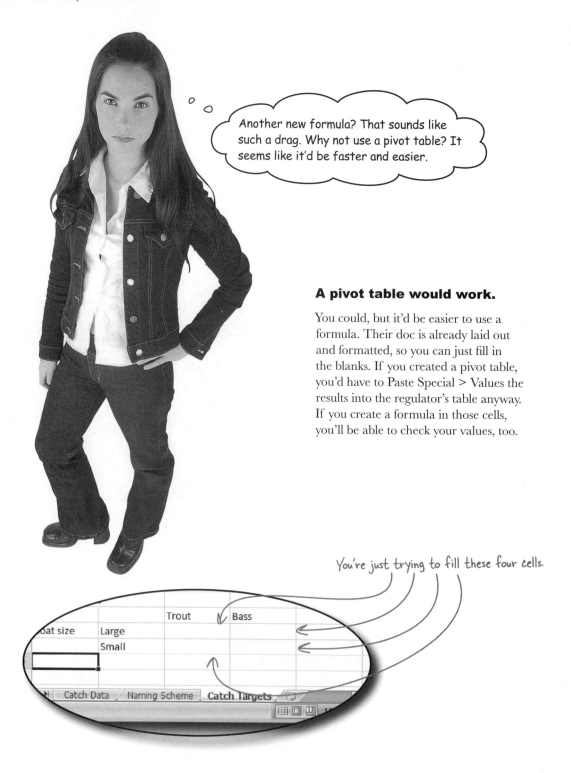

Another new formula? That sounds like such a drag. Why not use a pivot table? It seems like it'd be faster and easier.

A pivot table would work.

You could, but it'd be easier to use a formula. Their doc is already laid out and formatted, so you can just fill in the blanks. If you created a pivot table, you'd have to Paste Special > Values the results into the regulator's table anyway. If you create a formula in those cells, you'll be able to check your values, too.

You're just trying to fill these four cells.

		Trout	Bass	
oat size	Large			
	Small			

Catch Data / Naming Scheme / **Catch Targets**

Sharpen your pencil

In the Help files, find the COUNT formula that will count records based on a boat's type and size.

The COUNT functions are under the category of Statistical functions.

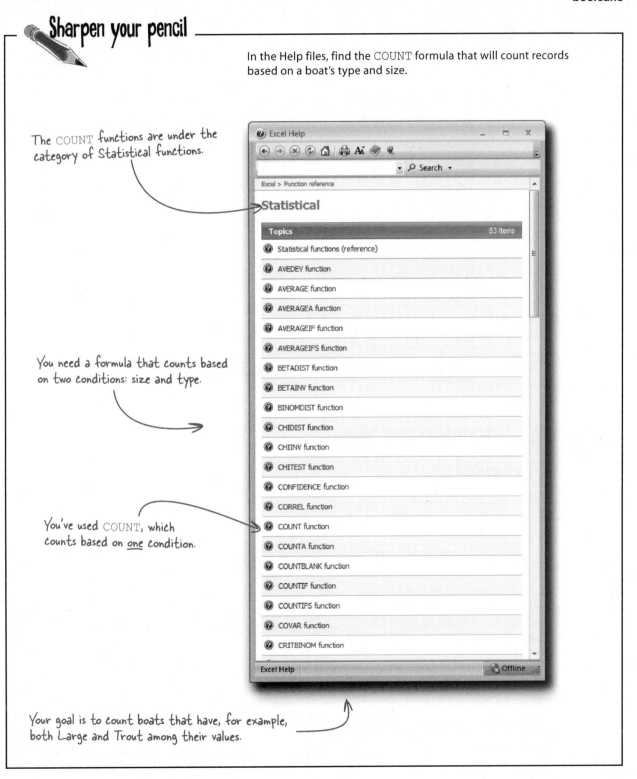

You need a formula that counts based on two conditions: size and type.

You've used COUNT, which counts based on <u>one</u> condition.

Your goal is to count boats that have, for example, both Large and Trout among their values.

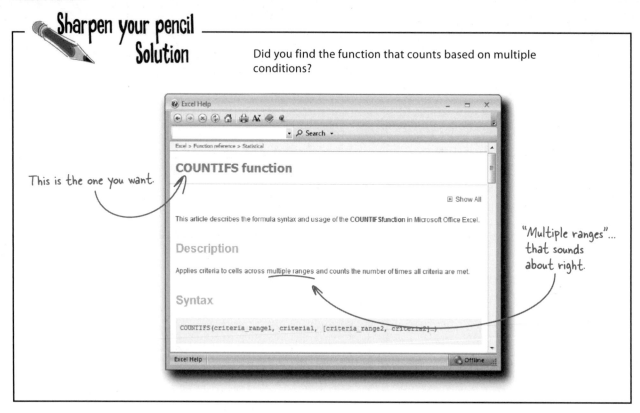

Sharpen your pencil Solution

Did you find the function that counts based on multiple conditions?

This is the one you want.

COUNTIFS function

⊞ Show All

This article describes the formula syntax and usage of the COUNTIFS function in Microsoft Office Excel.

"Multiple ranges"... that sounds about right.

Description

Applies criteria to cells across multiple ranges and counts the number of times all criteria are met.

Syntax

COUNTIFS(criteria_range1, criteria1, [criteria_range2, criteria2]...)

COUNTIFS is like COUNTIF, only way more powerful

COUNTIFS is a formula new to Excel 2007 that can count elements based on one or more criteria. Say you want to count the number of boats that have "Large" and "Trout" in their rows. COUNTIFS is the function you want.

It also can count based on single criteria, so it has all the functionality of COUNTIF and more. A lot of Excel users have stopped using COUNTIF altogether because COUNTIFS is so powerful.

COUNTIFS will handle the entire list for each boat.

Here are four Large Trout boats.

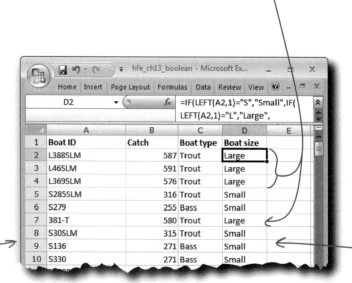

	A	B	C	D	E
1	Boat ID	Catch	Boat type	Boat size	
2	L388SLM	587	Trout	Large	
3	L46SLM	591	Trout	Large	
4	L369SLM	576	Trout	Large	
5	S285SLM	316	Trout	Small	
6	S279	255	Bass	Small	
7	381-T	580	Trout	Large	
8	S30SLM	315	Trout	Small	
9	S136	271	Bass	Small	
10	S330	271	Bass	Small	

D2 fx =IF(LEFT(A2,1)="S","Small",IF(LEFT(A2,1)="L","Large",

COUNTIFS is a straightforward formula, but implementing it here could get tricky. Your challenge is to create one formula that you can copy to the other three blanks in your Count of boats table. You'll need to use absolute references.

Your criteria values will be these cells.

Use references inside your COUNTIFS formula to point to these criteria values.

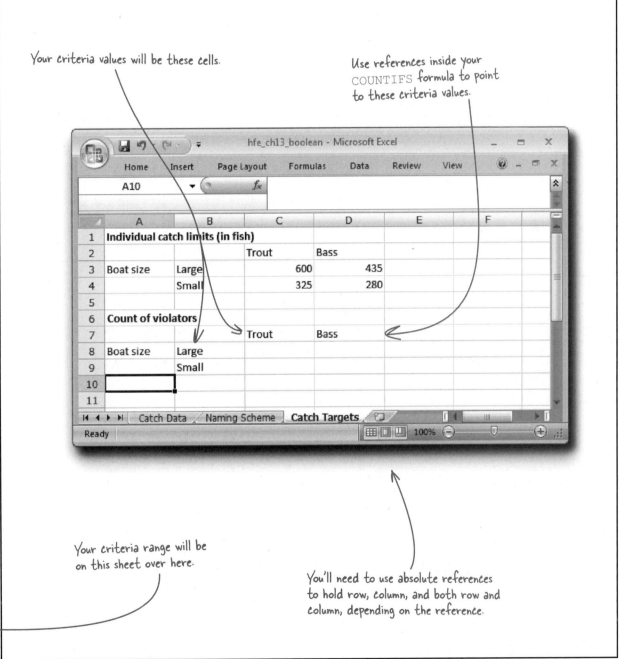

	A	B	C	D	E	F
1	**Individual catch limits (in fish)**					
2			Trout	Bass		
3	Boat size	Large	600	435		
4		Small	325	280		
5						
6	**Count of violators**					
7			Trout	Bass		
8	Boat size	Large				
9		Small				
10						
11						

Your criteria range will be on this sheet over here.

You'll need to use absolute references to hold row, column, and both row and column, depending on the reference.

Exercise Solution

You just implemented a COUNTIFS formula to count the number of boats in each category. What were your results?

This range refers to the Boat types values.

It's an absolute reference on row and column, because you don't want either to shift.

This reference is to "Trout" because you want to count the instances of the word "Trout."

=COUNTIFS('Catch Data'!$C$2:$C$393,'Catch Targets'!C$7, 'Catch Data'!$D$2:$D$393,'Catch Targets'!$B8)

This refers to the Boat size field.

Here's "Large."

Hold the row reference here...

...and the column reference here.

The formula copies and pastes smoothly for the other three blanks.

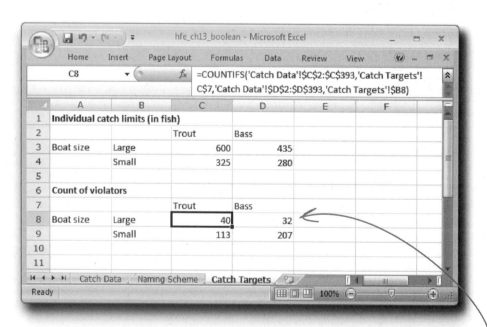

If your absolute references are correct, this is what you'll see.

Awesome! Now I just need that list of people who've violated their catch limits. Couldn't you write a Boolean formula or something to tag each boat "Violator" or not?

This could be tricky.

You **could** do it with about 50 nested IF formulas for each row. But imagine what that would entail! There must be an easier solution.

Here's the logic you'd need to encode into a big nested IF formula.

Wow, this would be a huge pain to implement.

There's got to be a way to break this problem down a little bit.

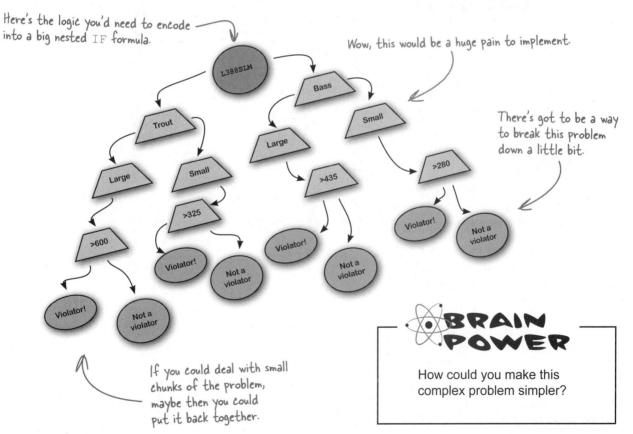

If you could deal with small chunks of the problem, maybe then you could put it back together.

🔬 **BRAIN POWER**

How could you make this complex problem simpler?

When working with complex conditions, break your formula apart into columns

You'd have an easier time if you just created a field for each item that said whether it was in violation of any of the four categories. Take boat L388SLM in row 2. You could create a formula that returned true if the boat is "Trout Large" and over its catch limit of 600.

And if you could copy that formula so that it evaluated every other combination (Trout Small, catch > 325, and so forth), then if L388SLM were in violation, at least one of the new cells would be true.

You want a formula here that returns TRUE if L388SLM is "Trout Large" and in violation.

It'd be nice if you could copy and paste the same formula for all these other cells.

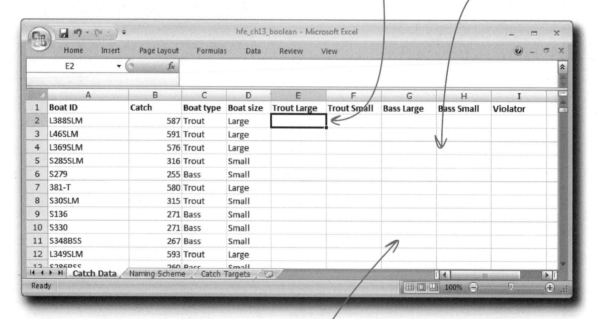

You know that L388SLM isn't a Bass Large, but as long as your formula returns TRUE only for the category Trout Large if it's in violation, you can ignore the FALSE values in the other columns. Then you can write a formula in column I that returns TRUE of one of the cells in columns E through H are TRUE.

Yes, it's a roundabout solution. But give it a shot. Excel ninjas are always thinking about how to solve complex problems in multiple simple steps.

That way, one of the values in columns E through H will be TRUE if the boat is in violation.

Exercise

Create a formula that returns TRUE if a boat matches one of the labels in E1:H1 and is in excess of the corresponding catch limit.

1 You're going to use the AND function in this case, which takes a series of Boolean expressions and returns TRUE only if all those expressions individually evaluate to TRUE. Take a look at AND in the help screens if you need more information.

2 Write an AND formula for each of these columns. The first one is partially done for you below, but you'll have to add dollar signs to create absolute references. Plus, the maximum catch amount is going to change for each of the four cells.

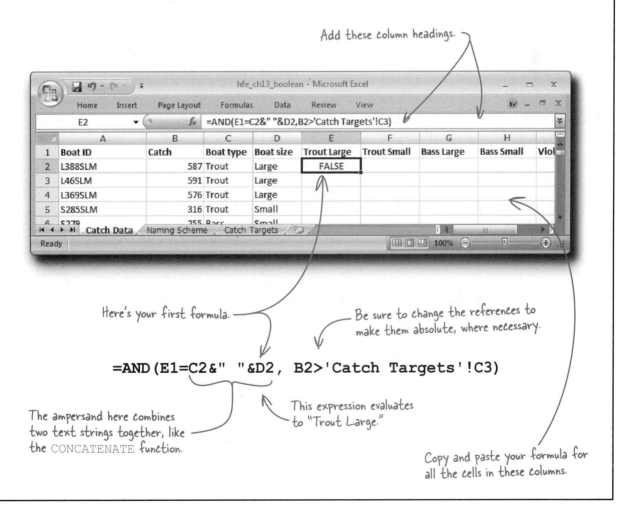

Add these column headings.

	A	B	C	D	E	F	G	H	
1	Boat ID	Catch	Boat type	Boat size	Trout Large	Trout Small	Bass Large	Bass Small	Viol
2	L388SLM	587	Trout	Large	FALSE				
3	L46SLM	591	Trout	Large					
4	L369SLM	576	Trout	Large					
5	S285SLM	316	Trout	Small					
6	S279	255	Bass	Small					

E2 fx `=AND(E1=C2&" "&D2,B2>'Catch Targets'!C3)`

Here's your first formula.

Be sure to change the references to make them absolute, where necessary.

$$=AND(E1=C2\&" "\&D2, B2>'Catch\ Targets'!C3)$$

The ampersand here combines two text strings together, like the CONCATENATE function.

This expression evaluates to "Trout Large."

Copy and paste your formula for all the cells in these columns.

Exercise Solution

You just created formulas to evaluate whether each boat is in violation of any of the categories. What did you find?

For the other three columns, you just need to change the reference to the catch limit.

`=AND(E$1=$C2&" "&$D2,$B2>'Catch Targets'!$C$3)`

Here's where the absolute reference dollar signs go for the formula in E2.

`=AND(F$1=$C2&" "&$D2,$B2>'Catch Targets'!$C$4)`

`=AND(G$1=$C2&" "&$D2,$B2>'Catch Targets'!$D$3)`

`=AND(H$1=$C2&" "&$D2,$B2>'Catch Targets'!$D$4)`

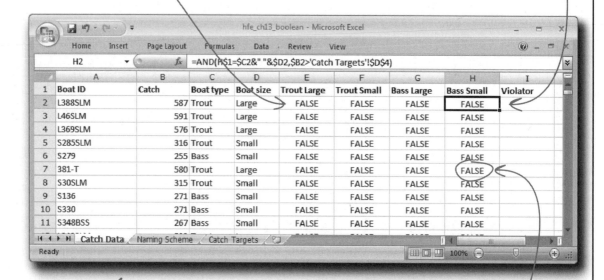

There are lots of FALSE values, but we're looking for needles in a haystack here, since there aren't a whole lot of violators.

This formula shows that it's FALSE that 381-T is both "Bass Small" boat and in violation of the Bass Small catch limit.

Now you have a grid of Boolean values. Combine the values for each boat using a _single formula_ that says whether the boat is a violator.

Exercise

Now you're ready to wrap up this assignment. Create the formula that will combine the Boolean values in columns E through H for each boat. That will tell you once and for all whether the boat is a violator. Then filter the list to show violators only.

1 Using the Help files, look up the logical function that takes a range of Booleans and returns TRUE if one or more of them is correct.

One of these functions returns TRUE if one or more of its arguments is TRUE.

2 Implement the function you've chosen for each boat. For example, for boat L388SLM, make the formula look at the Boolean values in cells E2:H2 and return TRUE if one of them is TRUE.

3 Filter the violators. Make your filter display only rows where the value in column I is TRUE.

Exercise
Solution

You just created formulas that return TRUE if the boat is a violator. Are there a lot of boats who are violators?

1 Using the Help files, look up the logical function that takes a range of Booleans and returns TRUE if one or more of them is correct.

The OR function is what you want to use.

If you want to get real fancy, you can nest AND, OR, and IF functions all inside each other.

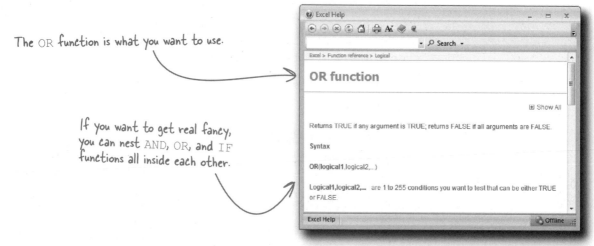

2 Implement the function you've chosen for each boat. For example, for boat L388SLM, make the formula look at the Boolean values in cells E2:H2 and return TRUE if one of them is TRUE.

You can write the formula in one of two ways.

$$=OR(E2,F2,G2,H2)$$

$$=OR(E2:H2)$$

This formula returns TRUE if one of its arguments is TRUE.

3. Filter the violators. Make your filter display only rows where the value in column I is TRUE.

Here's the filtered list.

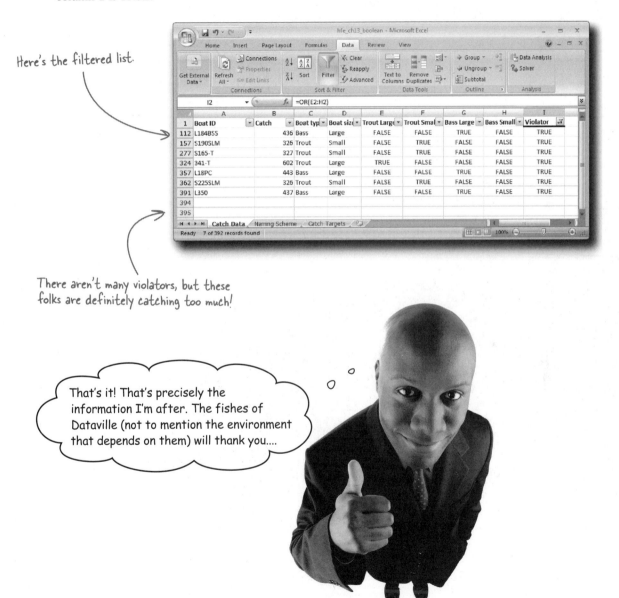

There aren't many violators, but these folks are definitely catching too much!

That's it! That's precisely the information I'm after. The fishes of Dataville (not to mention the environment that depends on them) will thank you....

Justice for fishies!

Using your analysis, violators were brought to justice. They paid a fine and promised not to take more than their share again. As a result, the ecology of Lake Dataville is in tip-top shape, with stable populations of very happy fish.

14 segmentation

Slice and dice

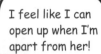

Get creative with your tools.

You've developed a formidable knowledge of Excel in the past 13 chapters, and by now you know (or know how to find) most of the tools that fit your data problems. But what if your problems *don't fit those tools*? What if you don't even have the data you need all in one place, or your data is divided into categories that don't fit your analytical objectives? In this final chapter, you'll use **lookup functions** along with some of the tools you already know to slice new **segments** out of your data and get really creative with Excel's tools.

You are with a watchdog that needs to tally budget money

Geopolitical Grunts is a swashbuckling group of policy geeks who advise businesses and governments on the most important macro trends of the day. They need your help doing some hardcore pivot table work.

The data set describes the spending of the U.S. federal government at the county level for the past couple years.

Thanks for coming aboard! I've got some beastly data here that I just can't make work for me. I know it has the information we need, I just don't know how to draw it out.

Government spending policy geek

Here's the graph they want

This doesn't seem like it'd be a problem.

From: G.G.
To: Head First
Subject: Data project

Dear Head First,

Guess what? I drew for you exactly what I'm looking for. If you can draw the graph below, you're done. It describes how much each agency spends per household on average.

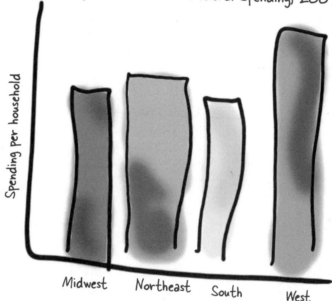

Average Per Household Federal Spending, 2009

No data? That's a problem.

Problem is, we don't have the data for this graphic. We don't have the per household spending, and we don't have our geography broken into these regional divisions.

We have something altogether different. Our data is big, and it's ugly. Be prepared to look at a bunch of zeros.

Wow, he wants the "impossible"....

Anyhow, if you can somehow make that data into the data to create this chart, that would be great. Can't you Excel gurus make the impossible happen?

—G.G.

Here's the federal spending data, broken out by county

The folks at Geopolitical Grunts sent you this database, which is a county-by-county summary of U.S. federal government spending over the past couple years. And because it's almost 50,000 lines, you might want to close other programs before loading it!

These fields describe the county.

These describe the state.

Here's the agency that spent the money.

You know this one.

How much they spent.

The number of households in that county.

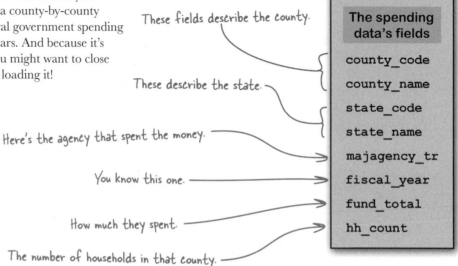

The spending data's fields

county_code

county_name

state_code

state_name

majagency_tr

fiscal_year

fund_total

hh_count

There's a lot of data in here.

Almost 50,000 lines...sheesh!

Load this!

www.headfirstlabs.com/books/hfexcel/
hfe_ch14_usaspend.xlsx

Sharpen your pencil

Look at the chart he wants. Can you create it from the data you have? Why or why not?

Here's your data.

	county_code	county_name	state_code	state_name	majagency_tr	fiscal_year	fund_total	hh_count
1								
2	13	Aleutians East Borough	2	AK	All other agencies	2007	$ 504,110	760
3	13	Aleutians East Borough	2	AK	Environmental Protection Agency	2007	$ 2,791,848	760

This means that the EPA spent $2.8 million in Aleutians East Borough in 2007.

There are 760 households in this county.

Look at both axes of this chart and say whether you can create those axes from the database you have.

Here's the chart they want.

Average Per Household Federal Spending, 2009

Spending per household

Midwest   Northeast   South   West

....
....
....
....
....
....

Write your answer here.

Sharpen your pencil
Solution

You just compared the data to the chart you've been asked to generate. How well do the two match up?

	county_code	county_name	state_code	state_name	majagency_tr	fiscal_year	fund_total	hh_count
1								
2	13	Aleutians East Borough	2	AK	All other agencies	2007	$ 504,110	760
3	13	Aleutians East Borough	2	AK	Environmental Protection Agency	2007	$ 2,791,848	760

You can probably calculate per household spending from these data points.

The data says county/state, but the chart they want says region.

There are going to be some problems making this work. First, the data is divided into states and counties, not regions. Alaska is "West," but that fact is not in the data set itself. Spending per household isn't in the data either, but we could probably create that figure with a simple calculation.

There is a lot going on here.

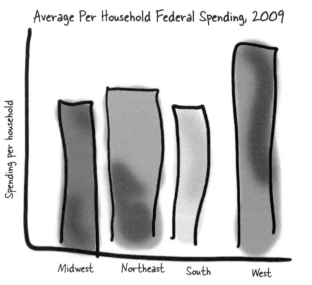

Average Per Household Federal Spending, 2009

Spending per household

Midwest   Northeast   South   West

Sometimes the data you get isn't enough

Data can be close to what you want without ever quite getting there. But that doesn't mean that you can't do your analysis. You can just transform the data you have into the data you need to have.

Region is the category you want.

Data outputs

New categories

Categorical summaries using numbers

Categorical summaries of numbers

Numeric calculations

States and counties are categories.

Transform it!

Data inputs

Categorical data

Numeric data

Spending totals and household counts are numbers.

You need to calculate fund total divided by household count.

ExerciSe

Go ahead and create the field you need: the spending per household for each agency in each county.

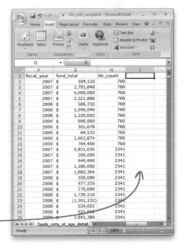

1 Convert your data to a table and name the table "SpendingData."

2 Create a column on the end called `Per_Household` and populate it with a function that divides the `fund_total` field by the `hh_count` field.

Put your Per_Household column here.

Exercise Solution

You just created one of the fields you need for your chart: spending per household. How did it go?

Create your table using the Insert tab.

1 Convert your data to a table and name the table "SpendingData."

Table Name:
SpendingData
Resize Table

If the colored bars annoy you, clean up the formatting of the table.

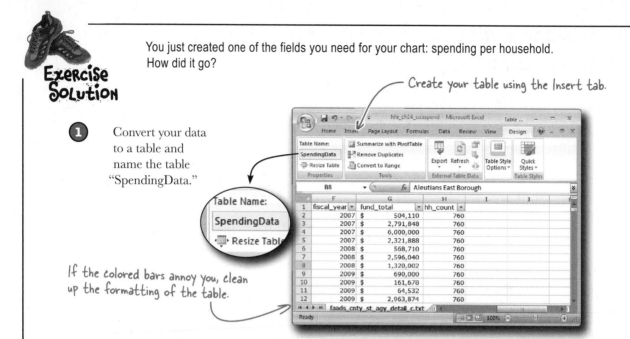

2 Create a column on the end called `Per_Household` and populate it with a function that divides the `fund_total` field by the `hh_count` field.

Add your column here.

```
=SpendingData[[#This Row],[fund_total]] /
       SpendingData[[#This Row],[hh_count]]
```

This calculates per household spending.

To get this, press "=", then click on fund_total, then press "/", then click hh_count.

Don't forget to format the data as currency.

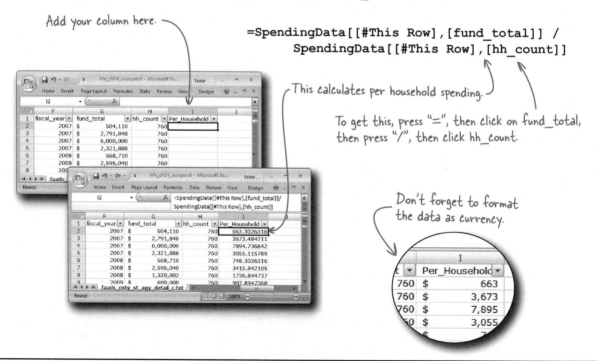

Your problems with <u>region</u> are bigger

Calculating the `Per_Household` figure was straightforward, because you had all the data you needed right there on the spreadsheet.

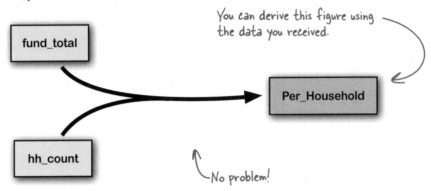

You can derive this figure using the data you received.

No problem!

But you're in a different situation with `Region`, since there's nothing implicit in the data that you can use to calculate `Region`. You need to **incorporate more data** in order to determine the region for each row.

You're going to need something else to make this work.

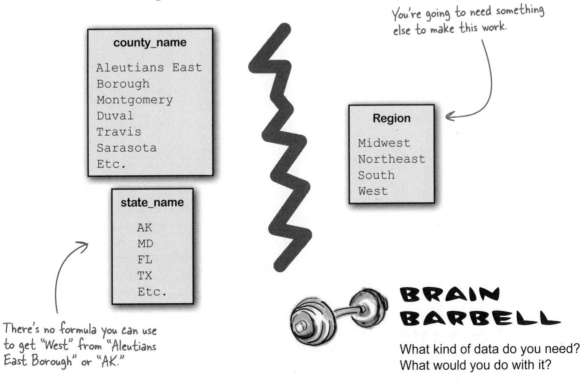

There's no formula you can use to get "West" from "Aleutians East Borough" or "AK."

BRAIN BARBELL

What kind of data do you need? What would you do with it?

Here's a lookup key

You can poke around in search
engines for a few minutes and find
data like this: a key that shows how
state names fit with regions.

Load this!

www.headfirstlabs.com/books/hfexcel/
hfe_ch14_state_region.xlsx

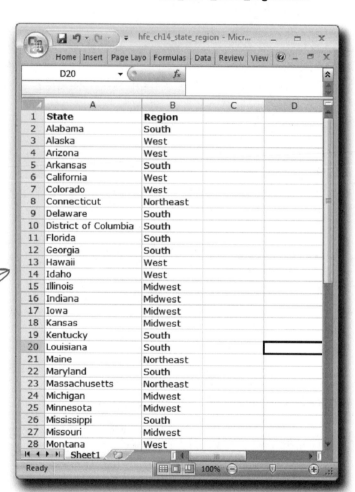

This key shows how State and
Region match each other.

Using this data, you can bring Region data
into your spending spreadsheet, which will
enable you to create that chart they want.

If your spreadsheet doesn't have the
data you need, maybe you can use another
data source to bring that data in.

VLOOKUP will cross-reference the two data sources

A particularly useful function in Excel is VLOOKUP. The V stands for *vertical*, and what the function does is look up a reference value in a vertical list and then return the value from another column that matches the position of the value in the vertical list.

Here's a reference to the table containing your lookup key.

VLOOKUP searches for lookup_value in the first column of table_array.

This number specifies the column of the table that contains the value you want returned.

=VLOOKUP(lookup_value, table_array, col_index_num, [range_lookup])

This is the value you're looking up in a lookup key data set.

This argument is optional.

col_index_num takes a numeric value, not a reference, to specify the column.

Table Array

Column 1	Column 2
AL	South
AK	West
AZ	West
AR	South
CA	West

Look at the bullet points for more info.

BULLET POINTS

- VLOOKUP searches for the `lookup_value` in the first column of the table_array.

- `col_index_num` asks for a number to point to the column containing the data you want returned, not a reference.

- `[range_lookup]` takes a Boolean argument.

- If you set the `[range_lookup]` to FALSE, VLOOKUP returns an error if there isn't an exact match, and your table_array doesn't have to be sorted.

- If you set `[range_lookup]` to TRUE, VLOOKUP returns a value near your `lookup_value` if there isn't an exact match, but your table_array has to be in order.

state_name will be your lookup value.

C	D	
code ▼	state_name ▼	maja
2	AK	All o
2	AK	Envi
2	AK	Dep:
2	AK	Dep:
2	AK	All o
2	AK	Dep:
2	AK	Envi
2	AK	Envi
2	AK	Dep:
2	AK	Dep:
2	AK	Dep:
2	AK	Dep:

It's a big function. Let's give it a shot....

Stop! The data doesn't match! In the new file, state names are spelled out, and in the original data, state names are abbreviated.

Oh, bother. So it looks like you're going to have to cross-reference the region to the state abbreviation, then use that abbreviation to cross-reference the region to your original data. Fortunately, VLOOKUP will make quick work of bringing these data sets together.

Load this, too!

**www.headfirstlabs.com/books/hfexcel/
hfe_ch14_state_abbrev.xlsx**

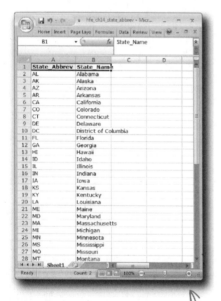

This spreadsheet matches state names with their abbreviations.

Copy the state_region data into your state_abbrev spreadsheet like this....

Now you'll have both data sets on the same sheet.

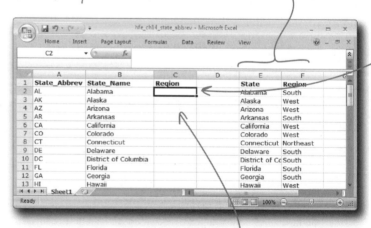

Let's put the region data into this column.

Pool Puzzle

Your **job** is to take formula elements from the pool and place them into the blank lines in the formula. You may **not** use the same formula element more than once, and you won't need to use all of them. Your **goal** is to make a VLOOKUP formula that puts Region and State_Abbrev into the same table.

Write the formula that would go here.

This is the value you're looking up.

=VLOOKUP(_____,_____,_____)

This reference contains the data your looking up.

This number specifies the column with the data you want returned.

Note: Each thing from the pool can be used only once!

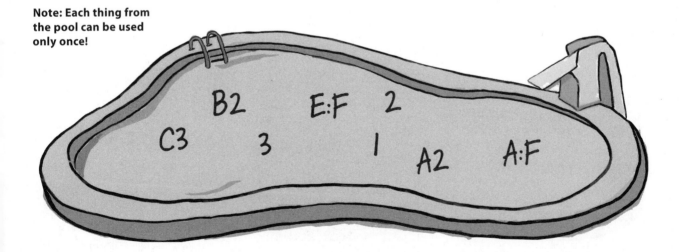

B2   E:F   2

C3   3

1   A2   A:F

Pool Puzzle Answers

You just wrote your first VLOOKUP formula to create a table that relates your Region field to your State_Abbrev field.

You want VLOOKUP to return the corresponding value in the second column.

	E	F
	State	**Region**
	Alabama	South
	Alaska	West
	Arizona	West
	Arkansas	South
	California	West
	Colorado	West
	Connecticut	Northeast
	Delaware	South
	District of Co	South
	Florida	South
	Georgia	South
	Hawaii	West

Here's where you're looking....

=VLOOKUP(B2 , E:F , 2)

In the first row, the value you're looking up is "Alabama".

	A	B	
1	**State_Abbrev**	**State_Name**	**Re**
2	AL	Alabama	
3	AK	Alaska	
	AZ	Arizona	
		Arkansas	

We don't have to use the [range_lookup] argument, since we know the state data is complete and in order.

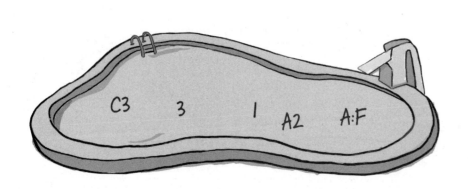

C3   3   1   A2   A:F

Do this!

If you haven't already, type this formula into your cell C2 and copy/paste it for each row. You'll use it in the next exercise.

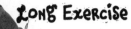

Long Exercise

You're just a step away from having all the data you need to create the chart the Geopolitical Grunts want. Create the VLOOKUP formula that will bring region data into your spending spreadsheet and then create the pivot chart your client wants.

1 Copy the lookup key sheet you've been working on in `hfe_ch14_state_abbrev.xlsx` into your original workbook. Right-click on Sheet1 and tell Excel to move the sheet into your `hfe_ch14_usaspend.xlsx` workbook.

Put the formula to look up your Region value here.

2 Add a Region column to your original data and then write the VLOOKUP formula that will look up the region field based on the state abbreviation in that row.

> **NOTE:** You will need to have the fourth argument of VLOOKUP be FALSE.

Here is the sheet you import from `hfe_ch14_state_abbrev.xlsx`.

3 Create the pivot chart that the Geopolitical Grunts want. Just click "Pivot Chart" rather than "Pivot Table" and let Excel create the chart. You **will** have to change the title and formatting to get the chart right.

Here is the chart they want.

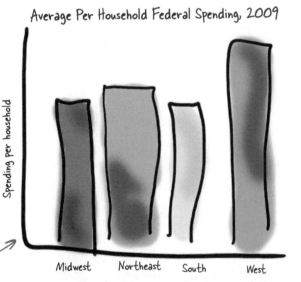

Average Per Household Federal Spending, 2009

LONG EXERCISE SOLUTION

You just added another column to your data set and then created a pivot chart. How does it look?

1 Copy the lookup key sheet you've been working on in `hfe_ch14_state_abbrev.xlsx` into your original workbook. Right-click on Sheet1 and tell Excel to move the sheet into your `hfe_ch14_usaspend.xlsx` workbook.

Here's what the "Move or Copy" dialog box looks like.

You get to it from right-clicking on the sheet's tab at the bottom of the screen.

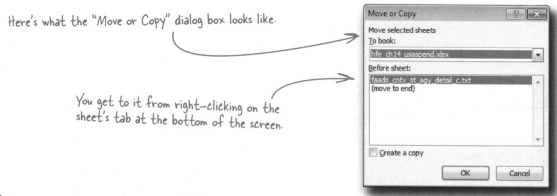

2 Add a Region column to your original data and then write the VLOOKUP formula that will look up the region field based on the state abbreviation in that row.

The second and third arguments point to the lookup table you created.

```
=VLOOKUP(SpendingData[[#This Row],[state_name]],Sheet1!A:C,3,FALSE)
```

Here's your formula.

Take a look at the help screens for more information on this argument.

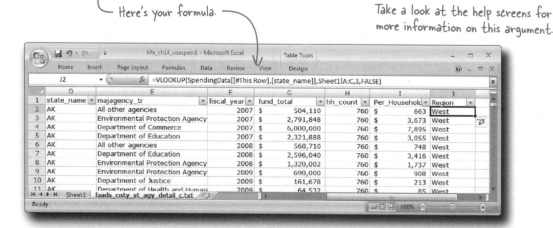

3 Create the pivot chart that the Geopolitical Grunts want. Just click "Pivot Chart" rather than "Pivot Table" and let Excel create the table. You *will* have to change the title and formatting to get the chart right.

Lots of things you need to do to clean this up....

These are the fields that you created.

Filter by fiscal year 2009.

Format the average as currency.

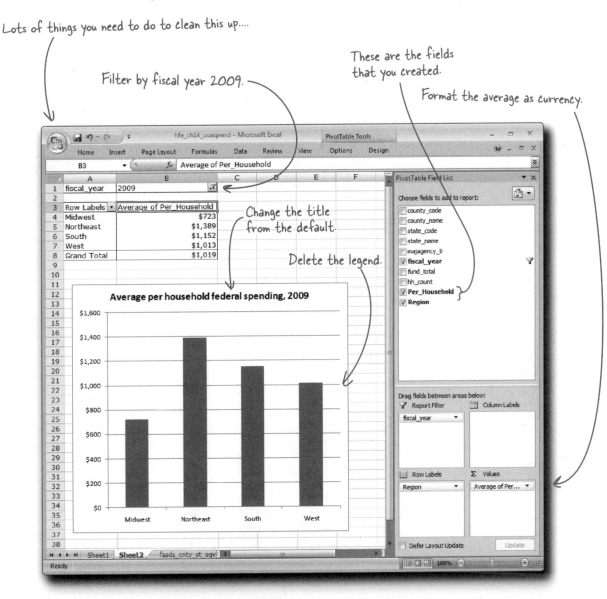

Change the title from the default.

Delete the legend.

Create segments to feed the right data into your analysis

The data you receive to analyze inside Excel is just a starting point. If that data doesn't do what you need it to do for your analysis, every tool of Excel is at your disposal to mutate the data into the form you need.

That's what slicing and dicing data is all about.

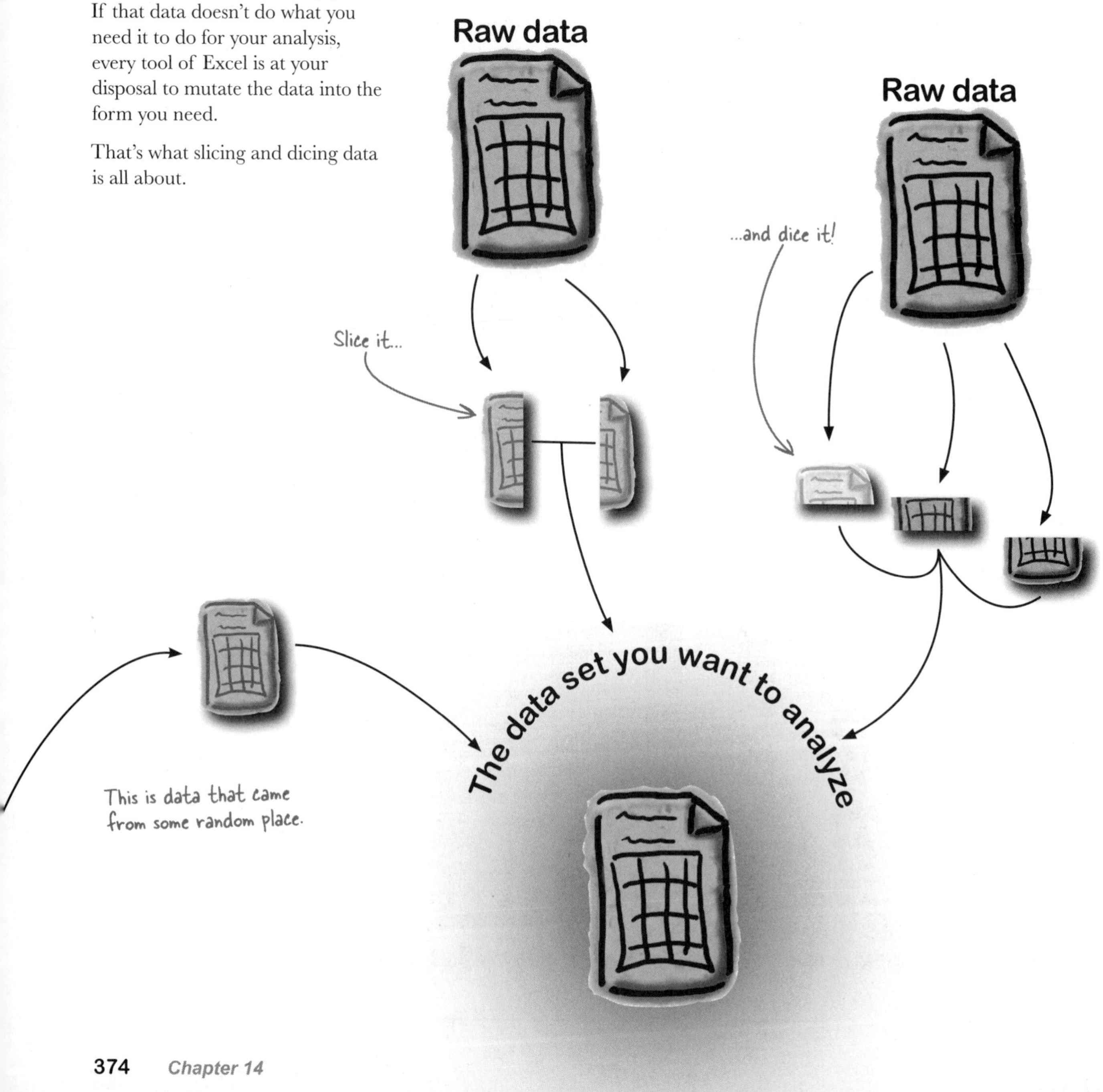

Raw data

Raw data

...and dice it!

Slice it...

The data set you want to analyze

This is data that came from some random place.

there are no
Dumb Questions

Q: Will I always use VLOOKUP to do this sort of thing?

A: By no means! VLOOKUP is powerful, but there are other lookup functions as well. There's HLOOKUP, which does horizontal lookups, as well as INDEX and MATCH, which are popular but slightly harder to understand.

Q: So there's a lot of versatility in Excel's functions when it comes to looking things up.

A: Absolutely. But you never know what formulas you'll be able to use to slice and dice data into the form you need. Remember, earlier in the chapter you used simple division to create a new field, which you graphed using a pivot chart.

Q: Now that I have lookup formulas and division, what else can I use to segment data points?

A: Boolean functions are big here. Say you wanted to tag all the records in your database that were Department of Defense programs in Maryland. It'd be easy to use a simple AND function to create a Boolean value.

Q: And I could take that Boolean value and use it with a formula like COUNTIFS to compare it with other values in my data set.

A: Or better yet, you could plug the Boolean value somewhere into a pivot table. Boolean functions are fantastic for segmentation, and they play really well with pivot tables.

Q: You know, this is kind of funny advice you're giving me. What you're basically saying is that there are a lot of different functions and techniques that can all do the same basic thing.

A: Right! Go on....

Q: And at the same time you're not giving me any quick and easy rules for how to use those functions and techniques for segmentation. Your advice is basically, "Look at the problem, and pluck an Excel feature out of thin air to solve it. Use whichever Excel feature is best."

A: That's a fair observation. But you've learned enough about the features of Excel that all the stuff you don't know consists of either super-advanced topics or subtle variations on the themes you've already picked up. At this point, your goal should be to play with the functions and think creatively about how to make them work for your specific problems.

Q: The student has become the master.

A: That might be overstating it a bit, but you're well on your way. Just as a book on Microsoft Word won't show you how to write the Great American Novel, a book on Excel can't teach you to create a brilliant spreadsheet.

Q: What can teach me how to do wild stuff in Excel?

A: You can certainly always be on the lookout for people's novel solutions to problems, but the best way to get good with Excel once you have a strong base of knowledge is just to learn as many functions as you can and experiment with making them work together. You'll inevitably surprise yourself with the creative ways you can use Excel.

Q: It probably wouldn't hurt to be good at math, either.

A: Definitely. A solid book on general data analysis or analysis for your area of expertise would show you some of the theoretical points that will make your spreadsheets smarter. But that's a whole different deal. In the meantime, let's see what your friend at Geopolitical Grunts has to say about your pivot chart.

Geopolitical Grunts would like a little more nuance

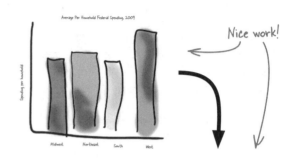

> Oh, wow, that visualization is fantastic. You know, you've got me thinking. What would be really nice would be to break out the department-level projects from everything else. Could you filter the data so that it only includes transactions where the word "Department" is in the majagency_tr field?

Nice work!

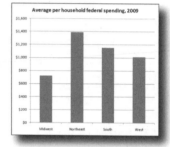

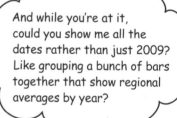

> And while you're at it, could you show me all the dates rather than just 2009? Like grouping a bunch of bars together that show regional averages by year?

Ah, clients.... What are you going to do? You flash a little skill, and once they know what you're capable of doing, they'll never leave you alone!

Exercise

Your client would like a little more detail in his chart. Looks like you're going to have to create a new segment....

1 Adding dates to your pivot chart is the easy part. Drag the date field out of the Filter box and into the box that will make the pivot show many bars representing region *and* year, not just region.

2 Your raw data rows need a tag to denote whether each transaction is from a department-level organization or not. Create a Boolean data field that contains TRUE if the word "Department" is in the **majagency_tr** field. If you need help, take a look at the hint below.

3 Head back over to your pivot table. Since you've added data to your data table, you'll need to press the button in the Ribbon to refresh your pivot table. Then add your new field as a filter, showing only data points where it's TRUE that the transaction is from a department-level organization.

> **Hint...**
>
> FIND() returns an error if the requested text substring is not found. ISERROR() returns TRUE if its argument is an error. NOT() returns TRUE if its argument is FALSE. Put these formulas together to create a big nested formula that returns TRUE if "Department" is in the substring you're looking at.

You just created a new segment to describe transactions originating from department-level
organizations. How did it go?

1 Adding dates to your pivot chart is the easy part.
Drag the date field out of the Filter box and into
the box that will make the pivot show many bars
representing region *and* year, not just region.

Drag fields between areas below:

▼ Report Filter   ▦ Legend Fields (S...

fiscal_year   ▼

▦ Axis Fields (Cate...   Σ Values

Region   ▼   Average of Per... ▼
fiscal_year   ▼

☐ Defer Layout Update   Update

2 Your raw data rows need a tag to denote whether each
transaction is from a department-level organization or
not. Create a Boolean data field that contains TRUE if
the word "Department" is in the **majagency_tr** field.

Add the year to the axis. —————

Imagine a cell doesn't have "Department" in it...

This formula will return an error...

Here's your formula. —————

=NOT(ISERROR(FIND("Department",SpendingData[[#This Row],[majagency_tr]])))

...this will return TRUE...

...and this will flip it to FALSE, since the cell doesn't contain "Department".

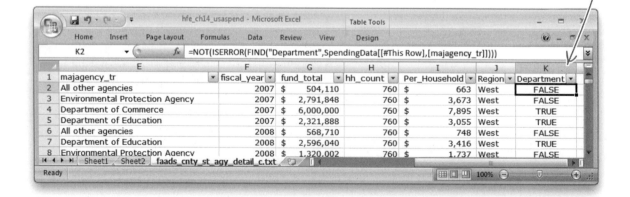

	E	F	G	H	I	J	K
1	majagency_tr	fiscal_year	fund_total	hh_count	Per_Household	Region	Department
2	All other agencies	2007	$ 504,110	760	$ 663	West	FALSE
3	Environmental Protection Agency	2007	$ 2,791,848	760	$ 3,673	West	FALSE
4	Department of Commerce	2007	$ 6,000,000	760	$ 7,895	West	TRUE
5	Department of Education	2007	$ 2,321,888	760	$ 3,055	West	TRUE
6	All other agencies	2008	$ 568,710	760	$ 748	West	FALSE
7	Department of Education	2008	$ 2,596,040	760	$ 3,416	West	TRUE
8	Environmental Protection Agency	2008	$ 1,320,002	760	$ 1,737	West	FALSE

K2 =NOT(ISERROR(FIND("Department",SpendingData[[#This Row],[majagency_tr]])))

Head back over to your pivot table. Since you've added data to your data table, you'll need to press the button in the Ribbon to refresh your pivot table. Then add your new field as a filter, showing only data points where it's TRUE that the transaction is from a department-level organization.

Click the refresh button to enable you to include your new field.

Here's your new chart!

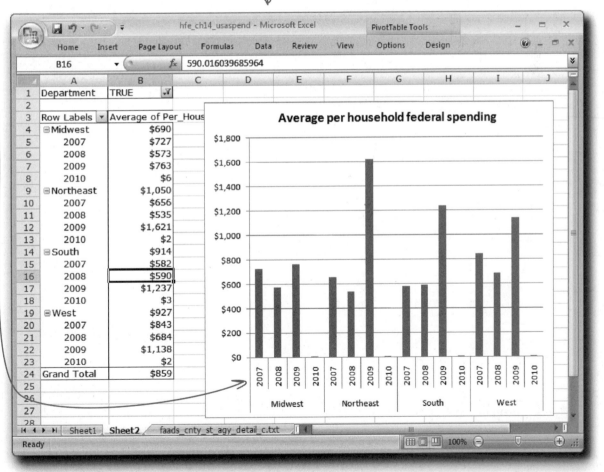

You've enabled Geopolitical Grunts to follow the money trail...

Which is a good thing, because there's a whole lot of it. So much of it, that it's hard to keep track of it all

Leaving town...

It's been great having you here in Dataville!

We're sad to see you leave, but there's nothing like taking what you've learned and putting it to use. You're just beginning your Excel journey, and we've put you in the driver's seat. We're dying to hear how things go, so ***drop us a line*** at the Head First Labs website, **www.headfirstlabs.com**, and let us know how data analysis is paying off for **YOU**!

appendix i: leftovers

The Top Ten Things (we didn't cover)

You're not finished yet, are you? But there is so much left!

You've come a long way.

But Excel is a complicated program, and there's so much left to learn. In this appendix, we'll go over 10 items that there wasn't enough room to cover in this book, but should be high on your list of topics to learn about next.

#1: Data analysis

It's one thing to be able to rock and roll inside Excel, but it's another thing altogether to be a good data analyst. **Data analysis** is a broad (and hot) field that encompasses knowledge not only of Excel and other software but of higher level topics like statistics and psychology.

Crack data analysts are omnivorous and voracious thinkers when it comes to data, and if you're interested in boning up on data analysis, might we suggest…

This book is more about analytic principles than software.

#2: The format painter

The **format painter** is one of those tools
inside Excel that you'll use all the time. The
format painter provides a super-quick way
to copy formatting attributes from one cell
to another. Just select the cell that has the
formatting you want to copy to another cell,
click the Format Painter button, and then click
on the cell or range where you want to apply
that formatting.

Try out this feature.

If you want to apply the formatting you've
loaded into the format painter to a number
of places in your spreadsheet (rather than
just one), double-click the button when the
cell whose formatting you want to copy is
highlighted.

You can also achieve the same results using
Paste Special > Formatting.

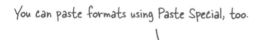

You can paste formats using Paste Special, too.

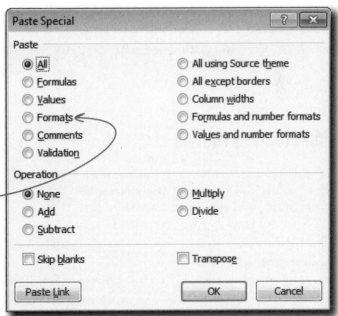

#3: The Data Analysis ToolPak

The Data Analysis ToolPak is a set of analysis tools that comes standard with Excel but isn't activated by default. If you need to use Excel for serious statistical operations like hypothesis testing, you'll want to take a look at this feature. Check out the Help files for information on how to activate it.

The Data Analysis ToolPak has a bunch of cool statistical functions.

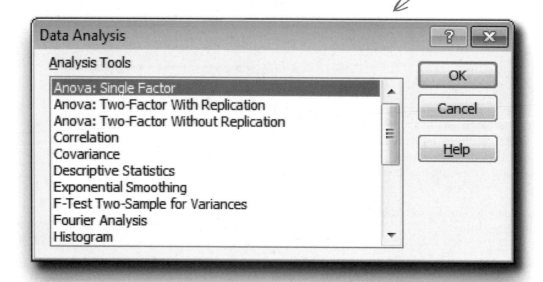

#4: Array formulas

Ever needed a formula to return more than one result? Does that question blow your mind? **Array formulas** are a conceptually difficult but programmatically powerful feature of Excel that push functions to the limits of their performance.

They're worth looking into if you're interested in taking your mastery of functions into a whole different dimension…literally!

#5: Shapes and SmartArt

Excel 2007 introduced a bunch of visual formatting tools, and this book has only scratched the surface of those tools. If you enjoy thinking visually, try poking around the Shapes and SmartArt features. They are a treasure trove for quick and easy yet elegant formatting options for flow charts and other visualizations.

You can draw all sorts of interesting diagrams inside Excel using Shapes and SmartArt.

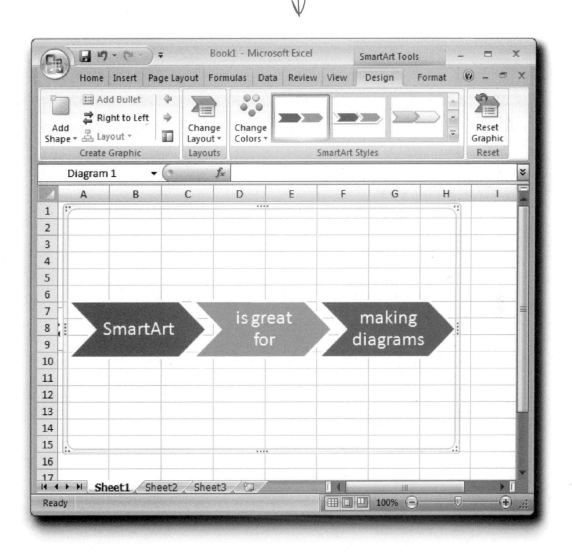

#6: Controlling recalculation and performance tuning

If your spreadsheet gets large and full of formulas, especially array formulas, you might experience slowdowns as all your formulas recalculate when you update data. If you suspect you're experiencing something like this, head over to the Options menu and play around with the settings that control Excel's recalculation and other performance behaviors.

Check out this window for performance tuning options.

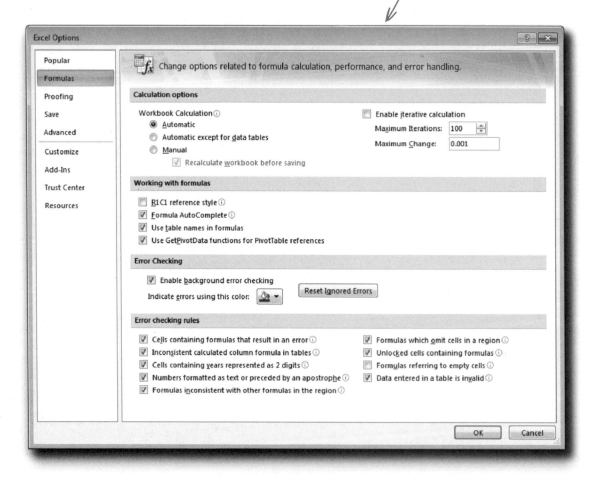

#7: Connecting to the Web

All of us spend time surfing the Web, so why not make
Excel and the Web work together? Excel has a number
of facilities for bringing web data into your worksheets
and exporting your spreadsheets for use on the Web.

#8: Working with external data sources

You can pull data into Excel from relational databases
like Microsoft Access and from a variety of other
external sources besides the Internet. Interfacing
databases with Excel pivot tables using OLAP (Online
Analytical Processing) technology is a particularly
powerful and cool way to analyze data.

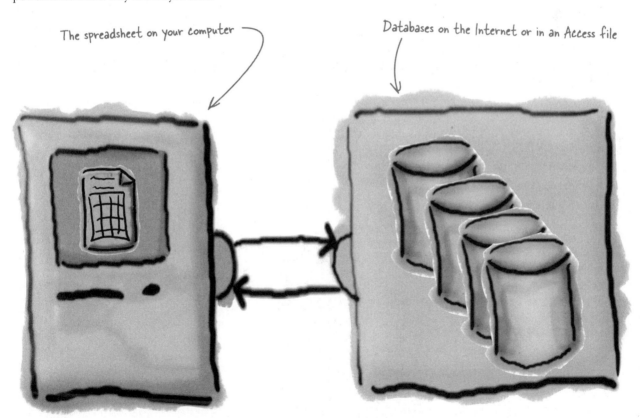

The spreadsheet on your computer

Databases on the Internet or in an Access file

#9: Collaboration

Excel's collaboration features like Track Changes
make working with other people on the same
spreadsheet a lot easier. To look at some of the
collaboration features, head over to the Review tab.

Look into collaboration options here.

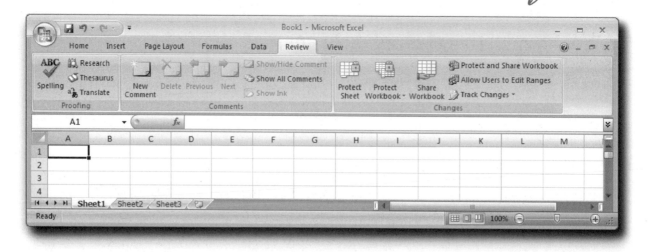

#10: Visual Basic for Applications

Have you learned most of
Excel's features, even the
super-technical stuff like
array formulas, and find
yourself demanding more?
Visual Basic for Applications
(VBA) is a full-blown
programming language that
you can use inside Excel to
create your own functions
and much, much more.

*Your spreadsheet dreams of
having its own VBA code.*

appendix ii:
install excel's solver

The Solver ✳

I want to optimize now! I don't want to have to install some add-in...

Some of the best features of Excel aren't installed by default.

That's right, in order to run the optimization from Chapter 10, you need to activate the **Solver**, an add-in that is included in Excel by default but not activated without your initiative.

Install Solver in Excel

Installing the Solver in Excel is no problem
if you follow these simple steps.

This is the Microsoft Office button.

1 Click the Microsoft Office button and select **Excel
Options**.

Here's Excel Options.

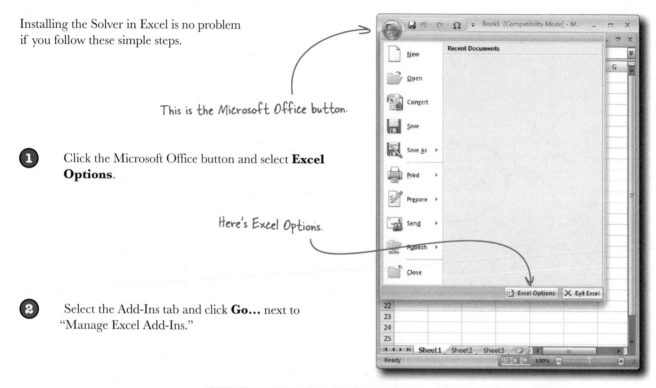

2 Select the Add-Ins tab and click **Go...** next to
"Manage Excel Add-Ins."

The Add-Ins tab

Click this button.

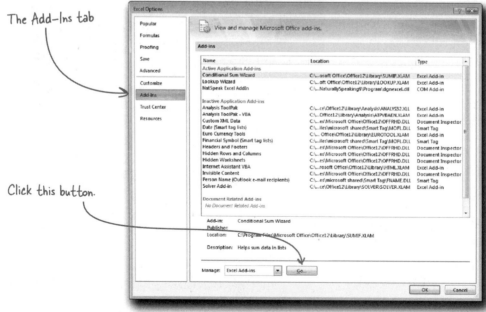

3 Make sure that the Solver Add-in box is checked, and then press **OK**.

Make sure that this box is checked. ———

4 Take a look at the Data tab to make sure that the Solver button is there for you to use.

Make sure that Solver can be seen under the Data tab.

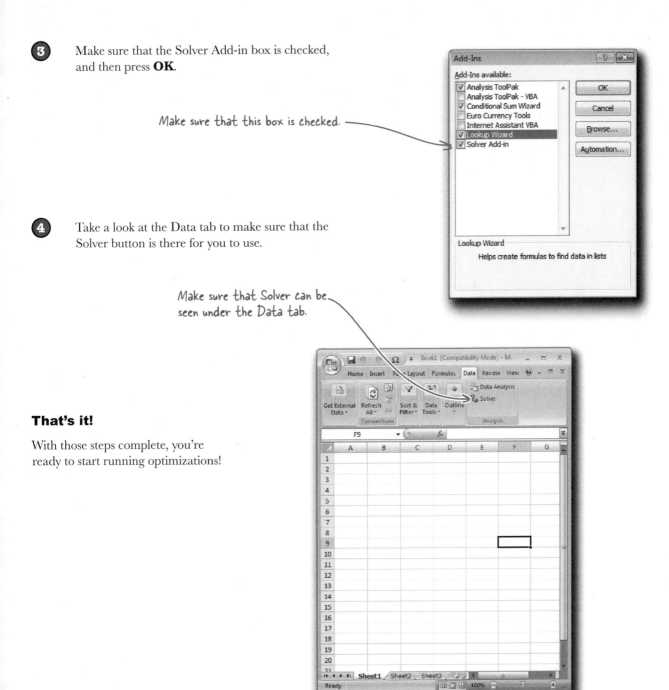

That's it!

With those steps complete, you're ready to start running optimizations!

Index

Learning for the Way Your Brain Works

Learning isn't something that just happens to you. It's something you do. But all too often, it seems like your brain isn't cooperating. Your time is too valuable to spend struggling with new concepts. Head First books combine strong visuals, puzzles, humor, and the latest research in cognitive science to engage your entire mind in the learning process.

 Also available:

Head First HTML with CSS & HXTML

Head First Web Design

Head First Software Development

Head First iPhone Development

Head First Design Patterns

You can't learn everything from a book.

Now that you're building your knowledge with this book from O'Reilly, why not polish your skills and advance your IT career in the unique interactive learning environment at the O'Reilly School of Technology?

- Work with expert instructors, one-on-one

- Learn at your own pace and set your own deadlines

- Create, compile, and test your programs in a real-world environment

- Earn a professional certificate from the University of Illinois

Our courses won't break your budget, and you can take a test drive with our 7-day money-back guarantee. To find out more, come take a campus tour at **http://oreillyschool.com**.

Certification available through

Get even more for your money.

Join the O'Reilly Community, and register the O'Reilly books you own. It's free, and you'll get:

- 40% upgrade offer on O'Reilly books
- Membership discounts on books and events
- Free lifetime updates to electronic formats of books
- Multiple ebook formats, DRM FREE
- Participation in the O'Reilly community
- Newsletters
- Account management
- 100% Satisfaction Guarantee

Signing up is easy:

1. **Go to: oreilly.com/go/register**
2. **Create an O'Reilly login.**
3. **Provide your address.**
4. **Register your books.**

Note: English-language books only

To order books online:

oreilly.com/order_new

For questions about products or an order:

orders@oreilly.com

To sign up to get topic-specific email announcements and/or news about upcoming books, conferences, special offers, and new technologies:

elists@oreilly.com

For technical questions about book content:

booktech@oreilly.com

To submit new book proposals to our editors:

proposals@oreilly.com

Many O'Reilly books are available in PDF and several ebook formats. For more information:

oreilly.com/ebooks

Spreading the knowledge of innovators   www.oreilly.com

Buy this book and get access to the online edition for 45 days—for free!

Head First Excel

By Michael Milton
March 2010, $34.99
ISBN 9780596807696

With Safari Books Online, you can:

Access the contents of thousands of technology and business books

- Quickly search over 7000 books and certification guides
- Download whole books or chapters in PDF format, at no extra cost, to print or read on the go
- Copy and paste code
- Save up to 35% on O'Reilly print books
- **New!** Access mobile-friendly books directly from cell phones and mobile devices

Stay up-to-date on emerging topics before the books are published

- Get on-demand access to evolving manuscripts.
- Interact directly with authors of upcoming books

Explore thousands of hours of video on technology and design topics

- Learn from expert video tutorials
- Watch and replay recorded conference sessions

To try out Safari and the online edition of this book FREE for 45 days, go to **www.oreilly.com/go/safarienabled** and enter the coupon code ZCZSOXA. To see the complete Safari Library, visit safari.oreilly.com.

O'REILLY®

Spreading the knowledge of innovators

safari.oreilly.com